Publications of
The Colonial Society of Massachusetts
Volume 51

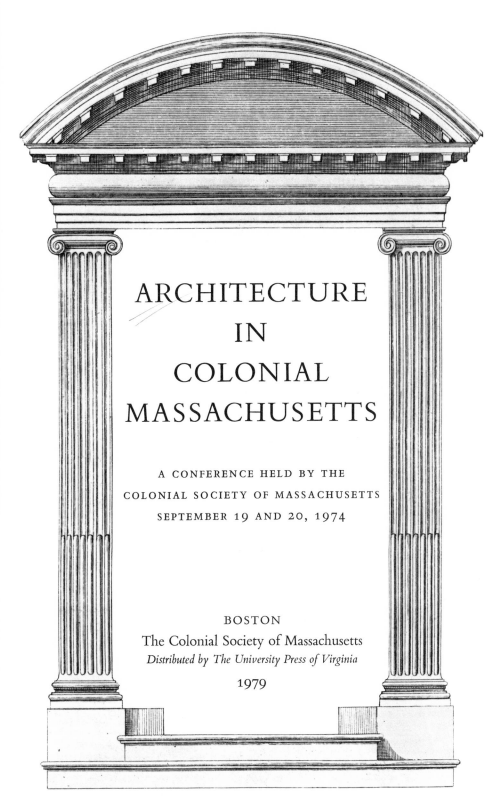

ARCHITECTURE
IN
COLONIAL
MASSACHUSETTS

A CONFERENCE HELD BY THE
COLONIAL SOCIETY OF MASSACHUSETTS
SEPTEMBER 19 AND 20, 1974

BOSTON
The Colonial Society of Massachusetts
Distributed by The University Press of Virginia
1979

COPYRIGHT © 1979 THE COLONIAL SOCIETY OF MASSACHUSETTS

LIBRARY OF CONGRESS CATALOGUE CARD NUMBER 79–51657

PRINTED FROM THE INCOME OF THE SARAH LOUISE EDES FUND

Title-page illustration from William Salmon,
Palladio Londinensis (London, 1734). See also Figure 6.

Contents

Foreword   xi
FREDERICK S. ALLIS, JR.

Introduction   xiii
ABBOTT LOWELL CUMMINGS

The Early History of the Paul Revere House   3
STEPHEN J. ROPER

The Royall House in Medford: A Re-Evaluation of   23
the Structural and Documentary Evidence
ARTHUR L. FINNEY
    with an appendix: "An Inventorey of the Estate
    of Isaac Royall"

Plymouth Colony Architecture: Archaeological   43
Evidence from the Seventeenth Century
JAMES DEETZ

The James Blake House: A Documentary Study   61
EDWARD ZIMMER
    edited by Matthew J. Kiefer

The Building of Trinity Church, Boston   75
JAMES B. PEABODY

Measured Drawings of the Hancock House by John   87
Hubbard Sturgis: A Legacy to the Colonial Revival
MARGARET HENDERSON FLOYD

Massachusetts and Its First Period Houses: 113
A Statistical Survey
ABBOTT LOWELL CUMMINGS

Appendices

    I. Summary abstracts of the structural history of   125
    a significant sampling of First Period Houses at
    Massachusetts Bay *by Abbott Lowell Cummings*

    II. Massachusetts Bay building documents, 1638–   193
    1726 *compiled by Abbott Lowell Cummings*

Index   223

Illustrations

1. Paul Revere house, North Square, Boston, Mass., before restoration. 5

2. Paul Revere house, North Square, Boston, after restoration. 7

3. Front facade and south brick end of the Royall house, Medford, Mass., showing outline of earlier building. 24

4. Garden facade, Royall house. 25

5. Schematic evolution of the Royall house prepared by John H. Hooper. 27

6. Frontispiece in the Ionic order. Plate XXIII, William Salmon, *Palladio Londinensis* (London, 1734). 28

7. Detail of frontispiece, garden facade of the Royall house. 29

8. Front facade with later wing, Royall house. 32

9. Exposed footings of Whaler's Tavern, Great Island, Wellfleet, Mass. 46

10. Conjectural structure of Wellfleet Tavern. 47

11. Wall plaster samples, showing lath impressions. Wellfleet Tavern. 49

12. Isaac Allerton site, Kingston, Mass. 50

13. Re-created post-hole house at Plimoth Plantation. 53

14. James Hall's plan of Standish site, Duxbury, Mass. 54

15. Ground plan of John Alden site, Duxbury, Mass. 55

16. Ground plan of R.M. site, Chiltonville, Mass. 57

17. Detail of Edward Everett Square, Dorchester, Mass., showing original and present locations of the Blake house. 64

18. Division map of John Blake and the heirs of Josiah Blake, April 22, 1748, showing the Blake house and barn. 68

19. Blake house before removal to new site. 70

20. Blake house after removal to new site and restoration. 71

21. Detail of the Price-Burgis *South East View* of Boston, Mass., as revised in 1743, showing Trinity Church. 84

22. Detail of "paster" with tower of Trinity Church minus spire. 85

23. Trinity Church. Wood engraving by Abel Bowen. 86

24. Residence of John Hancock, Boston, Mass. 89

25. South elevation, Hancock house. 90

26. North elevation, Hancock house. 91

27. East elevation, Hancock house. 92

28. West elevation, Hancock house. 93

29. Ground plan, Hancock house. 94

30. Chamber floor plan, Hancock house. 95

31. Interior details, staircase and window, Hancock house. 96

32. Hancock house. Detail of fireboard painting of Park Street Church, Boston (c. 1812). 97

33. Front hall and staircase in the Hancock house. 98

34. The Washington Room in the Hancock house. 100

35. West elevation and plan of attic, E. W. Hooper house (1872), 25 Reservoir Street, Cambridge. 103

36. Plan of ground floor, E. W. Hooper house (1872), 25 Reservoir Street, Cambridge. 103

37. A. A. Carey house (1882), 28 Fayerweather Street, Cambridge. 104

38. Plan of A. A. Carey house (1882), 28 Fayerweather Street, Cambridge. 105

39. Chimney breast (1872), E. W. Hooper house.   106

40. Chimney breast (1882), A. A. Carey house.   107

41. Staircase newel post (1882), A. A. Carey house.   108

42. Bedroom shutters (1882), A. A. Carey house.   109

43. Old Ship Church Parish House, Hingham, Mass.   110

44. Massachusetts State Building (1893), Chicago World's Fair, 1893.   111

45. Balch house, Beverly, Mass.   127

46. Stanbury house (The Old Feather Store), Dock Square, Boston, Mass.   130

47. Cooper-Frost-Austin house, Cambridge, Mass.   133

48. Fairbanks house, Dedham, Mass.   136

49. Capen house, Dorchester, before removal to Milton, Mass.   139

50. Story house, Essex, Mass.   141

51. White-Ellery house, Gloucester, Mass.   142

52. Whipple house, Ipswich, Mass.   158

53. Whipple house, Ipswich, Mass.   159

54. Peak house, Medfield, Mass.   163

55. Philip English house, Salem, Mass.   173

56. Gedney house, Salem, Mass.   175

57. Parkman house, Salem, Mass.   178

58. Probate division of Turner estate, Salem, Mass., 1769.   181

59. Turner house, Salem, Mass.   182

60. Boardman house, Saugus, Mass.   185

Foreword

THIS volume is the first publication of the Colonial Society of Massachusetts to be issued since the death of Walter Muir White-hill on March 5, 1978. Yet even though he is not here to see the book in finished form, it is still very much his volume. From the very beginning, the idea of holding conferences on various aspects of Colonial history and then publishing the papers given at those conferences was Walter's. It is, therefore, most appropriate to present this volume to the Society and to the public in memory of him.

Walter was Editor of Publications for our Society from 1946 to 1978 and during that time saw to the publication of sixteen volumes of *Transactions* and *Collections*. One might suppose that he would have eased up during his last years as Editor, but nothing could be further from the truth, for the decade of the 1970's has been the most productive one in the history of our Society. Walter always said that Colonial Society publications came in bunches, like bananas; certainly this was true in the 1970's. During the years 1973, 1974, and 1975 seven volumes appeared—two conference volumes, two volumes of *The Journals of Ashley Bowen*, one volume of *The Notebook of the Reverend John Fiske*, and two volumes of Harvard College Records. Though the Society has published nothing since 1975, no less than ten projected volumes, all conceived by Walter, are in various stages of preparation. When these volumes appear and are added to those already published, the whole corpus will be striking evidence of Walter's extraordinary productivity in his last years.

This volume, *Architecture in Colonial Massachusetts*, is the fifty-first to be published by our Society. It contains seven of the eight papers delivered at the conference on Massachusetts Colonial architecture held on September 19–20, 1974, at the Society's house at 87 Mount Vernon Street and at the Club of Odd Volumes. In addition to these papers the book contains as well two Appendices with abstracts of

the history of important examples of early Colonial houses and transcriptions of seventeenth-century building documents. To plan the
conference and to edit the volume of papers that it produced, the
Society was fortunate in obtaining the services of our fellow-member
Abbott Lowell Cummings, currently Executive Director of the Society for the Preservation of New England Antiquities and the leading authority on the conference subject. Abbott Cummings' productivity in the field of Colonial architecture is not limited to the present
volume, however; this same year the Belknap Press of the Harvard
University Press will publish his study entitled *The Framed Houses of
Massachusetts Bay, 1625–1725*. Taken together, these two volumes rep-
resent a distillation of over thirty years of dedicated research in the
field of Colonial architecture, starting with a Master's thesis at Ober-
lin College in 1946 and continuing down to the present.

Our Corresponding Secretary, Sinclair Hamilton Hitchings, has
also made important contributions to this volume. After his retirement from the Boston Athenæum, Walter Whitehill was free to
travel frequently, both in this country and abroad. During his ab-
sences from Boston, he needed a deputy to carry on the editorial
work of the Society. This function Sinclair Hitchings has performed
with rare sensitivity to editorial problems. When it comes to awarding
credits for the excellence of this publication, Sinclair deserves a generous share.

I know how proud Walter would have been of this volume. Let
us hope that succeeding ones will maintain the high standard of editorial excellence that he set for our Society.

FREDERICK S. ALLIS, JR.
Editor of Publications

87 Mount Vernon Street
Boston, Massachusetts
January 1979

Introduction

THE celebration in 1930 of the founding of the Massachusetts Bay colony, three centuries earlier, created a flurry of antiquarian researches and some historical writing as well. Despite, however, the continuing achievements in seventeenth-century studies of such distinguished scholars as Samuel Eliot Morison and such organizations as the Massachusetts Historical Society which published the Winthrop Papers between 1929 and 1947, the real explosion of interest in our first century of settlement did not occur until the decades following the Second World War. Concurrently, the leadership role fell increasingly into the hands of a newer, younger generation of scholars, many of them in the academic world, and they in turn have sparked a widespread general interest in the seventeenth century at the graduate and undergraduate level.

The proliferation of studies and the dynamics of shifting emphases which have dramatically altered traditional nineteenth-century attitudes about seventeenth-century architecture are reflected in the papers presented in this volume. At the same time there are necessary and vital links with earlier traditions in the house biographies prepared by Stephen J. Roper and Edward Zimmer, in each case a summary of much more extensive research projects. Candidates for doctoral degrees in Boston University's American and New England Studies Program and thoroughly representative of the emerging younger generation of seventeenth-century scholars to which we have referred, these writers rival the impressive efforts of nineteenth- and early twentieth-century antiquarians who sought to verify building dates and delineate the social history of a given structure, and surpass them in that they bring to their subjects the advantage of a thorough and professionally acquired knowledge of New England architectural history. The documents in one sense, as will be seen from a glance at the Appendices which form part of the Editor's contribution to this volume, are meaningless unless an explicit relationship to the building can be traced in terms of style as revealed through physical evidence. In this respect, a review of earlier scholarship concerning the Royall house in Medford, followed by a reading of Arthur L. Finney's careful re-evaluation of structural and documentary evidence, will reveal at once how successive generations of students can be seriously misled in the historical interpretation of important buildings—until the record has been set straight.

Verification of the raw data which form the core of so many recent studies devoted to quantitative analysis (which is the subject of the Editor's essay dealing with the dating of First Period houses in Massachusetts) continues to be central to the advancement of our knowledge of the field. "Colonial archaeology," on the other hand, unpracticed by an earlier generation, has all the burgeoning force of a wholly new discipline. For the first time in New England's history we are beginning to come to grips in a direct, systematic way with those aspects of material culture which have not survived or have been subject to radical change. James Deetz in discussing certain of the earliest structures in the Plymouth Colony as revealed through archaeological excavation enlarges our understanding of buildings heretofore glimpsed only imperfectly if at all through glancing references in the documents and provides as well a disciplined outline of current methodology in Colonial archaeology. Geoffrey P. Moran presented to the conference an equally interesting progress report on the results of investigation of seemingly ephemeral and unrecoverable features of Salem's early waterfront. We shall look forward to a completed study of this subject in the not distant future.

Essays by the late James B. Peabody and Margaret Henderson Floyd are concerned also with a somewhat later period in Colonial history. The Hancock house in Boston has been a leading source of enlightenment and inspiration to the romanticist, to the student of architectural and social history, to the preservationist (for whom it furnishes one of the initial guideposts), and now, as Mrs. Floyd explains, to the architects of the Colonial Revival. In the process, John Hubbard Sturgis, who made the first recorded measured drawings of an historic American building, emerges as an evocative link between Colonial and nineteenth-century New England. In 1863 Arthur Gilman published in the *Atlantic Monthly* a significant sampling of the original documents associated with the building of the Hancock house which marked, perhaps, the earliest conscious realization for New England that a building, though destroyed, can remain a living force or at least be rendered meaningful to students through extensive documentation. This principle has been clearly demonstrated once again by Mr. Peabody in his study of both the voluminous written records and the slim and somewhat tantalizing visual documentation which survive for the first Trinity Church in Boston.

The various subjects presented in this volume may seem diverse, even unrelated in some respects—skipping from Anglican churches to post-hole houses. The connecting thread, however, is visible and strong: as we move into the final two decades of the twentieth century and recognize the awesome challenge to contemporary historians of that volume of material from the last two centuries which marks our life as an independent nation, it is unarguable, nevertheless, that the subject of Colonial studies has a profoundly important role to play and continues to inspire the most dedicated and increasingly skilled efforts of serious and well-disciplined students.

ABBOTT LOWELL CUMMINGS
Editor

ARCHITECTURE

IN

COLONIAL MASSACHUSETTS

◄•◦ STEPHEN J. ROPER ◦•►

The Early History of the Paul Revere House[1]

T HE Paul Revere House, like any building, can be considered
from a variety of points of view. To millions of schoolchildren,
the house has something to do with that fellow on horseback
who rode about shouting that the British were coming. To innumer-
able hardened sightseers, it's that funny little house on the Freedom
Trail that we couldn't get a photo of. But to the architectural historian, the Revere House is a tremendously important Colonial artifact.

And a building is an artifact—a product of the needs, desires, and
resources of the man for whom it was built. A building is not, however, a stable artifact. As time passes, needs change, owners sell out or
die off, and an old building is altered to suit new purposes. An older
building becomes a sort of palimpsest showing, in layers, the evi-
dences of the men who have used it.

Two of the primary tasks of the architectural historian are the separation and identification of the layers of cultural history found incorporated in the fabric of an important building. Only as these tasks

1. This paper is in large part a distillation of two research reports prepared for the
Paul Revere Memorial Association which remain in manuscript form: "History of
the Property of Paul Revere Memorial Association," by William Lebovich, 1973; and
"The Early History of the Paul Revere House, North Square, Boston," by this author, 1974. Both reports are heavily documented; copies of both are available for reference at the Society for the Preservation of New England Antiquities. Material
drawn from these reports will not be specifically footnoted here; footnotes will be
limited to the identification of the sources of direct quotations and the documentation
of material not included in either of the earlier reports. Readers interested in a structural analysis of the Revere House (as opposed to the documentary study summarized
here) are referred to two reports prepared for the Paul Revere Memorial Association
by Frederic C. Detwiller, Architectural Historian, Consulting Services Group, SPNEA:
"Paul Revere Association Properties, 19–31 North Square, Boston, Massachusetts, Ar-
chitectural-Historical Analysis," Feb. 1976; and "Paul Revere House, Structure Report," 2 vols., July 1976. Copies of both are available for study at SPNEA.

are completed can the architectural historian begin to understand the evidence presented by a building. Only when he understands a great number of buildings in this way can he begin the critical task of discovering relationships and hypothesizing mechanisms of change.

The Paul Revere House in Boston's North Square is doubly significant to the architectural historian. Besides being one of only a handful of surviving First Period dwellings originally built in urban rather than rural contexts, the Revere House is the only known wooden dwelling of the First Period still standing on Boston's Shawmut Peninsula. Potentially, then, the Revere House has much to tell us, not only about our earliest urban architecture, but also about the possible early role of Boston as a New England style center.

To date, however, the tremendous potential of the Revere House has been only partially tapped, the reason being that the earliest layers of the Revere House "palimpsest" have long resisted separation and identification. Estimates of the building's date of erection have ranged from 1650 to 1681.[2] While some authorities have thought that the original owner was John Jeffs, others, after more thorough research, have found the evidence inconclusive.[3] The exact original configuration of the building is also in doubt. Are the main house and the peculiarly angled ell the unified product of a single building campaign? Is the ell a fragment of an earlier house to which the larger section facing North Square was later added? Or is the ell, instead, a

2. Joseph Everett Chandler, the architect who restored the house in 1907–1908, speculated on purely physical evidence that the house was built sometime between 1650 and 1680. See his "Notes on the Paul Revere House," in the *Handbook of the Paul Revere Memorial Association* (Boston, 1950), p. 18. Later historians, benefiting from documentary research, have usually placed the date between 1676 and 1681. Among the most authoritative of these: Hugh Morrison, *Early American Architecture* (New York, 1952), pp. 59–62, says c. 1676; while Esther Forbes, *Paul Revere and the World He Lived In* (Boston, 1942), p. 169, Harold Comer Read, "A Brief History of the Paul Revere Memorial Association and the Paul Revere House," in the *Handbook of the Paul Revere Memorial Association* (Boston, 1950), p. 5, and Walter M. Whitehill, *Boston: A Topographical History*, 2nd ed. (Cambridge, Mass., 1968), p. 15, all say about 1680. Another recognized authority, Fiske Kimball, does not include the Revere House in his *Domestic Architecture of the American Colonies and the Early Republic*, reprint ed. (New York, 1966), presumably because it failed to meet his rigorous standards for documentation.

3. Forbes and Morrison both suggest John Jeffs as the original owner; Chandler, Read, and Whitehill hazard no guesses.

1. Paul Revere house, North Square, Boston, Mass., before restoration. Photo, Wilfred A. French, c. 1880, courtesy Society for the Preservation of New England Antiquities.

later addition to the main house? Each of these theories has been seriously advanced at one time or another.[4] While the single-build explanation is now favored by most experts, the validity of that theory has not been conclusively demonstrated; nor has it been shown that either of its rivals can be safely eliminated.

In an effort to shed some new light on these unsettled questions of date, original ownership, and original form, the Paul Revere Memorial Association has sponsored a program of intensive research into the early history of the Revere House. William Lebovich began the documentary portion of this research in 1972–1973, and I completed it the following year. While the documentary study has turned up little information concerning the building's original form,[5] it has produced relatively solid answers to the questions of date and original ownership. The documentary evidence in these two areas and the conclusions which it supports are the subject of this paper.

The architectural historian's first line of research is the title chain. A completed title will provide the names of the original and all subsequent owners of a property; it will usually establish a rough date for a building's erection, and it may provide clues to the dates of later remodelings. As the first step in the Revere House research project, William Lebovich undertook a thorough search of the property's title. Mr. Lebovich was able to run a solid chain of title back to November 2, 1681. On that day, Capt. Daniel Turell, Sr., anchorsmith, and Sgt. Thomas Walker, brickmaker, both of Boston, sold to the Boston merchant Robert Howard "All that peece of Land and the dwelling house that stands upon part therof Scituate at the North

4. Chandler, in his "Notes," suggests that the ell predates the main house; Morrison, in *Early American Architecture*, assumes the ell to have been a later addition; and the staff of SPNEA, in the two reports for the Paul Revere Memorial Association mentioned in note 1, assumed the main house and ell to have been built in one campaign. This was also the consensus reached by the approximately twenty members of the New England Chapter, Society of Architectural Historians, who examined the Revere House during a special meeting held there on Dec. 3, 1974.

5. What information was turned up on the question of original form supports the single-build theory (see note 21 and the section of text to which it pertains for a discussion of this material). A final answer to this question, however, will probably have to await either the discovery of some conclusive structural evidence in the house itself, or the development of a satisfactory dendrochronological sequence for New England, by which means the timbers in the two sections of the house can be accurately dated.

2. Paul Revere house, North Square, Boston, after restoration. Photo courtesy Society for the Preservation of New England Antiquities.

end of Boston near the New Meeting house."[6] At this point the title chain falters, and might have come to a premature end, save for the existence of one extremely important clue—the Rev. Increase Mather of the Second Church is said to have once lived on the Revere House site. Following this lead, Mr. Lebovich was able to locate a deed in which the Second Church purchased a house and land from one Anthony Chickley in 1670. The land described in this deed can be positively identified as the Revere House lot in North Square.

The discovery of the 1670 deed created an eleven-year gap in the title chain—a gap Mr. Lebovich was not able to fill. The land and probate records are silent concerning the links between the Second Church, which bought the Revere House lot in 1670, and Turell and Walker, who sold it in 1681. There is no recorded conveyance of the property out of the Second Church, no recorded conveyance of the property to either Turell or Walker, and no indication in the 1681 deed that Turell and Walker might have been acting as anything other than private individuals.

While the land and probate records provide no answers to our questions concerning the ownership of the Revere House property from 1670 to 1681, some rather convincing evidence has been discovered in other documentary sources. This evidence strongly indicates that the property was owned throughout this eleven-year period by the Second Church, and that Turell and Walker were acting on behalf of the church when they sold the property to Robert Howard in 1681. The evidence supporting these conclusions falls in two areas. That in the first area establishes that the Second Church owned the Revere House lot until at least November of 1676. That in the second establishes that Turell and Walker were both Second Church members, and very likely members of a church committee charged with negotiating the sale of the Revere House property in 1681.

The principal sources of evidence in the first area are the diaries and family records kept by the Rev. Increase Mather. Mather recorded the births of each of his ten children in the family Bible, noting in each case the house in which the child was born. The first four

6. Suffolk County Deeds, XIII, 86, Nov. 2, 1681, Turell and Walker to Howard.

children, born between 1662 and 1669, were all delivered in the house of John Cotton (Mather's father-in-law) where the family lived for eight years. The fifth child, however, born November 8/9, 1671, entered this world in "that house which was bought of Mr. Anth. Chickley."[7] This corresponds nicely with the Second Church's recorded purchase of the Chickley property in North Square in December of 1670.

The Chickley House was Mather's home for less than seven years. Though he records that his sixth child was born in this house in August of 1674, the next birth on Mather's list, that of Abigail in April of 1677, is described as having occurred in "that House which was Capt. Bredons formerly."[8] The family's removal to Thomas Bredon's house is graphically explained by the following entries in Mather's rough diary for 1676:

[November 27, 1676]
This was the Fatal and dismall day, when the Meeting House and Houses hereabouts, and mine amongst the Rest, were burnt with fire. The services of the day were such that I could doe nothing at my study. I and my wife and several of my children were kindly entertayned at Mr. Richards. The Lord reward him.

[November 29]
A.M. Time spent in drying my Bookes and taking care about another house et. P.M. Removed things to C. Bredons House.

[December 5]
Removed from mr. Richards to that House which was Capt. Bredons.[9]

The move to Capt. Bredon's was not a permanent solution. Exactly one year later, Increase Mather bought an empty lot on Hanover Street. Within a year, a house had been raised on this lot, and Mather's last three children were all born "in that House which was built for me."[10]

7. Increase Mather Family Records, in the John Cotton Bible, Special Collections (Massachusetts Historical Society).

8. Increase Mather Family Records.

9. Increase Mather, "Diary, 1675–6," Massachusetts Historical Society, *Proceedings*, 2nd ser., XIII (1900), 373–374.

10. Increase Mather Family Records.

In summation: as Increase Mather is known to have occupied the Chickley House at least as late as August of 1674; as there is no record of Mather buying any real estate or owning a house of his own before 1677; and, as there is no evidence to indicate that Mather moved out of the Chickley House before the fire of November 27, 1676, it is therefore assumed that the house from which the Mathers were driven by the fire was, in fact, the Anthony Chickley House. It should follow, then, that the Second Church owned the Chickley/ Revere House property until at least November 27, 1676.

The second body of evidence supports an attempt to close the eleven-year gap in the title chain from the opposite end. The goal here was to identify positively the individuals, Daniel Turell and Thomas Walker, and then to discover the relationship between them which led to their being co-grantors of the Revere House property in 1681. This has been accomplished; the critical relationship between the two appears to have been the active membership of each in the Second Church.

The identification of Capt. Daniel Turell, Sr., anchorsmith, was relatively simple. The only other man to bear the name in seventeenth-century Boston was the anchorsmith's son, who was usually identified as "Jr.," who seems never to have borne a military title, and who appears in the Colonial records chiefly as the alleged father of an illegitimate child. Daniel Turell, Sr., on the other hand, was a man of some prominence in early Boston, rising eventually to a captaincy in one of the military companies, and being voted a Selectman for a number of years.

Sgt. Thomas Walker, brickmaker, was not so easily identified. There were at least three, and possibly as many as six men who bore the name Thomas Walker in seventeenth-century Boston. After extensive genealogical research, the grantor of the Revere House property has been identified as the Thomas Walker, Jr., who married Susanna Collins in 1662, and who died a wealthy man in 1725/26. This particular Thomas Walker is the only one who fits all of the identifying characteristics supplied in the 1681 deed, and he also appears to have been the only one of that name active in Boston during the period between the late 1660's and the mid-1680's.

Once Turell and Walker had been identified as individuals, an attempt was made to relate them to the Revere House property and to each other. The results are strongly suggestive. I found no direct connection between the Revere House property and either man, save for the 1681 deed in which the pair sold it. There is no recorded conveyance of the property to either one. I found no deeds to properties adjoining the Revere House lot which named either Turell or Walker as abutters. I found nothing in any Boston town records, including tax records, to associate either man with any property in North Square. On the contrary, there is evidence in both land and tax records to indicate that Turell was living on the harborfront, and Walker next to the mill-pond, during at least part of the period in question. I did, however, find two ways in which Turell and Walker were related to each other. The two men were named in the 1678 will of Nathaniel Blague, brickmaker, as overseers of Blague's estate. Also, Daniel Turell, Sr., is known to have been, and the correct Thomas Walker almost certainly was a member of the Second Church in the 1680's.

The connection through Nathaniel Blague appears to have no direct bearing on the question at hand, as Blague does not seem to have been related to the Revere House property in any way. Blague's naming of his "very good friends Mr. Daniel Turin and Mr. Thomas Walker"[11] as overseers of his estate, however, does establish that Turell and Walker not only knew each other and shared at least one good friend, but that the two had worked together in a semi-official capacity at least once prior to the 1681 conveyance of the Revere House property.

The second connection between Turell and Walker is much more to the point. Capt. Daniel Turell, Sr., was an extremely active member of the Second Church from the 1670s on; a Thomas Walker, who is almost certainly the man we are interested in, became a member of that church in 1680. While Thomas Walker's name appears only infrequently in the Second Church records, Capt. Daniel Turell

11. Suffolk County Probate Records, New Series, II, 352, Dec. 12, 1678, will of Nathaniel Blague.

was regularly named to positions of responsibility within the church. Significantly, Turell's first major church appointment was to the committee of five brethren charged with rebuilding the meeting house after the disastrous fire of 1676. At a church meeting held in December of that year it was "Voted and agreed that Brother[?] Richards, Brother Collicot, Brother Philips, Brother Tyril, Brother Hudson, be appointed as a C[omm]ittee in order to the Rebuilding of a Meeting House, for the comfortable attending the Publick worship of god."[12] Turell must have proved his worth on this initial undertaking, for his name reappears on each of the several committees formed to supervise repairs to the new meeting house over the next two decades. These included a committee of four to see about either casing its roof with lead or adding a shingled roof in 1681, and a committee of three appointed in 1691 to "inspect the condition of the Meeting-House, as to any want of Repairs in it, and act accordingly."[13]

Daniel Turell's services to the Second Church were not limited to his participation on the various committees charged with overseeing the meeting house. At a church meeting held on January 15, 1678/79, the members voted that

Brother Turil, Brother [. . .]our and Brother Hudson should be desired to receive[?] the weekly Contribution, and dispose of it according to the churches order. Consequent to this vote it was declared that Deacon Philips should deliver the church Books, and what Moneys are in his hand belonging to the church unto the Brethren Mentioned Who were also desired to take care about providing for the Lords Table and to attend in [. . .] the bread and wine at the Administracon of the Lords Super.[14]

In essence, Capt. Daniel Turell was voted onto the "Board of Trustees" of the Second Church in 1678/79.

All of the foregoing evidence points strongly toward the following conclusion: that Capt. Daniel Turell, virtually a Trustee of the Second Church and a fixed member of its "property committee," and

12. "Records of the Second Church," MS, III (Massachusetts Historical Society).
13. "Records of the Second Church," MS, IV.
14. "Records of the Second Church," MS, III.

Thomas Walker, a church member who had worked with Turell before, were ideally suited to act as agents of the Second Church in the disposal of the Revere House property in 1681. I have found not one scrap of evidence which would contradict the conclusion that Turell and Walker were, in fact, acting as a committee of the Second Church in that transaction.

Given what is now known of the backgrounds of Turell and Walker; given the evidence presented by the Mather family records; and given the absolute lack of evidence to the contrary, I believe that it is safe to conclude that the Second Church owned the Revere House property continuously from 1670 to 1681. The gap in the title chain is thus closed.

This leaves us in a somewhat curious situation, for one now recalls that while the Anthony Chickley House burned in November of 1676, the 1681 deed to Robert Howard was to a piece of land "with the dwelling house" standing thereon. The inference must be that the Second Church was responsible for the erection of a new house on the Chickley lot sometime between November of 1676 and November of 1681. And, presumably, it is the skeleton of this new dwelling which survives as the original seventeenth-century core of the Paul Revere House.

Thus far we have established two major points: first, a dwelling house was erected on the Chickley/Revere lot sometime between November 27, 1676, and November 2, 1681; and second, this dwelling house must have been built at the direction of the Second Church, which owned the property throughout this five-year period. We have not established, however, what specific motive prompted the Second Church to erect this new building. The one which immediately suggests itself, that the new dwelling was built to replace the Chickley House as the residence of Increase Mather, has already been eliminated. Mather, as detailed above, removed first to Capt. Thomas Bredon's house, and then to a new house which he had built on Hanover Street. The Revere House, it seems, was not built for Mather's use.

A second plausible motive is suggested by the fact that ministerial duties in Puritan churches were divided between two men—a pastor to exhort, and a teacher to instruct. Given the magnitude of the 1676 fire (it destroyed about forty-five houses) there would appear to be a good chance that Mather's colleague at the Second Church was also burned out. If this were the case, the church might have built the new house for that minister's use. This motive, too, can be quickly eliminated—Increase Mather was the only minister of the Second Church between the retirement of John Mayo as pastor in 1673 and the ordination of Mather's son, Cotton, as teacher in 1685.[15] Even the suggestion that the church might have provided their retired pastor with a new house if his own had been destroyed can be easily dismissed—Mayo had moved from Boston to Barnstable in 1670 and he died on the Cape in May of 1676, six months before the great fire leveled North Square.[16]

With the two most obvious motives for the Second Church to have erected the Revere House thus removed, we are forced to consider some less obvious possibilities. Let us begin by recalling the situation faced by the Second Church at the end of 1676. The fire of November 27 had destroyed their meeting house, Mather's dwelling, and about forty-five other houses in the North Square area. Some seventy to eighty families were homeless. Many if not most of these people were undoubtedly members or attendants of the Second Church. In this situation, the church could have found at least two motives for the erection of a new house on the Chickley site: to bolster its overburdened treasury through the rent or sale of a new dwelling house, or to provide housing for some of its burned-out members. The two possibilities are not mutually exclusive; in fact, there is evidence to suggest that both may have figured in the Second Church's decision to rebuild on the Chickley site.

Support for a purely financial motive might be discovered in several places. To begin with, the Second Church is known to have built and rented several shops and tenements on church-owned land in Ship Street early in the eighteenth century. Knowing that the

15. Chandler Robbins, *A History of the Second Church, or Old North, in Boston* . . . (Boston, 1852), and Increase Mather, "Autobiography," American Antiquarian Society, *Proceedings*, LXXI, pt. II (1962), 300–301, 310.

16. Elna Jean Mayo, *Mayo Genealogy* . . . (Pueblo[?], Colo., 1963), pp. 2–3.

church initiated one early real estate development scheme, would it not be logical to suppose that it might have undertaken a somewhat similar project between 1676 and 1681? Consider, also, that Robert Howard paid the rather stiff price of £300 for his house and lot in 1681. From what is known of North End property values and construction costs in the 1670's and '80's, it appears that the Second Church either built a very expensive house, or realized a tidy profit on its redevelopment of the Chickley property.[17] It may have done both.

Concerning the second motive (the provision of housing for burned-out church members)—a small body of indirect evidence suggests that the Second Church may have built the new house in North Square specifically for a particular homeless member of its congregation—Robert Howard. This theory, which is based partly on Howard's known connections to the Second Church and to the North Square area, and partly on the surprisingly expensive character of the new house, is tantalizingly logical. The earliest evidence to support it is found in the fragmentary Boston tax lists of 1674. These indicate that as early as that year a Robert Howard was living on the western side of North Square.[18] There were only two known Robert

17. The contract for a house of comparable size built for John Williams in the North End in 1678/79 (published in the "Records of the Suffolk County Court, 1671–1680," pt. II, Colonial Society of Massachusetts, *Collections*, xxx [1933], 1125–1126) was taken at £130 "current mony of New England." Assuming the construction cost of the Revere House to have been roughly similar, that leaves perhaps £150–£170 of Howard's £300 purchase price to be accounted for by the value of the land and/or the profit of the church. It does not seem that the land alone could have been worth much more than £100–£125. Consider that the Revere House lot, as Howard purchased it in 1681, contained roughly 3000 sq. feet, with 30 feet of frontage on North Square. In comparison: in 1683, Howard purchased an adjoining interior lot containing about 4000 sq. feet with no buildings upon it, for £65 (Suffolk County Deeds, XIII, 84, July 19, 1683, Martin heirs to Howard); and, in 1689, Howard purchased the parcel next north of the Revere House, containing some 2000 sq. feet with a 20-foot frontage, *and with a dwelling house with leanto standing upon it*, for £110 "current money of New England" (Suffolk County Deeds, XXVIII, 182, May 22, 1689, Paine and Woodbry to Howard). The inference I am drawing is that land values on the west side of North Square were not particularly high in the 1680's; the Second Church seems to have gotten a pretty good price for its house and lot.

18. There is a very slight possibility that this man was lodging with Increase Mather; more probably, he was renting the house next north to Mather's. See pages 29–33 of my report to the Paul Revere Memorial Association for a thorough discussion of this point.

Howards in Boston in 1674—the merchant who later purchased the Revere House, and the man who was probably his father, a notary public. As the notary is clearly identified in these tax lists as residing in one of Boston's southern precincts, it is almost a certainty that the man living in North Square in 1674 was the same Robert Howard who bought the Revere House seven years later.

Now, surely, if Robert Howard, merchant, were living in North Square in the 1670s he would have been an attendant of the Second Church (whose meeting house stood across from his own front door, and of which he became a full member in 1682/83). Surely, he would have known Daniel Turell, Thomas Walker, and the other leaders of that church. If Howard were still living in North Square in 1676, then he was almost certainly burned out in the fire of November 27. Might Howard have signified to the leaders of the Second Church his desire to stay in the North Square area after the fire? Might he have even worked out with them an arrangement whereby the church would build and sell to him a new house on the site of Increase Mather's old one?

Further support for this theory can be found in the expensive nature of the house which the Second Church built. As remarked above, the £300 which Howard paid for this house and land seems notably high. Even allowing for the church to have made a substantial profit on the deal, a purchase price of £300 should indicate that the new house was a relatively large and elaborate one. This deduction is confirmed by the Boston tax schedules of 1687.[19] In this detailed listing of the taxes assessed in that year, about a thousand Bostonians were assessed under the heading "Houseing, Mills and Wharfs." While the inclusion of mills and wharfs, and the use of lump sum figures for the taxes of individuals owning more than one building, makes it difficult to determine the exact tax assessed against any particular dwelling house, this can be done in many instances. Such a figure, once determined, can be compared to the average tax levied

19. Boston Record Commissioners, *First Report: Boston Tax Lists etc., 1674–1694,* 2nd ed. (Boston, 1881), pp. 91–133, gives the complete 1687 tax schedules for all eight Shawmut precincts and the two outlying precincts at Muddy River and Rumney Marsh (now Brookline and Chelsea, but then parts of Boston).

against all assessed buildings (a highly approximate figure, I will admit) to obtain a rough indication of that particular dwelling's relative worth. This has been done for the Revere House and the results are quite revealing.

Prior to 1689, Robert Howard, merchant, is only known to have owned one building—the Paul Revere House. It is therefore assumed that the 20d. tax entered against Howard's name in the "Houseing, Mills and Wharfs" column in the 1687 tax schedules was figured solely on the value of the Revere House. In comparison, the average tax assessed under the "Houseing, Mills and Wharfs" head in 1687 was roughly 7d. Amongst the thousand-odd Bostonians assessed under this category, Robert Howard was one of only sixty-two (roughly 7% of the whole) whose assessments were listed at 20d. or higher.[20] And even amongst the members of this elite group there must have been many whose higher assessments resulted from the ownership of several buildings, none of which, individually, were taxed at anywhere near the 20d. which Howard paid on the Revere House.

All of this evidence supports the conclusion that the Paul Revere House was one of the finer houses of its day in Boston. Would the Second Church have undertaken the construction of such a house on pure speculation?[21] I rather doubt it. I suspect, instead, that the church

20. I included the figures from Muddy River and Rumney Marsh in my calculation of the town-wide average tax figure, but I purposely left out the Precinct 6 figures, as there seems to have been some confusion in those records. (The figures in the "Acres" and the "Houseing, Mills and Wharfs" columns appear to have been reversed in some sections of Precinct 6.) The deletion of the Precinct 6 figures lowered the total number of individuals taxed for buildings by perhaps 150–170, and similarly lowered the total of those taxed 20d. or more by about 20. If these dubious Precinct 6 figures had been included, they would have had a negligible effect on the 7d. average tax-assessed figure, and would have raised the percentage of individuals taxed 20d. or more by about one percentage point.

21. As a check against the possibility that Howard might have bought a rather modest house from the Second Church and then radically enlarged or improved it between 1681 and 1687, an attempt was made to determine which of the thirty-two other individuals assessed for exactly 20d. under the "Houseing, Mills and Wharfs" head in 1687 could be satisfactorily demonstrated to have owned just one dwelling house in the late seventeenth century. An attempt was then made to establish the price that each of these individuals had paid for that specific house and lot. I am reasonably confident that this procedure has succeeded in two instances—those of William Coleman in Precinct 1, and Isaac Walker in Precinct 3. Coleman purchased his house and land for £260 "current money of New England" in 1679 (Suffolk County Deeds,

built the house for a specific client—one who could afford to pay a premium price for a large and fashionable dwelling. While the identity of this supposed client is far from certainly known, the leading candidate can only be Robert Howard.

So, while the documentary evidence has identified the Second Church as the original owner of the Revere House, it has also suggested that the church may have erected the building with the specific intention of selling it to Robert Howard. If this is so, then it must be presumed that Howard was actively involved in determining the size, layout, finish, and all of the other myriad details involved in the construction of the house. In fact, if this line of reasoning is correct, it may have been Howard, rather than any committee of the Second Church, who exercised that direct control of the design and construction process which is the normal role of the original owner. It just might be that Robert Howard, who purchased the Revere House in 1681 and lived in it until his death thirty-six years later, was the single individual most responsible for the original seventeenth-century character of the Paul Revere House. Who, then, was Robert Howard?

"Robert Howard, of Boston, merchant." The name appears here and there among the Colonial records of Boston; never a description of the man, never very much information in any one place, but enough bits and pieces to begin to sketch the character of a highly successful seventeenth-century merchant. The sketch lacks depth, for very little is known of Robert Howard before 1681. We know that by that date he was married, had at least one child, and was living in Boston. It appears that he was the son of Robert Howard of Dorchester, later of Boston, a notary public, but this is not certain. Of the rest of the merchant's background, virtually nothing is known.

In fact, Robert Howard doesn't really emerge from the documents as an individual until the mid-1680's. The image which forms then is

---

XII, 24, Sept. 29, 1679, Thacher heirs to Coleman), and Walker paid £300 "lawful money of New England" for his in 1675 (Suffolk County Deeds, IX, 187, May 5, 1675, Edwards to Walker). These prices are right in line with the £300 "current money of New England" paid by Howard, and suggest that, in 1687, Howard's house remained largely as constructed by the Second Church.

primarily that of an active and prosperous merchant. Though Howard in his later years rose to positions of prominence within both the Second Church and Boston's town government, these appear as short-lived incidents—society's marks of respect offered to a man who had spent most of his life in the successful pursuit of commercial gain. Briefly, then, I will summarize what is known of Howard's commercial affairs.

Surviving documentary evidence indicates that Robert Howard was one of late seventeenth-century Boston's principal West Indies traders. He had particularly strong connections in Barbadoes, and did a considerable business in Antigua and Jamaica as well. He is also known to have traded to Newfoundland, Amsterdam, and Virginia, but apparently with less frequency. He may have increased his transatlantic ventures in the late 1690's, for he is known to have registered a number of large, ocean-going vessels just at the turn of the century.

The cargoes carried on Howard's vessels remain largely unknown. Specific mention is made only of logwood (the source of a dye) carried from the West Indies to Amsterdam, rum from Barbadoes to Boston, and tobacco from Virginia to Newfoundland. There is strong evidence that he dealt in fish, and at least one indication of an interest in the New Hampshire ships-timber trade.

Through the Bailyns' analysis of the surviving portion of the Massachusetts Shipping Register (covering the period 1697–1714) we are able to establish Howard's relative position among the maritime traders of late seventeenth-century Massachusetts. Of the 332 individuals who owned shares in the 171 vessels comprising the Massachusetts fleet of 1698, only 17 invested in more than 4 vessels—Robert Howard was one of those seventeen. The Bailyns went on to compute a "total-tonnage-per-owner" figure for sixty-nine of the leading investors. These figures show Robert Howard tied for the ninth-largest tonnage-interest in the 1698 fleet. And, finally, the Register shows that Howard invested in four new vessels in 1699, including two large ships of 100 and 110 tons. If the Bailyns had been able to analyze the Massachusetts fleet at the end of 1699, they might well have found that Robert Howard was one of the five heaviest investors in it.

Howard's business success allowed him to enjoy luxuries unavailable to most of his fellow townsmen. While most Bostonians, then as now, probably raised bitter complaints about the taxes on their real estate, Robert Howard was one of a relatively small handful of seventeenth-century Bostonians who could also complain about the taxes on his trade, his cow, his horse, and his Negro servants. By 1687, the man was ranked among the top 2% of Boston's taxpayers. Robert Howard was distinctly well-off.

In light of Howard's prominence as a merchant, it is perhaps surprising that absolutely nothing has come to light concerning his political views. His terms as Selectman (1702–1704) are his only known (and quite uneventful) ventures into politics at any level. Though Howard signed a number of petitions concerning fish, shipwrecks, convoys, and the prevention of fire, he is not known to have come out on either side of any of the important contemporary political issues. In only two instances did he even come close to taking a political stand. First, he evaded the Navigation Acts (but so, presumably, did nearly every other Colonial merchant). And second, he was on the jury which acquited Increase Mather of slandering Edward Randolph in 1687. It appears, however, that Randolph didn't have much of a case, and Howard might well have been predisposed to favor his own minister against the despised Collector of Customs whether he agreed with Mather's politics or not.

In conclusion, the picture which emerges of Robert Howard is that of an active and highly successful merchant. Politically cautious, he apparently believed that the surest way to survive in Colonial Boston was to mind one's own business. Respected by his townsmen, Howard was chosen Selectman for several years, and sat on at least two committees to arbitrate differences among them. A staunch member of the Mathers' congregation, he served on a number of church committees and was named, essentially, a Trustee of the Second Church toward the end of his life.

So there the case rests. A fairly solid body of evidence indicates that the Revere House was built sometime between 1676 and 1681 upon the orders of the Second Church. A less substantial body of evidence suggests that the church was acting in accordance with an agreement made with the wealthy merchant Robert Howard. Although these conclusions cannot be regarded as definitive, they are the end product of two years of intensive documentary research. I believe that they come very close to the truth about the early history of the Paul Revere House.

◀◦ ARTHUR L. FINNEY ◦▶

The Royall House in Medford: A Re-Evaluation of the Structural and Documentary Evidence

IT has long been thought that the Royall House in Medford was enlarged to its present size approximately ten years after the death of Isaac Royall, Sr., in 1739 by his son, Isaac Royall, Jr.[1] Isaac Royall, Sr., had moved from Maine to Antigua in the West Indies in the first quarter of the eighteenth century. He made a fortune in sugar, rum, and in the slave trade, and produced both a son Isaac, Jr., and a daughter Penelope (who became Mrs. Henry Vassall of Cambridge). Owing not only to a succession of poor crops, but chiefly because he wished his children to be educated in a different climate, he bought Ten Hills Farm in 1732, the 600-acre property which had once belonged to Gov. John Winthrop in what was then Charlestown. On the estate was a two-and-one-half-story brick farmhouse, erected either by Mrs. Peter Lidgett who acquired the property in 1677, or by Lt.-Gov. John Usher who succeeded to the title in the 1690's.

According to tradition, Isaac Royall engaged his brother, a merchant of Boston, to supervise the construction of his mansion. The farmhouse was used as the nucleus, and the brick end wall on the south side of the present mansion shows clearly its original outlines (Fig. 3). The rest of the bricks used were made of the fine clay from the banks of the river, which was used until recently in extensive brickworks in Medford.

---

1. Fiske Kimball, *Domestic Architecture of the American Colonies and of the Early Republic* (New York, 1922), pp. 283–284.

3. Front facade and south brick end of the Royall house, Medford, Mass., showing outline of earlier building. Photo, Arthur C. Haskell, 1934, courtesy Society for the Preservation of New England Antiquities.

Royall was constrained by the ceiling heights of the farmhouse, and by the narrowness of the hallway, which, according to the elegance of the carved detail and the elaborate staircase, would otherwise have inspired more spaciousness. But in his extension of the structure beyond the thick rear wall of the farmhouse, he heightened the West Parlor ceiling in a manner better suited to the sophisticated architectural detail, thus requiring a step up into the "Marble Chamber" above it. The designation "Marble Chamber," found in the 1739 inventory of the house, refers unquestionably to the painted marbleizing of the woodwork, in addition to which fragments of a

4.   Garden facade, Royall house. Photo courtesy Society for the Preservation of New England Antiquities.

hand-painted leather covering were found on the walls above the dado. The carving in this room is the work of a highly skilled craftsman.

The exterior facades are remarkable examples of the Georgian style, doubtlessly inspired by the imported English architectural books of the day. The east front is clapboarded and the windows heavily framed with handsome moldings. The series of windows on each side of the three floors were given a columnar effect, tied together by broad flat panels, unique, I believe, in Colonial New England architecture, but known to have precedents in English Georgian architecture.

The west facade, facing what was originally a cobbled courtyard with an elaborate garden beyond it, is a superb example of rustication, flanked by broad fluted pilasters, surmounting tall paneled plinths. The first- and second-floor windows are pedimented, and the wide door is surmounted by an arched pediment (Fig. 4). The whole effect is Palladian. As the date of the building of the west facade had been subject to question—some having claimed that it was actually an enlargement by Isaac Royall, Jr., of a pre-existing leanto attached to the original brick farmhouse (Fig. 5)[2]—it was decided, at the advice and under the actual supervision of Abbott Lowell Cummings, to settle the question through an examination of the underlying construction. At a point of junction with the level of the presumptive leanto, a beveled block of the rustication was carefully removed disclosing that the entire three-story wall of the west facade as it now stands is of one build. The construction is, in fact, somewhat unusual, if not ingenious. Massive studs infilled with brick and clay in a continuing seventeenth-century tradition form the underlying structure of the wall, to which wide horizontal sheathing boards have been nailed. Overlying the sheathing at regular intervals are narrow vertical furring strips to which, in turn, the two-inch-thick rustication has been affixed. In this way the builders have provided (and apparently with conscious deliberation) for circulation of air which may well be the reason why the rustication is now, some two hundred and thirty

2. Ibid., p. 39.

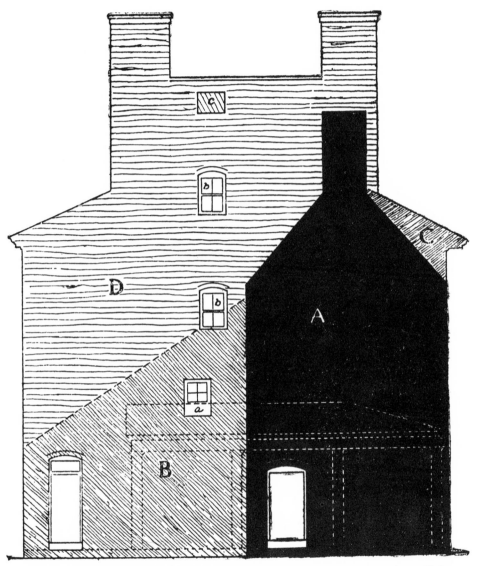

5.   Schematic evolution of the Royall house prepared by John H. Hooper. *The Medford Historical Register*, III (1900), 142.

6. Frontispiece in the Ionic order. Plate XXIII, William Salmon, *Palladio Londinensis* (London, 1734).

7. Detail of frontispiece, garden facade of the Royall house. Photo, Mary H. Northend Collection, courtesy Society for the Preservation of New England Antiquities.

years later, in such uniformly sound condition. The chief grounds for supposing that the wall of the west facade had been raised was a statement in 1900 by the local historian, John H. Hooper. On either side of the west entrance, he reported, there were cracks caused by the shrinkage of finish around the door which revealed "underneath the panel work that now forms the outside of the present building . . . the ends of clapboards that once formed the outside" of the presumptive leanto wall.[3] There is no such evidence now, and no trace of clapboards or an earlier wall were found when the wall was opened. One must assume that Mr. Hooper was incorrect in his interpretation of whatever it was he observed through the "cracks" around the entrance.

When, then, was the west facade completed, and is it contemporary with the east or street facade? The answer is to be found in the documents. The house required four or five years to remodel, and in 1737 the Royalls came to live in it. They brought with them from Antigua at least thirteen slaves, who according to tradition lived in the brick "Out Kitchen" built at the same time as the mansion, although the 1739 inventory indicates that some of the slaves slept in the main house. In 1739 Isaac Royall, Sr., died only two years after moving into the house. As was customary at the time, a most complete inventory was made and filed, and it is on the basis of this inventory which describes all major rooms in the house as it now stands that we can safely hypothesize, in conjunction with the structural evidence, the completion before 1739 of both facades. The west entrance, incidentally, is almost certainly modeled on plate XXIII of William Salmon's *Palladio Londinensis*, which had just been published in London in 1734 (Figs. 6–7). The inventory is thorough and of such importance that it has seemed wise to include a complete transcription of the document as an appendix to this paper.

Isaac Royall, Jr., lived on in the house after his father's death, becoming an important and well-liked citizen of Medford. Each Sunday he drove in his coach-and-four to King's Chapel in Boston. It

3. John H. Hooper, "The Royall House and Farm," *The Medford Historical Register*, III (1900), 143.

was on a spring Sunday in 1775 that General Gage confronted him with the refusal to allow him, as a Loyalist, to return to his Medford property which was within the rebel lines. Consequently he went to Salem, then to Halifax, and eventually to England. Although he was most anxious to return to his home in Medford, he was never able to do so. His affection for New England was shown by the provision in his will which led to the creation of the Royall Professorship of Law at Harvard.

On Royall's departure, the estate was confiscated by the General Court. The house was used during the early months of the Revolution as headquarters for Generals Stark, Lee, and Sullivan, and was visited by General Washington for consultations with them. After the Revolution, General Washington's secretary, Colonel Cary, bought the property and lived in it for two years. The house then passed through several hands, and in 1811 was bought by Mrs. Jacob Tidd, the sister of William Dawes who had, like Paul Revere, ridden to give warning in Middlesex County of the approach of British troops on the night of April 18, 1775. Mrs. Tidd's family was so large that it was necessary to extend the house toward the north. As old photographs show, this was a large addition, built without the slightest concern for architectural integrity (Fig. 8); it was later destroyed by a fire that stopped short of damaging the eighteenth-century house.

In the late nineteenth century the house fell into sad disrepair, but was purchased by Miss Kate Gear, from whom it was bought in 1908 by the Sarah Bradlee Fulton Chapter, Daughters of the American Revolution. The Royall House Association was then established, and has maintained it ever since. A 1912 article in *The Medford Mercury* concerning the restoration that was then under way noted that many fireplaces had been bricked up to accommodate stoves. Marble mantels had been installed; on removing these and the bricks, original Delft tiles were discovered (though those in the West Parlor were introduced at the time of restoration). Through volunteer work, the Association has furthered the work of restoration and preservation of the Royall House, and has acquired very choice furnishings of the period in order to bring the rooms back as closely as possible to their eighteenth-century appearance.

8. Front facade with later wing, Royall house. Heliotype opposite p. 119, Samuel Adams Drake, *Historic Fields and Mansions of Middlesex* (Boston, 1874).

The formal garden beyond the courtyard was noted for its beauty. A long allée led due west. The focal point was an octagonal gazebo, mounted on two circular terraced levels, under which ice was stored. The structure consisted of seven arched windows and an arched door, all flanked by fluted pilasters with Ionic capitals; the roof was a graceful bell-shaped dome, surmounted with a cupola. Above was a carved wooden life-sized figure of Mercury which the Association now displays nearly intact. It stood on one foot, and may conceivably have been mounted to turn as a weather vane. A photograph and two watercolors of the complete gazebo made before its demolition indicate that it must have been an outstanding garden structure. One wall of the gazebo has been preserved by the Sarah Bradlee Fulton Chapter, D.A.R., and stands in the present garden as a memorial to General Washington.

An Inventorey of the Estate of Isaac Royall Esqr taken by us the Subscribers this twenty Ninth Day of July 1739[4]

In the Best Room (viz)

1 peer Looking Glass	55: 0:0
1 p^r Large Sconsces	60: 0:0
a marvel table wth Iron frames	35: 0:0
2 p^r brass Armes @ 40/	4: 0:0
a Jappaned tea table	7: 0:0
a Sett of Cheney for the Same	13: 0:0
a Large mahogeney table	10: 0:0
a Small Ditto	7: 0:0
a Doz of wallnut Chares wth Leather bottomes	30: 0:0
a p^r of brass And Irons	3: 0:0
a fier Shovel & tonggs	1: 0:0
a Turkey Carpitt	40: 0:0

265

In the Front Room Next to medford

1 peer Looking Glass	55: 0:0
1 Sconce	15: 0:0
1 mahogeny tea table	3: 0:0
a parcell of Cheney for the Same	3: 0:0
a Black wallnut Desk	6: 0:0
an Easey Chear Covered wth Blew	7: 0:0
a Green Cheney Bead	30: 0:0
1 wallnut Cheare	2:10:0
1 doz burnt Cheney plats	7: 0:0
1 doz of blew and white D^o	6: 0:0
3 Cheney Dishes @ 60/	9: 0:0
2 Small Cheney Bowles	2:15:0
1 Glass Decanter	10:0
1 Coffe mill	1: 0:0
a Case of Bottles Small	1: 0:0

4. Middlesex County Probate Records, 1st ser., docket no. 19545.

1 doz burnt Cheaney plats	7: 0:0
8 Cheney Dishes @ 30/	12: 0:0
1 fruit plate	10:0
6 wine Glasses & Nine tumblers	3: 0:0
1 Iron back	2
5 Custard Cups 3/	15:0
2 blew and white Cheney Dishes	3: 0:0
6 Cheney Salvers	3: 0:0
1 p^r Brass Armes	2: 0:0
1 Glass Salver	1:10:0
	183:10:

In the Dineing Room

a Large Sconce	£30: 0:0
a Mahogoney table	8: 0:0
1 Smal ditt^o	5: 0:0
8 Leather Chears 25/	10: 0:0
a wooden Arm Chear	10:0
1 p^r Brass And Irons	3: 0:0
a fier Shovel and tonggs	1: 0 0
2 p^r brass arms 40/	4: 0 0
2 fowling pices @ £7	14: 0 0
1 Iron back	2: 0:0
1 doz of burnt Cheney plats	7: 0:0
1 Glass Decanter	2:6
2 Glass Salts	8:0
1 Tubler [sic]	4:0
1 p^r of tobacco tonggs	1: 0 0
	86: 4 0

In the Star Case 1 Clock	60: 0:0

In The Marble Chamber

1 Sconce	30: 0:0
a Crimson Silk Damask Bed wth Counterpin feather bead Bolster Blankets Sheets & pillow wth an Easey Chear of the Same & Cushing	200: 0:0
3 wallnut Chears	7:10:0
a Turkey Carpet	30: 0 0
1 p^r brass arms	2: 0 0
a blew hair trunck	3: 0 0
a Feather Bed	10 0 0
	282:10:0

In The Blew Chamber

a Blew Cheney Bed wth Feather Bed &^a	40: 0
1 mahogoney Chest of Draws and Chamb^r table	60: 0 0
1 Large Sconce	30: 0:0
1 Small Ditto	15: 0 0
2 Chairs	10:0
	145:10:0

In the Green Chamber. viz

1 Large Sconce		30: 0:0
1 Dresing Glass		9: 0 0
a Bewro table		10: 0 0
a Red Cheney Bed wth feather Bed &^a		40: 0:0
1 p^r Blankets		4: 0:0
11 p^r Sheets @ 5£		55: 0 0
1 p^r of New holland D^o		12: 0 0
1 p^r Old D^o		3: 0 0
17 Dowlass pillowbeers @ 7/		5:19:0
6 holland D^o	15/	4:10:0
5 Blankets	20/	5: 0 0
1 Rugg	40/	2: 0:0
1 Sealskin trunck		12:0
1 Leather D^o		10:0
		181:11 0

In the Kitching Chamber.

1 Looking Glass		8: 0:0
1 p^r Andjrons Shovel & tonggs		2: 0 0
a Cloeths horse		1: 0 0
a Close Stool		1:10:0
3 Chares		10 0
a Seal Skin trunck 12/ a Leather D^o 12/		1: 4:0
2 Negros Beds and Beding @ 40/		4: 0 0
a pine table & folding Board		2: 0 0
2 brushes		8:0
1 doz Diaper table Cloths		36: 0 0
5 D^o @ 10/		2:10 0
6 Breakfast D^o		4:10:0
6 Damask knapkins @ 10/		3:
9 ordinary D^o	5/	2: 5:0
12 towells	5/	3: 0 0
		71:17:0

In The Spinning Garrat

2 Bedsteds	1:10:0
a Spinning wheel	15:0
2 feather beads Small	10: 0:0
a Negro bed Gradle [sic] & two Blankets	3: 0:0
an Ovel Table	2: 0 0
	17:05:0

In the Front Garrats. viz

7 blanketts	10:10:0
1 Rugg	4: 0:0
1 Ditto	4: 0 0
1 Old Chest	13:0
1 Bedsted pillow & Bolster	6:
1 Small Glass	1:10:0
1 Bed and Bolster	10: 0:0
1 turkey Carpit	10: 0 0
1 Chest	2: 0 0
1 Small Bed Blanketts and Sheets	6: 0:0
1 Bedsted	1:10:0
4 Chears	8:6
1 fier Shovel and tongs	1: 0:0
	57:13 6

In the Kitching

a Large table	3: 0 0
a warming pan	4: 0:0
a Jack and furniture	8: 0:0
a Brass Stand for plates	2: 0 0
1 Iron Chafeing Dish & Stove	1:10:0
a Bread Toaster	8
a brass Chaffin Dish	1: 0 0
2 Bellmettle Skilletts	3:10 0
1 p^r Bellows	5:0
1 p^r Andjrons	1:10 0
fier Shovel tongs fender & Slice	1: 5:0
an Iron Dripping pan	3:
a Large Bellmettle Skellet	4: 0 0
One Iron pott & Kettle & tramle	2:
17 Brass Candlesticks & Snuffers	3: 0 0
a Brass flower Box	8:0

a Brass Candle Box	1:10 0
2 tin Dish Covers 2 Cake pans & 1 tin pudding pan	1:10 0
1 Iron Skillet	10 0
2 Gridjrons	1: 5:0
1 Spitt and wheele	15:0
a Brass Skummer & Ladle	1: 0 0
6 Chairs @ 3/6	1: 1:0
1 p^r Small Stilliards	10 0
1 Copper Kettle w^t 46^lb @ 5/	11:10 0
1 Brass D° 39	6: 0 0
1 Large Iron D°	4: 0 0
1 Small Iron pott	10 0
2 Iron tramells @ 15/	1:10:0
1 frying pan	1: 5:0
1 Iron Kittle	1
1 Churn	1
a percell of tubbs tables & Stools and Other wooden ware	5: 0 0
1 p^r Anjrons & tonggs & Slice	3: 0 0
a wartering pot	15:0
18 milk pans	18:0
5 Negroes Beds and Beding	15: 0:0
115 [lb.] pewter @ 4/6	25:17:6
1 Iron bar	15:0
	124:17:6
609½ oz of plate @ 30/	914: 5:0

a Cattalogue of Books

Echard^s Hist^r England	1 Vol.	2: 0:0
Rapins D°	2 Vol.	12: 0:0
Chambrs's Dictionary	2	20: 0:0
Tiletsons works	3:	10: 0:0
Malls Gephey [sic]	1	3: 0 0
Burnits Hist.	2:	8: 0 0
Locks works	3:	8:10 0
Hist of knights of Malta	2:	1:10 0
Prallaves [sic] works	2:	2: 0 0
taylors Life and Deth of the Holey Jesus	1	3: 0:0
Falthams Resolves		12:0

Tacitus	2 Vol	1: 5:0
province Lawbook		1:10.
Burnetts Hist Reformaton	2	1: 5
Tryall Earl macklesfield		1: 0:0
Lawrances Agrevelture [sic]		15:0
Duke of malboroughis Life	3:	1:10 0
Sences morralls		1: 0 0
Spectale [sic] of Nature	3:	1:16:0
Ground Reson of the Christian Relidgon		12 0
Defence of Christianity		10 0
Vindication of D^o	2 Vol	1:10:0
Doct^r Souths works	6	5: 0 0
Establishment of Brittans		
among ye Gauls	2 Vol	1: 0 0
Hist. of the Revolutions of		
ye Romans Republick	2 Vol.	1:10 0
Hist. of ye Revolution of portugal		12
Shakespears works	3 Vol^s	2: 0:0
Religeous Phylosephers	1 & 3 Vol^s	1:10 0
Life and Hist^r of Lewis 14th	2 Vol	1:10
Doct^r Bulls works	2 Vol	1:10:0
Bradly's agraculture	4	2: 8:0
Sr Wm Temples Letters to y^e		
king	3	1: 0 0
Reign of Quen Ann		12 0
mortimors art Husbandry		10:0
Travels of Robert morden		10
Bocrhaves [sic] Elements of Chemistry		3: 0:0
Gazetteers		15:0
Wilsons Tregenometry		10 0
Euclids Elements		1: 0 0
Princes Crenolegy	2 Vol.	12 0
Catos Letters	4 Vol^s	2: 0:0
Phillips way of teaching		6:0
Ancient & modern Languages		10:0
Life of Doct^r Ball		5:0
Roman Hist^r	5 Vol.	3:10:0
Clarendens Hist^r of Civil		
wars	6	6: 0 0
present State of Grate Brittane	2.	18:0
Hist^r Europe		10:0
Sydenhams works		1: 0:0

Baxters Infant Babtism	3 :0
Hist^r Europe in 1705	15 :0
Continuation of morning Exersise	15 :0
Littletons Dictionary	2:10 0
works of the Author of the hole Duty of man	4: 0 0
Country Justice	1: 0 0
Hugh Grotious on War & peace	6 0
Shaftsburys works 3 Vol.	3: 0 0
	136: 0:0

Cattle viz

20 Cows @ £10	200: 0:0
2 bulls 8	16: 0 0
1 Steere	12: 0 0
2 Yoak Oxen 28	56: 0:0
2 heffers 7	14:
4 Calves 2	8: 0:0
a mair & 2 Colts	20: 0:0
5 Score Sheep @ 18	90: 0:0
1 Cart horse 16	16: 0:0
14 Swine 2	28: 0:0
4 Coach horses	200: 0:0
a Charriot and 2 p^r harnesses	300: 0:0
2 Carts	12: 0:0
9 Negro Men Named Fortune, Barron Peter, Ned, house peter, Robin, Quamino, Cuffe, Smith, Phillip	900: 0:0
4 Negro Women Named Ruth, Trace, Sue, & Ionto,	300: 0:0
	2172: 0:0

Dwelling house	4000: 0:0
Out Kitching	200
Pidgen house	50. 0.0
Corn hous	100 0 0
Coach house and Stable	200: 0 0
2 old Barns	100: 0 0
1 New barn	200: 0:0
1 Old D^o	60 0 0
Clevelands house & Barn	600: 0.0
2 Smal D^o of Cleavland	500: 0 0

532 Acres of Land @ 35£	17620	[sic]
42 Acres of wood Land	600	0 0
13 Acres D° @ 12£	166	0 0
	24396:	0:0
	£ 29094:	3:6

The Execut^{rs} now add
One large boat   £150
1 Garding Stone   6
Sam.^{ll} Cary ⎫
Jn^a Foye   ⎬ Apprizers
James Russell ⎭

◄◊ JAMES DEETZ ◊►

Plymouth Colony Architecture: Archaeological Evidence from the Seventeenth Century

T HE contribution which archaeology may make to the study of early vernacular structures in New England is of a limited but very special nature. By its very definition archaeology deals only with that part of any building which was either below ground or which would leave evidence within the ground to be recovered and studied by the archaeologist. Such a limitation immediately rules out a major portion of the data normally used by students of early buildings. On the other hand, the archaeological remains of buildings are much more durable and less subject to loss over time as long as the site on which they are located is not disturbed. Furthermore, there is some evidence in the ground for structures earlier than those which have somehow survived the passage of time, and, in the Plymouth area, for buildings quite different from any known on the basis of surviving examples.

There are no standing structures known in the area that was Plymouth Colony which can be confidently dated to the first half of the seventeenth century, and only a few which might be assigned to the third quarter of that century. As a result, study of the earlier building traditions of the Old Colony has always had to rely on documentary evidence of a variety of types, from references to buildings or parts of them in the court records to a rich body of probate data which at least gives a feeling for the number and uses of rooms in these early dwelling houses. Within the past twenty-five years, an increasing interest in the archaeological study of Plymouth Colony has resulted in the excavation of some twenty-odd sites, some of which have produced architectural data of a limited but unique nature. This paper

43

will examine these data and demonstrate how they shed additional light on the story of architectural development in the Old Colony and raise new questions.

The precise form of archaeological evidence of an architectural nature can be thought of in terms of both its *focus* and its *visibility*. By focus is meant the degree to which archaeological features can be read clearly and unambiguously. The visibility of an archaeological feature is primarily a function of the quantity of material which is observed. Some examples will make these concepts clear. A house which was occupied briefly and had no later modifications might leave a set of footings, chimney base, and cellars to be excavated by the archaeologist. Such a feature has clear focus as well as high visibility. On the other hand, if the structure had no cellars, and footings which were set on the ground and later removed, its visibility would be much less to the archaeologist, consisting only of a chimney base as an archaeological feature. Houses which underwent successive builds, with walls cutting walls, might have a very high visibility, but the focus of the feature would be quite low, having been affected by later developments. Factors which affect both focus and visibility fall into three broad classes; duration of occupation, manner of destruction or removal, and type of construction. Generally speaking, longer occupations lead to higher visibility and poorer focus. Houses which burned in place have sharper archaeological focus than those which were moved or dismantled. Construction which intrudes below grade enhances both focus and visibility. The ideal feature for archaeological study would be a house which was built with wall trenches, deep chimney base, and cellars, was occupied for a relatively brief time, and was not added to in any way, and which burned in place. The least useful type of feature would be the remains of a house which was occupied briefly, had no cellars or other below-ground features, and was systematically dismantled in situ, with all of its building materials carted off for reuse elsewhere. Sites of both extreme types and intermediate forms have been excavated in the Plymouth Colony area.

From an architectural standpoint, the two most significant sites to have been excavated in the Old Colony are a whaler's tavern located on Great Island, Wellfleet, Massachusetts (Ekholm and Deetz, 1971), and the Isaac Allerton dwelling house in Kingston, Massachusetts. One is of late seventeenth-century date and of specialized function, the other is the earliest single source of archaeological architectural information thus far studied from Plymouth.

The whaler's tavern on Great Island was excavated by a Plimoth Plantation archaeological party during the summers of 1969 and 1970. In terms of both focus and visibility this site is the most productive yet to be studied. While its period of use coincides in part with a time from which we have standing structures elsewhere in the Plymouth Colony area, the date of initial erection, circa 1690, is quite early for Cape Cod, and thus provides important late seventeenth-century architectural information for that area. The building was definitely abandoned and removed by circa 1735, and there was no later construction of any type on the site. The limiting dates for this site are based on artifactual dating. The pipestem interior bore diameter curve peaks in the period 1710–1750, suggesting that the most intensive occupation of the site took place during the first half of the eighteenth century. Ceramic dates permit a refinement of this date to a considerable degree. The initial date of 1690 is based on the occurrence of both North Devonshire Sgrafitto ware, which occupies a late seventeenth-century date range where it is found elsewhere in the country (Watkins, 1960), and Frechen stoneware in the form of Bellarmine jugs, also a seventeenth-century type. Further support to a 1690 beginning date is provided by late seventeenth-century wine glass stems and seal-top spoons with fig-shaped bowls. A termination date of circa 1735 is based on somewhat less secure data, but the total absence of white Staffordshire stonewares and the prevalence of the dipped stonewares from the same region argue strongly for such a date (Mountford, 1971).

The tavern was a large structure, fifty feet in length and thirty feet in width (Fig. 9). The front entrance was central and faced south. A roughly paved walkway led to the door. Both the focus and visibility of this structure were excellent, primarily because Great Island, being a vast sand dune, has no stones occurring naturally. Thus all stone encountered archaeologically could safely be assumed to have been brought in for construction. The chimney had been of brick; only the base survived, and it was located in the traditional position in the center of the building with the door coming in just opposite the chimney breast. Large quantities of brick were found in one of the cellars and scattered over much of the site. A tentative ground plan for this building would indicate two large rooms flanking the chimney, with at least one other room to the rear beneath some type of lean-to (Fig. 10). It is impossible to determine whether the building had been of one or two stories. A two-story arrangement is suggested by the function it clearly served, that of a tavern for shore whalers working from the Great Island beaches. Each of the main front rooms had a cellar beneath its floor. That beneath the east room was small (8′ x 10′) and lined with rounded beach cobbles set with sand-and-clamshell mortar. It was entered by way of a set of stone stairs from within the house, presumably through a trapdoor in the floor. Its low height, under five feet, suggests that it functioned as a food storage

9. Exposed footings of Whaler's Tavern, Great Island, Wellfleet, Mass.

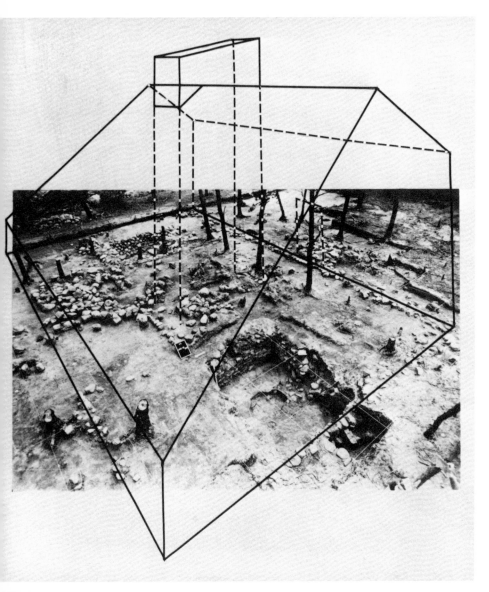

5. Conjectural structure of Wellfleet Tavern.

cellar. A remarkable artifact found on the floor of this cellar was probably connected with food processing: a large cervical vertebra of a whale made into a chopping block, possibly for meat. The cellar beneath the west room was larger (9′ x 10′) and slightly deeper. At one time it had been entered through a bulkhead from the west exterior side of the building, but by the time of abandonment this entrance had been walled up and entrance must have been through a floor trapdoor, as in the east cellar. The west cellar was also lined with a very different kind of stone, flat rectangular pieces laid in rather even courses. This cellar was also probably primarily for food storage.

Numerous architectural details were provided by artifacts recovered in and around the foundation and its cellars. Window glass fragments numbered in the thousands, and sufficient pieces of lead cames were recovered to indicate diamond-paned windows. Nails were even more numerous than glass shards.

Interior wall plaster was also abundant. This material provided some specific information on the framing and sheathing of the house. Almost every one of the thousands of pieces of wall plaster bears an impression of the wall to which it once was attached (Fig. 11). Impressions of laths are very clear, showing the grain of the wood and the placement of lathing nails. These impressions in every case demonstrate that the laths were attached to vertical planks rather than to studs. The grain of the planks shows clearly, confirming the possibility of exterior vertical plank siding rather than stud construction. Had the laths been attached to studs, the plaster would have compressed between them and encountered no surface behind them. The resulting impression in such a situation would show no form or impressions between the lath impressions such as occur on the examples in question. If the tavern *was* sheathed in this fashion, it would stand as a good early example of this style, which Candee (1969) has suggested to be a Plymouth Colony diagnostic, and the easternmost occurrence of the technique.

The ultimate fate of the Wellfleet tavern is unknown. Local traditions hold that it was floated across the harbor and erected somewhere in the town of Wellfleet. This possibility has not yet been proven to be true, but it is certain that the building was removed, whole or in parts, rather than burned. No evidence was found suggesting a fire. On the other hand, the large quantity of nails, bricks, and plaster fragments strongly suggests at least a partial dismantling of the structure, if not a complete razing. However it met its end on that site, there was no other construction or occupation on the location for the following two centuries. The only artifacts found which did not relate to the occupation period cited above were the casual leavings, such as whiskey bottles, of people who had dug randomly in the ruin in this century in search of coins or bottles.

11. Wall plaster samples, showing lath impressions. Wellfleet Tavern.

Archaeological remains of Plymouth Colony's earliest dwelling houses are extremely scarce. It is now certain that the main reason for this rarity is that such buildings were of a sort which resulted in archaeological features of very low visibility. Goods were scarce in the Colony's early years, there was little in the way of disposable refuse, cellars seem to have been rare if nonexistent, and construction techniques were of a type to leave little readable evidence for the archaeologist. Thus it was unusual when, in the summer of 1972, Plimoth Plantation archaeologists found and excavated a house which almost certainly was constructed in 1630, and which had been destroyed by the middle of the seventeenth century. Even the discovery of this site was largely a matter of luck. A Kingston, Massachusetts, man planned to build a house on a vacant parcel of land. By fortunate coincidence, his architect had some knowledge of seventeenth-century artifacts, and finding a few in a freshly plowed garden he brought them to the Plantation for identification. They proved to be of a very early date and subsequent investigation of the plowed area suggested that the remains of some kind of building might be there. An extensive excavation program which occupied most of the summer resulted in the recovery of a ground plan which had very sharp archaeological focus, although the visibility was quite low.

During the 1630's, the parcel of land was the property of Isaac Allerton, one of the Colony's financial agents. It is known that Allerton had moved to Kingston, and presumably built a dwelling house there as early as 1630. The artifacts recovered from the site are totally

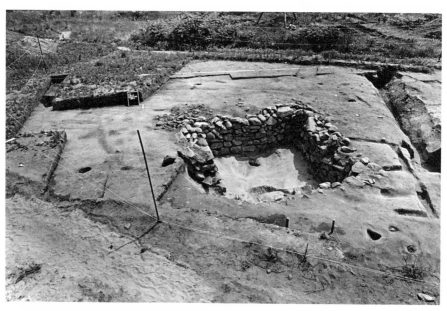

12.   Isaac Allerton site, Kingston, Mass. Palisade trench to right. Cellar in center is from post-1650 house; hearth of 1630 post-hole house cut by cellar at upper left corner.

consistent with such a date. The house was a small structure, twenty by twenty-two feet square, of post-hole-type construction (Fig. 12). Each corner of the house was occupied by a massive post, possibly eighteen inches square, set four feet into the ground. These posts carried plates and girts, and probably studs which in turn supported wattle and daub walls. Any evidence of these studs was unrecoverable, since they were usually not set deeply into the ground, and years of cultivation had thoroughly disturbed the upper foot of the site. A rectangular hearth occupied one end of the house, laid directly on the ground, and made from cobbles set without mortar. This hearth measured seven feet by slightly more than three. It showed evidence of intensive use, the stones being thoroughly blackened and fire cracked.

Parallel to the house at the end opposite the hearth ran a palisade, probably of contiguous poles some eight feet high. The palisade began at the house and ran some three hundred feet to the south, at which point it simply stopped. Since the palisade did not enclose anything, it almost certainly was never finished. The reason for this is not known, nor will it ever be; one can surmise that perhaps the need for which it was being built no longer existed before it was complete, or that Allerton tired of the project before finishing it. At regular intervals along the palisade, faint evidence of other structures was found. These were presumably outbuildings. Support for this identification comes mainly from artifacts found in the palisade trench adjacent to each location. It is fairly certain that sometime around 1650, the dwelling house and outbuildings were torn down, as was the partially completed palisade. The palisade must have been dismantled first, since at regular intervals the open trench was filled with structural debris and artifacts. Only that part of the palisade trench adjacent to the dwelling house contained a full domestic assemblage, with a variety of ceramics, food refuse, smoking pipes, glass, and tools. One of the concentrations consisted almost solely of redwares and may relate to a dairy adjacent to the palisade at that point. Time and construction schedules did not permit the full investigation of all of these loci. The testing that was done on them strongly suggested special functions for the other buildings.

The dating of this earliest construction period is supported by pipe-stem data, preponderantly of the period 1620–1650, and ceramics, which included Cologne stonewares typical of the early years of the century, white sandy wares, also common at that time but absent in the second half of the century, and small amounts of the more elaborate blue on gray Westerwald wares of the same period. A seal-top spoon with the short seal most common from the late sixteenth and early seventeenth centuries and a coin and lead fur-bale seal from the reign of King James I also support the assigned dates.

Sometime later, probably in the third quarter of the seventeenth century but possibly at the same time as the first complex was destroyed, a second more elaborate house was constructed on the same site. This structure was represented archaeologically only by a cellar twelve feet square with dry laid stone walls and a sand floor. This low visibility probably resulted from subsequent destruction of this house and the disposition of the footing stones in the cellar. Some twenty-five tons of stone were removed from the cellar when it was excavated. No chimney base could be located; it may have been removed in the course of the construction of the modern house now occupying the site. This second house was removed from the site circa 1725, a date based on artifacts found in the cellar fill. No later occupations occurred on the site until the construction of 1972. The cellar belonging to the second house cut the corner of the hearth of the first, providing a clear sequence for the two buildings.

The earlier component of the Allerton site is very important since it is the only direct evidence for post-hole construction in Plymouth Colony. In his history of the Plantation, William Bradford suggests such a construction type in his description of the hurricane of 1635: "It took off the boarded roof of a house which belonged to this Plantation at Manomet, and floated it to another place, the posts still standing in the ground" (Morison, 1952).

If the post-hole-type house was a common form in early Plymouth and these houses were constructed, as was the Allerton house, without cellars, it is little wonder that locating such early sites is so difficult. Both the visibility and focus of sites of this type are of such a low order on the surface that they must be discovered by chance.

Removal of the topsoil enhances the picture, but in view of the pau-
city of artifacts and refuse in this early period they are difficult to
detect from the surface.

The excavations at the Allerton site formed the basis for the recre-
ation of an early post-hole-type house at Plimoth Plantation in the
summer of 1973. Using only traditional tools, techniques, and materials, Professor Henry Glassie, a folklorist at the University of Indiana,
designed and directed the construction of this building. It probably
bears a close resemblance to the house which Allerton built in Kingston in 1630 (Fig. 13).

13. Re-created post-hole house at Plimoth Plantation.

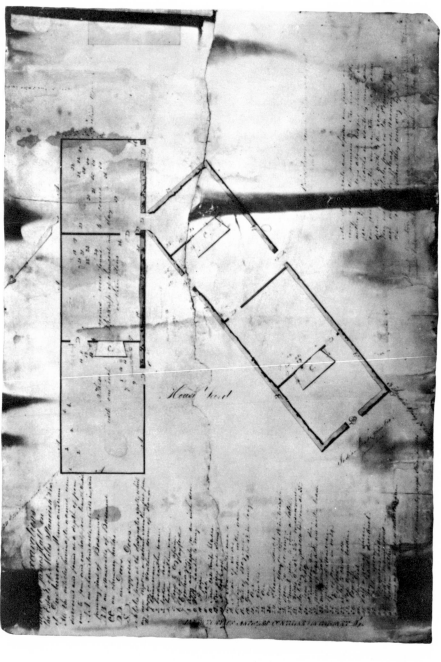

14. James Hall's plan of Standish site, Duxbury, Mass. Courtesy Pilgrim Society, Plymouth.

The existence of the post-hole-type house in Plymouth Colony has been demonstrated by archaeological excavation and analysis. Yet another house type, also not represented in the surviving structures of the Old Colony and possibly as early as the post-hole type, is strongly suggested by two excavations, one done in the nineteenth century on the Miles Standish homesite in Duxbury, and the other done in 1960 on John Alden's first Duxbury house. The Standish excavation is truly remarkable. Done by James Hall in the 1860's, it stands as the earliest known example of controlled archaeological excavation done anywhere in the world (Fig. 14). Hall's work stands as a model to this day; careful notes, the establishment of a control datum point, and proper cataloguing of artifacts all attest to a careful worker. The site map and the remnants of the artifact collection are today the property of the Pilgrim Society, Plymouth, Massachusetts. Hall uncovered a long structure represented by both wood and stone footings, with a cellar at one end. The building measures sixty by fifteen feet, a length-breadth ratio of 4:1. On the basis of the artifacts which have survived, this house was probably built by Standish at the same time that Allerton was newly living in Kingston. Roland Robbins' work at the Alden site, also in Duxbury, produced a remarkably similar ground plan (Fig. 15). In this instance, the house was shorter (forty feet) and narrower (ten feet) but also had an end cellar, and the length-breadth ratio is identical. Such long, narrow structures are not known from later surviving Plymouth examples. Just what English antecedents relate to them is unclear, although some of the

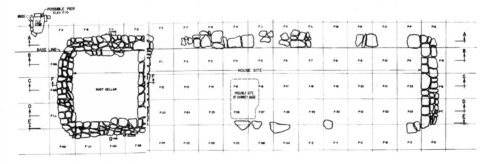

15. Ground plan of John Alden site, Duxbury, Mass. Courtesy Pilgrim Society, Plymouth.

buildings at Jamestown, from a somewhat later date, are similarly elongated. The R.M. site in Plymouth, Massachusetts, excavated by Henry Hornblower in 1940, is that of a house which was occupied for perhaps as long as forty years (1635–1675); as a result, the focus of the features excavated is of a low order. Further complications at this site resulted from intensive plowing of the site over a long period and large quantities of natural stone in the area. Yet when one examines the relationship between the cellar and a pair of hearths which were exposed, a long, narrow ground plan best accommodates these features (Fig. 16). It is not possible to make any definitive statements concerning these somewhat ambiguous examples, except to note that along with the Allerton site they suggest at least two different building traditions of early Plymouth, both different from those which a study of later examples would suggest. It is noteworthy that Abbott Cummings has suggested a date of circa 1660 as the end of the earliest phase of New England building. Such a date provides time for a single generation to have come of age in New England, and thus for the beginnings of an indigenous American cultural configuration. This same date has been suggested as marking the end of an initial English period of development of material cultural pattern and use as seen in ceramics (Deetz, 1973). It is reasonable to argue that for the first generation, newly arrived English immigrants would have built in a variety of styles which reflected their English regional origins. After circa 1660, this variation would have been sharply reduced, with one modal style of building emerging as characteristic of the new "home-grown" American Colonial tradition of the later seventeenth and early eighteenth centuries. Thus it is that the later part of the "first period" of New England building shows a greater architectural homogeneity than that which may well have prevailed in the initial years of the settlement of New England. The Plymouth data, limited as they are, strongly suggest such a model of development and change.

All of the data outlined above are reasonably firm and clear. It is important to note that there are many other sites which have been excavated which have provided little of significant architectural importance. All too often, one can locate cellar and chimney base, but

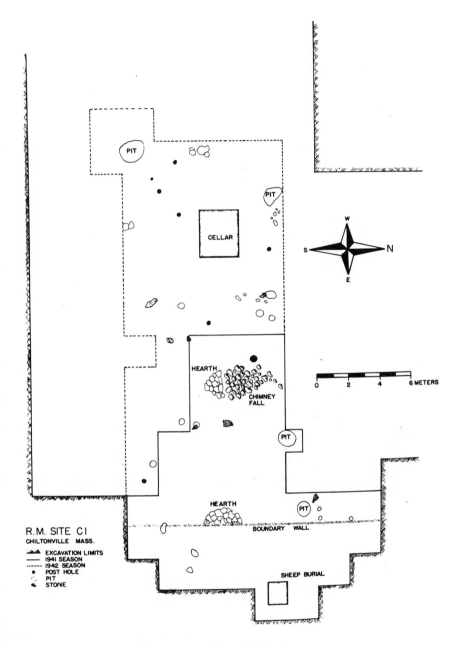

16. Ground plan of R.M. site, Chiltonville, Mass.

evidence for footings and locations of walls is sadly lacking or so obscured by natural stone in the New England soil that a clear ground plan is impossible to determine.

The most frustrating site encountered by Plimoth Plantation archaeologists was that of Edward Winslow's first house in Marshfield, Massachusetts. That it was an early site was certain. Its existence, like that of the Allerton site, was known from random artifacts coming from a vegetable garden. Six weeks of hard and careful work produced enough artifacts to hold in two hands and a red smear of decomposed brick which presumably marked the base of the chimney. Beyond these tantalizing bits of evidence, there was nothing. It is very likely that the house which once stood on the site was systematically disassembled for materials, leaving almost nothing behind. The Winslows built a much more elaborate house just adjacent to this first one, and excavation on this site produced a very rich collection dating to the second half of the seventeenth century.

Archaeology, then, is not a consistently rewarding source of architectural data on seventeenth-century vernacular building. For every Allerton dig there are ten which produce a muddled maze of disturbed stones, brickbats, and partially preserved cellars. Yet in view of the fact that it requires but one site such as that of the Allerton house to produce truly new and unique data for the Colony's earliest houses, work will continue, and new insights are bound to come, albeit slowly.

BIBLIOGRAPHY

Richard Candee, "A Documentary History of Plymouth Colony Architecture 1620–1700," *Old-Time New England*, Vol. 60, No. 2, 1969.

James Deetz, "Ceramics from Plymouth, 1635–1835: The Archaeological
Evidence," *Ceramics in America* (Winterthur Conference Report 1972,
University Press of Virginia for Winterthur Museum, 1973).

Erik Ekhom and James Deetz, "Wellfleet Tavern," *Natural History*, Vol.
80, No. 7 (August–September 1971).

Samuel E. Morison, ed., *Of Plymouth Plantation* (New York, 1970).

Arnold Mountford, *The Illustrated Guide to Staffordshire Salt-Glaze Stone-
Ware* (New York, 1971).

Malcolm Watkins, "North Devon Pottery and its Export to America in
the Seventeenth Century," *Contributions from the Museum of History &
Technology* (U.S. National Museum Bulletin 225, Smithsonian Institution, Washington, D.C., 1960).

◀ EDWARD ZIMMER ▶

Edited by Matthew J. Kiefer

The James Blake House:
A Documentary Study

T HE relatively small number of extant seventeenth-century
houses in Massachusetts and the even smaller number which
predate 1660 make a thorough investigation of each critical to
an understanding of seventeenth-century Massachusetts architecture.
The 1650 construction date traditionally assigned to the James Blake
House in Dorchester, placing it within the first generation of New
England houses built by carpenters born and probably trained in
England, makes the house particularly worthy of scholarly attention.

This brief review of surviving documents relating to the Blake
House examines published sources, public records, photographs, and
other relevant documents for information concerning the house's
construction date, its ownership history, and the sequence of physical
changes leading up to and including its restoration by the Dorchester
Historical Society beginning in 1895. Though it fails to confirm or
refute a 1650 construction date, this study positively links the house
to the Blake family in the seventeenth century, establishes an un-
broken chain of ownership from the Blake family to the Society,
and reveals the origins of the house's 1650 attribution.

THE PUBLISHED TRADITION

The generally accepted 1650 construction date is the product of a
published tradition over one hundred and twenty years old. Its first-
known mention is in 1857, by Samuel Blake (a descendant of the
builder of the house), who cites "tradition . . . and . . . the most
careful examination of old documents" as evidence that the house

61

was built by James Blake, but gives no source for his contention that "the house was doubtless built previous to 1650."[1] A second source of the same year confuses the house with another, also owned by James Blake; hence the 1680 date of this source may be disregarded.[2]

Of these two contemporaneous accounts, most subsequent writers have adhered to the former's 1650 date. Such books as Ebenezer Clap's 1859 *History of the Town of Dorchester, Massachusetts* and William Dana Orcutt's *Good Old Dorchester*, published in 1893, repeat the 1650 date without either challenge or corroboration. Thus, by the time of acquisition of the house in 1895 by the Dorchester Historical Society, the date had become generally accepted—in spite of the scant evidence supporting it.

An account written for the Society by James H. Stark in 1907 quotes an excerpt from the Dorchester Town Records of 1669, when at a general meeting the town voted to build a new house for the minister "to be such an house as James Blaks house is. . . ."[3] It then describes the house in dimensions which closely correspond to the present-day house, thus providing the first documented evidence of the building's age.

A final explanation for the 1650 attribution date is offered in a 1960 pamphlet published by the Society on the subject of its three houses, which states that "it was probably in anticipation of a marriage that James Blake built his house."[4] Though the date of this event is apparently not recorded, it is known that the first child of James and Elizabeth (Clap) Blake was born in 1652.

OWNERSHIP HISTORY

The James Blake House has been owned and maintained for over eighty years by the Dorchester Historical Society which, following authorization from the Board of Aldermen and mayoral approval,

1. Samuel Blake, *The Blake Family: A Genealogical History of William Blake of Dorchester and His Descendants* . . . (Boston, 1857), pp. 15–16.
2. Thomas C. Simonds, *History of South Boston* (Boston, 1857), pp. 31, 264.
3. James H. Stark, *The History of the Old Blake House* (Boston: Dorchester Historical Society, 1907).
4. Mrs. George A. French, *The Dorchester Historical Society and Its Three Houses* (Boston: Dorchester Historical Society, 1960), p. 18.

acquired the house in late 1895 from the City of Boston and moved it to its present location in Richardson Park. Interestingly, this is the first recorded instance in New England of a historic building being moved in order to prevent its demolition.

The City had acquired the house on its original site—just west of Massachusetts Avenue about four hundred yards to the northwest of its present location (Fig. 17)—from George J. and Antonia Quinsler in September of 1895, for $8000. The conveyance included nearly 11,000 square feet of land, adjacent to other parcels the City was acquiring for clearance to build municipal greenhouses.[5]

Antonia Quinsler had gained title to the land in June of 1892 from Josiah F. Williams,[6] who had inherited it upon his mother's death the previous year. Jane Williams' inventory lists her estate as consisting of a "House, barn, and about 11,000 feet of land," valued at $2000.[7] Jane's husband, Caleb Williams (1802–1842), a tanner, died intestate; however, an 1843 inventory describes his "House and land situate in Dorchester[,] land ten feet wide around the House and right of passage way to the same,"[8] valued at $450.

This extremely small lot was enlarged by his widow the following year through a purchase from the Trustees of the Hawes Fund of a "doughnut-shaped" lot eighty by one hundred feet in extent which surrounded but did not include the houselot itself.[9] This parcel of land had descended to the Hawes Fund through Benjamin Hawes, who had acquired it from his uncle, John Hawes, in 1828.[10]

Jane Williams' 1843 inheritance of the house and 1844 purchase of the surrounding land ended a period of nearly one hundred and thirty years when the east and west halves of the house and the land surrounding its immediate lot had all been under separate ownership. The process of consolidation had actually begun in 1832, when Caleb Williams purchased from his brother Charles, a laborer, for the sum of $150 "one undivided half part of the land under and ten feet

5. Suffolk County Deeds, vol. 2305, p. 30.
6. Ibid., vol. 2066, p. 303.
7. Suffolk County Probate Records, vol. 650, p. 210.
8. Norfolk County Probate Records, docket no. 20436, inventory dated Feb. 4, 1843.
9. Norfolk County Deeds, vol. 151, p. 113.
10. Ibid., LXXXVI, 167, and LXXXVII, 235.

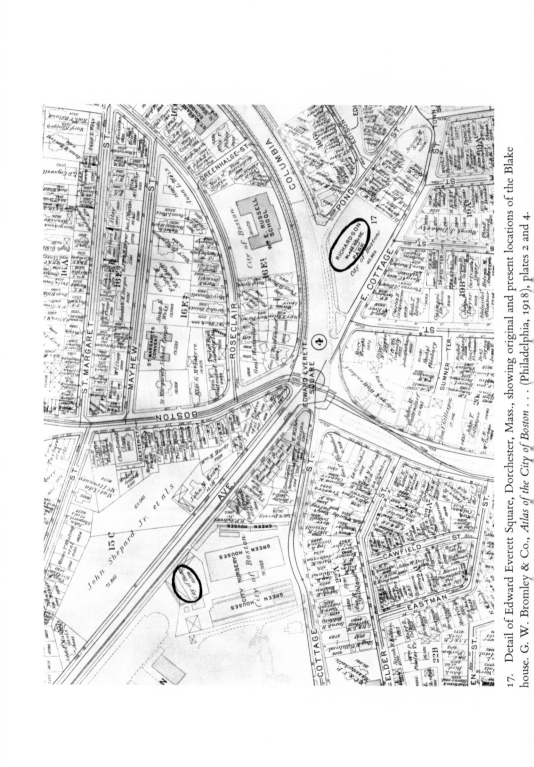

17. Detail of Edward Everett Square, Dorchester, Mass., showing original and present locations of the Blake house. G. W. Bromley & Co., *Atlas of the City of Boston* . . . (Philadelphia, 1918), plates 2 and 4.

around the dwelling house at present occupied by the said Caleb . . . with all the privileges of passing to and from and around said house and barn, as reserved in a certain deed from Ebenezer Blake to Elisha Clap conveying the other land around said house, and which other land is now owned by the heirs of John Hawes."[11]

John Hawes therefore owned not only the land surrounding the house, ultimately sold to Jane Williams in 1844, but also a part of the house itself. His 1819 will, probated upon his death in 1829, mentions each of these pieces of property separately. Clause number 14 of this will devised to his nephew Benjamin Hawes "the use and improvement of the dwelling house in Dorchester, which I lived in last before I removed from Dorchester to South Boston, with the land adjoining said dwelling house, being about nine or ten acres (excepting such part of the premises, as is herein devised to Eunice Williams). . . ."[12]

The following clause of the will states, "I give and devise to Eunice Williams, wife of Caleb Williams, my part of a dwelling house, situate on the land described in the clause last preceding, now occupied partly by the said Caleb Williams, and partly by Elizabeth Fearn and Rachel Blake, together with the land under said house, and a right of passage to the same suffiecient for a Cart way as is now used, with the privilege of the well, and a passage ten feet around the house. . . ."[13] Eunice and Caleb Williams were the parents of Caleb Williams, the tanner whose widow, Jane, subsequently bought the first-mentioned parcel from Hawes' estate.

The portion of the house not bequeathed in the above will, but mentioned as being occupied by Elizabeth Fearn and Rachel Blake in 1819, was purchased by the senior Caleb and his wife, Eunice Williams, in 1825 for the sum of $100 from Rachel Blake.[14] The deed reserves to Rachel Blake the right to occupy the house for the term of her natural life—which, as fate would have it, was approximately one month. Thus at the time of the execution of John Hawes'

11. Ibid., XCVII, 199.
12. Suffolk County Probate Records, vol. 127, p. 339.
13. Ibid.
14. Norfolk County Deeds, XCVII, 198.

will in 1829, the entire house was under the ownership of Caleb and Eunice Williams, who had occupied half of it since at least 1819.

It is at this point that the path of ownership becomes somewhat more labyrinthine. The portion of the house owned by Rachel Blake until 1825 will be traced first, in order to help illuminate the more complicated Hawes side.

Rachel Blake was born in 1741, one of five children of John Blake, cordwainer, and Abigail (Preston) Blake. Upon her father's death in 1772, the absence of a will caused his estate, which included the subject house and barn, as well as some thirteen acres of surrounding land, to be divided equally among his children.[15] Each of the individual shares of the surrounding land was sold off separately at different times, and by surviving her four siblings Rachel ultimately gained full possession of the house. Elizabeth Fearn, mentioned in Hawes' will as a co-occupant of the house, was Rachel's widowed sister and the last of her siblings to pre-decease her, dying in 1817.

John Hawes, the previously established owner of the remaining half of the house in 1819, purchased it in 1784 from the heirs of his wife's former husband, Elisha Clap, who had died nine years earlier.[16] In 1772, Clap had purchased from Ebenezer Blake, a weaver, for 200 pounds, "my easterly end of a dwelling house and a shop adjoining thereto [,] . . . and my easterly end or half of the barn standing being upon [a piece] of land which peice containeth seven acres one quarter and twenty two rods . . . allowing and reserving out of this piece of land for my uncle Mr. John Blake his heirs and assigns forever Convenient yard room about his part of the house for laying his wood and other necessities and the use of the way from the house to the highway and barn where it is now used. . . ."[17]

It should be noted that these rights reserved by Ebenezer Blake for his uncle remained attached to later conveyances of the property (in slightly modified form) until at least 1825, after which they were specified to be a distance of ten feet around the house. This remained

15. Suffolk County Probate Records, LXXII, 33, and LXXIV, 16.
16. Suffolk County Deeds, vol. 143, p. 53.
17. Ibid., vol. 121, p. 143.

the bounds of the houselot until Jane Williams enlarged it in 1844.

The above-quoted deed is also significant for its reference to John Blake as the owner of the remaining half of the house, which establishes a familial link between the two separate ownership shares in the house.

Ebenezer Blake had inherited his half of the house and barn from his father, Josiah, a weaver, who died intestate in 1747, and whose inventory lists his interest in the house and surrounding land as being valued at 700 pounds.[18] Josiah was the brother of John Blake mentioned in the above deed; hence the house was under the split ownership of two brothers prior to 1747.

John and Josiah were the two youngest of seven children of John Blake (1657–1718), who died intestate with an inventory listing his "Dwelling House" as valued at 50 pounds. The administration of his estate divided the house between his two surviving sons, with sisters Hannah and Elizabeth given occupancy rights until their marriage, when the entire estate would revert to the male heirs.[19]

John Blake was one of six children of James and Elizabeth Blake. Thought to be the original builder of the house which now stands in Richardson Park, James' 1700 will devises to his son John "my Dwelling House and Barns, Orchard, Yard, Garden, and ten acres of land adjoining. . . ."[20] This is the earliest-known reference in the deed or probate records which can confidently be linked to the same house.

James Blake was born in Pitminster, England, in 1624, the son of William and Agnes Blake, who, according to tradition, brought their family of five to America on the *Mary and John*, which landed in Dorchester in 1630. William Blake, who is mentioned in the Dorchester Town Records for the first time in 1637, died there in 1663, his wife in 1678. William Blake's will, written in 1661, simply divided his estate in half, assigning one part to his five children, and the other to his "beloved wife." The 1663 inventory of his estate includes only

18. Suffolk County Probate Records, XLI, 451.
19. Ibid., XXI, 555.
20. Ibid., XIV, 192.

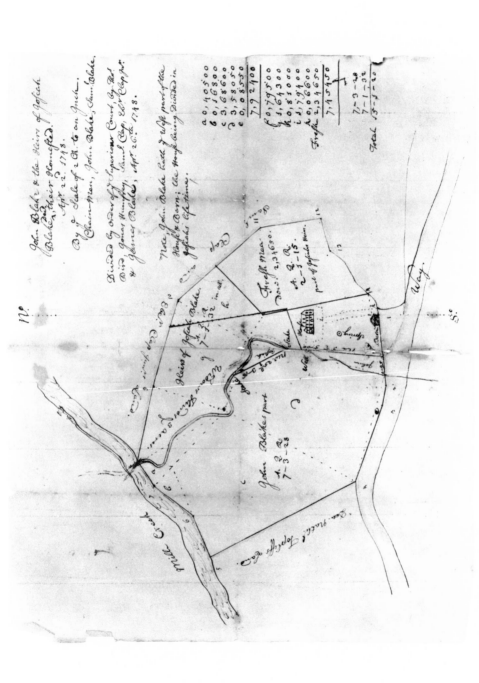

18.   Division map of John Blake and the heirs of Josiah Blake, April 22, 1748, showing the Blake house and barn. Courtesy Dorchester Historical Society.

the simple listing: "his house and lands," valued at 154 pounds and 15 shillings.[21]

No further records have yet been discovered to describe this house more precisely, or document its passage to James Blake, one of four possible heirs. Although the Town Records do make occasional reference to lands granted to or owned by William Blake or, after 1657/8, James Blake, their topographical references are no longer decipherable. It is therefore impossible to say whether the present house was built by James, or inherited from his father's estate, and the earliest documented mention of the present-day house remains the 1669 reference in the Town Records to building a minister's house "to be such an house as James Blaks house is."[22]

STRUCTURAL HISTORY AND RESTORATION

A somewhat sketchy structural history of the Blake House has been pieced together from published records, photographs, prints, and other documents. In particular, the records of the Society yield some interesting information about the restoration of the house and the difficulties resulting therefrom.

The precise measurements which follow the aforementioned reference to the house in the Dorchester Town Records confirm that it was originally a simple, four-square structure basically the same in appearance and plan as it is today. The earliest-known graphic representation of the house is a thumbnail sketch in 1748 on a division map of the lands of John Blake and Josiah Blake's heirs (Fig. 18). This clearly shows not only a two-story ell at the left-hand end of the house, with a pitched roof and separate entrance, but also the suggestion of dormer windows in the front slope of the main house roof. Structural evidence of facade gables, which apparently had survived until 1748, still remain in the attic of the original structure.

Samuel Blake's account in 1857 contains the next extant representation of the house, a print which shows no facade gables and, in addition to the ell at the left, a story-and-a-half gable-roofed ell

---

21. Samuel Blake, *The Blake Family*, pp. 12–13.
22. *Fourth Report of the Record Commissioners of the City of Boston, 1880, Dorchester Town Records*, 2nd ed. (Boston, 1883), p. 162.

19. Blake house before removal to new site. Photo, William H. Halliday Collection, before 1896, courtesy Society for the Preservation of New England Antiquities.

20. Blake house after removal to new site and restoration. Photo, William H. Halliday Collection, c. 1896, courtesy Society for the Preservation of New England Antiquities.

at the right end as well which the author claims "has been added within the last quarter of a century."[23] The outline of the house on an 1874 real estate atlas clearly shows it to have an ell projecting from each end. A series of photographs in the collections of the Society for the Preservation of New England Antiquities and the Dorchester Historical Society, several of which were taken shortly before the relocation of the house, confirm that it retained both of the ells until the time of acquisition by the latter Society (Fig. 19).

The Dorchester Historical Society, which had been incorporated in 1891 and held its first meeting in 1893, undertook the preservation of the Blake House as the first major project of a fledgling organization. Introduced to the plight of the house in June of 1895 by a letter from Doctor Clarence Blake (presumably a descendant of the builder) who offered $500 toward the cost of moving it to a safe location, the Society had within four months secured an agreement with the City of Boston granting the Society the house and the right to move it to nearby Richardson Park at its own expense.[24]

A major subscription drive (destined to be long-lived) was begun to raise funds for the undertaking. By January of 1896 the house had been moved and re-silled—with both ells having been removed in the process—by a local building mover for $295. The move was accomplished, according to Dr. Blake's recollection twenty years later, by dismantling the chimney and jacking up the house onto a horse winch.[25]

Although the name of the moving company and some of the craftsmen involved in the subsequent restoration are identified in the Society's records, the director of the restoration is unclear. Dr. Blake mentions the assistance of a Mr. Hodgson, "a well known Dorchester architect. . . ." This seems to have been Charles Hodgson, an active member of the Society, who lived near Richardson Park between 1895 and 1907, after which he moved to New Rochelle, New York.

23. Samuel Blake, *The Blake Family*, pp. 15–16.
24. Minutes of the Dorchester Historical Society, MS, I, 44–45, 50–51.
25. "Dorchester's Settlement Appropriately Celebrated," *Dorchester Beacon*, undated clipping (June 1916?) in the collections of the Dorchester Historical Society.

Dr. Blake gives some indication of the actual restoration process in the following passage:

We then tried to have the material in the house duplicated as near as possible to the original material and it was necessary to even send to Holland for the glass in the windows because there was none of its kind in this country. The windows were of the lattice type and on close examination it will even be found that the shingles in the roof are fastened by the original nails which will give you a fine idea of how well built the houses were in those days. The same hinges are even on the doors.[26]

Because of continuing difficulties in raising funds to pay off debts incurred during the moving and gradual restoration, the Society voted in September of 1898 to float a $1000 bond issue to cover its $800 debt and advance the restoration. However, the Society's continued difficulty in paying off its debts suggests that the bond issue was a less than raging success. Not until 1907 do the records indicate the Society's indebtedness to have been discharged.

The actual physical changes to the house resulting from this restoration effort can be partially deduced from contemporary accounts and photographs. In addition to removing both side ells, then-existing double-hung sash windows were replaced with diamond-leaded casements (which may have been shortened slightly); wood shingles replaced clapboards; and a panelled door was removed in favor of a batten door "in the ancient pattern." The house was placed on a stone foundation, with the front sill raised about one foot above grade in the front.

Structural evidence indicates that then-existing door openings between the house and ell on the present left end of the house, probably enlargements themselves of original windows, were re-converted to windows after the ell was removed. Finally, it should be noted that the pre-restoration chimney, which was apparently later than the house itself, may have remained partially intact during the moving process. Arrived at the new site, this masonry feature underwent repairs, including a new foundation, at which time also recessed arches were added to the front and back of a newly created chimney top.

Although the exterior restoration had been accomplished fairly

26. Ibid.

quickly, restoration of the interior of the house proceeded gradually, beginning with the two ground-floor rooms. It was not until 1910 that the two upstairs chambers were completed and opened to the public. All that can be said of the details of the interior restoration process, based on documentary evidence, is that it included the stripping, staining, and polishing of exposed oak framing; the replacement of most of the structure's sills and the bottoms of the posts with new oak which was stained and chamfered to match the original timbers; and the "restoration" of the "antique fireplaces."

Any further determination of exactly how much of the present-day fabric of the house is original and how much the result of this early and well-intentioned restoration effort must be based on careful physical analysis. It is hoped that the claim of a *Boston Herald* reporter in 1911 that "every piece of old material that could be kept is still in use" will prove true.[27]

27. "Blake House Is Restored," *Boston Herald*, Boston, Mass., July 3, 1911.

◆᷾ JAMES B. PEABODY ᷾◆

The Building of Trinity Church, Boston*

TRINITY CHURCH was the last in the trinity of Episcopal churches to be built in Boston in Colonial times. King's Chapel in the central part of town was largely built in 1688, although the first services were probably not held there until June 30, 1689. Christ Church, Salem Street, in the North End had its cornerstone laid on April 15, 1723, and it was opened for worship at the end of that year. Things took longer in the South End. There the cornerstone of Trinity Church was laid on April 15, 1734, six years after land bounded by Summer Street and Bishop's Alley, later called Hawley Street and now the site of Filene's basement, was deeded to build a church. It was not for another ten years that we can say that the church was completed. Of these buildings only Christ Church remains standing today as the oldest ecclesiastical building in Boston still in use. The original wooden structure of King's Chapel was torn down in 1749 when the present fine Palladian stone edifice designed by Peter Harrison was erected on its site. After nearly a hundred years the first Trinity Church was also torn down and replaced by a Gothic stone building on the same spot in 1829. This structure in turn became a victim of the great fire of 1872, almost exactly forty-three years later, but after planning had already begun for the third church edifice in Copley Square, one of the key monuments of American architecture in the Romanesque style designed by H. H. Richardson, where the sixteenth Rector of Trinity was installed by the Bishop on the 6th of October, 1974.

It may be helpful to begin by describing Trinity Church's first

---

* Mr. Peabody's paper, as presented here, was prepared for publication before his untimely death on March 22, 1977.

75

building in a verbal sense, by which is meant the construction of the church as we can follow it in the original records of the Proprietors and the Vestry.[1] It will then be appropriate to discuss the building in a substantive sense, in the course of which the reader can ponder some descriptions of the outside as well as the inside of the church taken from the written accounts of people who visited the building, and also pictorial representations by people who presumably saw it.

If one understands how the church was built, he will learn more about a versatile and fascinating but unfortunately obscure Bostonian called William Price. Turning to the Church Records one finds that a majority of the purchasers of the land, bought in order to build the church, selected, at a meeting in Luke Vardy's tavern in Boston on October 17, 1733, five trustees to be a building committee. This committee consisted of Peter Luce, merchant; Thomas Child, distiller; Thomas Greene, merchant; William Price, cabinetmaker; and Leonard Vassall, a wealthy landowner, who was chosen treasurer. All these men were prominent members of King's Chapel, and it may be mentioned that William Price, who was born in 1684 in England and died in Boston in 1771, was a particularily ardent churchman who retained pews in all three Episcopal churches, was at various times a Warden and Vestryman in both Christ Church and Trinity, and was a generous contributor to all three churches. In his will he left a sum of money for a lectureship to King's Chapel, which eventually passed to Trinity, the principal sum of which amounted to $1,309,965 as of December 31, 1973.

The first question one might well ask is: Was there a plan drawn by an architect, or anyone else, for the first Trinity Church? This is a particularly apt question because to William Price has sometimes been ascribed the drawing of the plans for Christ Church, Salem Street, and Trinity Church in Newport, Rhode Island. Nothing has been found in the Church Records to show that a plan for the church was drawn in advance by anyone, although there is considerable evi-

1. The Colonial records of Trinity Church are being published at the present time by The Colonial Society of Massachusetts in its regular series of publications. The page proofs of the records are at the printers, and it is, therefore, impossible to give page and volume references to the selections quoted from these records.

dence in the same documents showing that various plans for different parts of the building were made as the work proceeded.

On November 6, 1733, the Building Committee noted the following: "We sent for John Indicott and Conversed with him about the most Proper Methods for carrying on the work. Agreed that there be 44 Large Windows and 16 small windows." On November 8, 1733, it was:

Agreed that there be three doors in front of the church and one door on the East side of the alter to answer to the Eastermost Ile. That there be one small window made in the front over the ceiling. That Mr. John Indicott having received an Account of everything that is to be done, be desired to give in an Account what he will do the Work and find the Stuff for.

So an account or description, not a plan, was apparently given to John Indicott, master carpenter and housewright, and from this description he must have prepared his own plan. It was John Indicott who built the first steeple for Christ Church, Salem Street, in 1740, probably after a draught by William Price. Indicott also built the school in School Street for the Wardens and Vestry of King's Chapel in 1748 when they were getting ready to build the present King's Chapel.

Although a contract was signed with John Indicott for the carpentry work the Building Committee made a separate contract containing specific measurements with Mr. John Goldsmith for the masonry work involved in the foundations, and on April 15, 1734, the cornerstone was laid by the Reverend Mr. Roger Price, Bishop's Commissary and Rector of King's Chapel.

On April 30, 1734, the Building Committee "Voted that there be one Seller door made in Bishop's alley . . . and that there be another door made under the Great Window that is over the Alter to go into the Seller." The word "alter" in the Church Records frequently means that part of the chancel where the wooden altar table was to be placed.

On June 25, 1734, there is recorded a significant change in the original concept of the Building Committee: "Voted that there be air holes left in the wall instead of the Windows we formerly agreed for." This suggests that a third tier of windows on both sides of the church was omitted at this point from the original plan.

On August 4, 1735, it was:

Voted that Mr. John Indicott be ordered to clear everything out of the Church and to pull down the old House and lime Shed that are before the Church as quick as Possable and that he be desired to erect a Pulpit a Reading desk and a Desk for the Clerk and to make as many Ruff Benches as shall be convenient.

On August 15, 1735, the first religious service was held in the church in the presence of the Royal Governor, Jonathan Belcher, and a dinner was provided afterwards by Mr. Withered, mine host at the Bunch of Grapes, the most popular punch house in town.

Even though the first service had been held the church was still far from finished. Glass didn't go into the windows until October and the first pews were not built nor was the inside of the church plastered until August of the following year.

On June 12, 1738, we find this interesting entry in the records of the Building Committee:

Voted that the Ceiling of the Alter be done after the Moddle made by William Price. Voted that John Indicott do woodwork for the Arching part, purchase Stuff for the same, and for fluted columns, floor and Rails for the alter as cheap as possible.

And on October 4, 1738, the Building Committee recorded that "We drew the plan on the spot for the steps, floreing and rails at the alter with the pillasters and gave Indicott directions to do work conformable to said plan."

On February 22, 1738, William Price was desired: "to treat with a carver about the Corinthian Capitols." A few days later, on February 28, Mr. Price reported that

he had been with Mr. Redding the Carver about the Cappitals, who said he would not Carve them well under Ten Pounds a piece. Therefore voted that Mr. William Price be desired to agree with said Redding for the Corinthian Cappitals and that he be paid £30 for them by a Note on a good Shop. The rest of the trustees desired Thomas Greene to treat with Mr.

Robert Kenton about Plaistering the Remaining Part of the Alter and make report as soon as possible.

At a meeting of the trustees at Mr. William Price's on March 5, 1738,

Thomas Greene reported that he had tawlked with Robert Kenton about his finishing the Plaistering of the Alter. His answer was he could do it as well [as] Any man in Boston. Upon which Thos. Greene was desired by the rest of the Committee to employ said Kenton immediately to do said work with all convenient speed and said Greene is hereby impowered to provide Stuff for said Kenton and likewise to Direct Mr. Indicott to Provide Proper Scaffolds.

On June 1, 1739, the Building Committee "Voted that Mr. John Indicott be desired to make a Table for the Alter of Pine to be five feet long and three feet broad," and within two weeks' time, on June 17, 1739, the records of the Vestry, which had been elected in April of that year in order to select a minister for the church, report that Sunday June 17th being Trinity Sunday the Holy Communion or Sacrement of the Lord's supper was administered in Trinity Church (being the first time) by the Reverend Addington Davenport, the Revd Mr. Saml Seabury assisted.

Earlier in this same year the Church Wardens had noted in a memorandum to their agent in London, to whom they were writing to seek assistance from the Society for the Propagation of the Gospel in Foreign Parts to help pay the salary of the minister they had not as yet chosen to be their Rector, that Trinity Church was far from being finished. "The Church wants," they wrote, "a Tower spire [and] Bell besides inner work."

Although the church was not finished, the members of the Building Committee delivered all their papers to the newly elected Vestry on May 8, 1740. There still remained to be built a permanent pulpit, reading desk, clerk's desk, and a sounding board. In addition there was the vestry room and a gallery around the interior of the church to be supported by fluted columns with carved Corinthian capitals on which additional pews would be built. On September 1, 1740, William Price was desired to give his advice with respect to the gallery. On October 13 "a draft for the galleries, pillars and arches was laid before the Vestry," and an agreement was made with John Indicott to do the work.[2] The work on the gallery, the vestry room, and two extra pillars under the organ loft was completed by May 4, 1742. A successful subscription having been completed that year, the Church Wardens ordered from London in early 1742 a pipe organ to be made for them such as "Dr. Berkely (now Bishop of Cloyne) presented the Church in Rhode Island which has mett with great approbation." They also sent the following measurements to London for the benefit of the organ builder:

a Church which is of the following dementions viszt. 90 feet in length 60 in width 28 feet high in the Stud besides an Arch 10 feet high and 28 broad which makes the whole hight from the floor to the top of the Arch 38 feet. The Organ Gallery is 12 feet from the floor and from the Gallery floor to the top of the Arch is 25 feet, the front of the Organ Gallery is 15 feet and 12 foot deep.

The organ, made by Abraham Jordan and tested by the great Handel in London, arrived in Boston early in 1742. It was soon set up, and Peter Pelham, Jr., became in that year Trinity's first organist.

In August of 1742 Governor Shirley delivered the handsome George II church silver he had received from the King's bounty for

---

2. A summary account in the Church Records entitled "The Cost of the Building of Trinity Church" contains the following entries for 1741:

for Building the Gallery	
viz. Jno. Indicott & Will More their Bill	
wholle Work & Stuff per agreement	[£]1057. 0.0
Will Coffin 31m⁰ lath nails	17.12.6.
Will Hunstable plaistering 430 yds	
@1/9	
hair and nails 8:11/	46. 3.6.
Thos. Fillebrown 150 bush. Lime & Lath	33.15
Johnson Jackson 50 bush lime @ 2/9	6.17.6.
Cash for Carting £4.15.6 lath & timber	
9:4/6	14. 0.0
Willm. Price cutting freeze for Organ	
loft	6.
Willm. Burbank Carving Capatols	152. 0.0
	[£]1333. 8.0

the church as well as a "large Royall Bible," prayer books, altar and pulpit cloths, and "cushons of Crimson Damask."

By 1744 one can confidently conclude that Trinity Church was substantially complete, just ten years after the cornerstone had been laid and sixteen after the land had been bought. It was calculated by the church authorities that the expense had been £2087 sterling. But still in the minds of the Vestry the church was not complete; and it is appropriate to mention briefly a few important additions and changes to the building that occurred or were contemplated by the Vestry in the latter part of the eighteenth century.

First of all it appears that a change of taste was registered in the vote of the Vestry on July 17, 1753, when it was:

Voted that we proceed on to painting the inside of the Church of Mahogany Collur, the pillars marble, the Capitols guilt and the alter decorated as farr as the Money Subscribed will go at the discretion of the Comitee to be chose.

Previous accounts in the Church Records reveal substantial sums paid for whitewashing the church. No indication is given of any other color being used.

On December 11, 1759, it was:

Voted that a Bell Col. George Williamson of his Majesty's Regiment of Royal Artillery hath Brought from Quebeck (which he took at the reduction of that place last Summer) that it be purchased and erected on this Church as soon as may be [and] that a Subscription be made for the payment of the bell.

As a substantial bill was paid that year to Mr. William More, partner of John Indicott, for "work and Stuff framing and hanging the same," it appears certain that, at least for some years, perhaps until the Revolution, Trinity Church had a bell in some sort of a belfry on its roof.

In July 1784 it was voted to recover the outside of the church with new clapboard and to paint it a stone color, and on May 17, 1789, a very handsome clock was presented to the church which was "fixed up in the front of the Organ Gallery."

In the last decade of the century the Vestry, apparently sensing a certain lack of dignity or grandeur in the exterior of their church, appointed a committee "to get a Plan of a porch or Portico with a colonade for the South End of the Church." On April 28, 1793, the

Plan for a colonnade for the South End of the Church was laid before the Proprietors and approved. But in answer as the expense of carrying the same into effect is estimated at three thousand dollars which sum appears to be more than can be easily raised.
Voted that the matter subside for the present.
Voted to make suitable returns to Mr. Bullfinch for his elegant and much admired plan.
N.B. Mr. Bullfinch refused to accept any pecuniary reward for his trouble.

Having traced the construction of Trinity Church in its records it is illuminating to read the descriptions left by people who actually saw the building in the eighteenth and early nineteenth century before it was torn down. These descriptions, do not, curiously, tally with some contemporary pictures of the church, which show Trinity as the proud possessor of an elaborate tower and steeple, architectural elements the first Trinity Church probably never possessed.

On the 9th of September, 1750, Francis Goelet of New York, Captain of the "Tarter Galley" put into Boston to repair damage done by a storm to his vessel before proceeding on to London. During his stay of almost three months he kept a diary in which he noted on October 14, 1750:

went to Trinity Church and was introduced by Mr. Coffin into his Piew. The Parson Mr. Hooper Gave us an Excellent Discourse on the following text (the Fear of the Lord is the Beginning of Wisdom). This build is very Plain without, with Large Sash Windows, But within Verry Neat and Comodius, the Architect Modren, with a Very Neat Little Organ Prettily Embellished. This Church having no steeple looks more like a Prespetarian Meeting House.[3]

Nor was there a steeple to be seen in 1817 when Charles Shaw described Trinity Church as

a large plain wooden building. . . . The inside has a show of the Corinthian style, but the building has nothing to recomend it but its roominess and

---

3. *New England Historical and Genealogical Register*, XXIV, 55.

convenience for worship. . . . The chancel is ornamented with some handsome paintings, and the choir is furnished with a large, well toned organ. It has three doors in front, without porches, and has no bell nor steeple.[4]

Finally, turning to the iconography of Boston, we find in the so-called "Price-Burgis View of Boston as revised, 1743" a clearly marked tower and steeple for Trinity Church even taller and more prominent than the tower and steeple of Christ Church, Salem Street (Fig. 21). On an impression in the British Museum of the first state of this plate, now believed to have been made in 1723, there are paper "pasters" altering the skyline as it might have been in 1736. One "paster" shows Trinity with a prominent tower but no spire, suggesting the progress being made in the construction of the church (Fig. 22). On the other hand, two views of Boston by James Turner, which appeared in the same month that William Price first advertised the 1743 view just mentioned, do not show a spire for Trinity Church.[5] These views show the spires of the three churches in the South End which it is known did have spires, namely the Old South Meeting House, still standing, the New South Meeting House at the junction of Summer Street and Blind Lane, and the Hollis Street Meeting House toward Boston neck. To deepen the mystery, however, both Paul Revere's "Prospective View of Boston of 1770" and his "View of the Town of Boston in 1774"[6] as well as an engraving from a drawing supposedly done by Governor Thomas Pownall before the Revolution from Castle William[7] seem to show four steeples in the South End. Two possible answers to this unsatisfactory iconography are either:

1) a confused perspective, or

2) the fourth steeple belongs to the Irish Meeting House located near the corner of Summer Street and Marlborough Street opposite Winter Street.

4. Charles Shaw, *A Topographical and Historical Description of Boston* (Boston, 1817), p. 265.
5. "Boston Prints and Printmakers, 1670–1775," Colonial Society of Massachusetts, *Publications*, 46 (1973), 43–44.
6. Ibid., pp. 46–49.
7. Samuel G. Drake, *The History and Antiquities of the City of Boston* (Boston, 1854), opposite p. 654.

21. Detail of the Price-Burgis *South East View* of Boston, Mass., as revised in 1743, showing Trinity Church (third from right). Courtesy American Antiquarian Society.

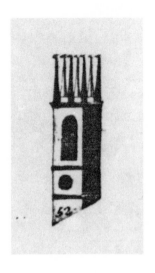

22.   Detail of "paster" with tower of Trinity Church minus spire, added in 1736 to the 1723 state of the Price-Burgis *South East View* of Boston.

What seems fairly certain is that in the Price-Burgis view of 1743 the clearly marked pictorial representation of Trinity Church, with its handsome tower and steeple, is only an exuberant expression of the hopes and dreams of Mr. William Price, cabinetmaker, printmaker, musician, and Vestryman of Trinity in 1741 and 1751, and Junior Warden of Trinity from 1745 to 1750.

The early nineteenth-century woodcut of the first Trinity Church by Abel Bowen (Fig. 23) may confirm in some minds the following judgment of the Reverend Phillips Brooks, ninth Rector of Trinity, that "the old pictures of it show us an exterior of such exemplary plainness, as would delight the souls of those who grudge the House of God the touch of beauty."[8]

Without venturing further aesthetic judgment one may suppose that William Price, from whatever heavenly cloud he may be looking down upon his beloved Trinity Church, is undoubtedly much gratified by the present church's great imposing central tower and

8. Phillips Brooks, *Trinity Church in The City of Boston 1733–1933* [Historical Sermon] (Boston, 1933), p. 32.

numerous turrets, almost gleaming today in their original splendor. And, if we listen carefully, we may hear him as he wafts gently by, carefully avoiding the obtrusive John Hancock Tower, plucking the strings of his celestial harp to the tune of "O How amiable are Thy dwellings, Thou Lord of Hosts."

23. Trinity Church. Wood engraving by Abel Bowen. Proof from printer's scrap-book as published in *The American Magazine of Useful and Entertaining Knowledge*, vol. 1, no. 1 (Boston, 1834), p. 18.

Measured Drawings of the Hancock House
by John Hubbard Sturgis:
A Legacy to the Colonial Revival

ONE of the first great battles for historic preservation was waged over the Hancock House on Beacon Street in Boston in 1863 (Fig. 24). Was the one-hundred-and-twenty-six-year-old stone mansion, home of the first governor of the Commonwealth, to be destroyed or preserved? The matter of the Hancock House came to a head during the Civil War, and with public attention divided between battles on the field and battles in the legislature, historic preservation would appear to have lost the first skirmish. A fire-engine-red six-foot-high auctioneer's poster (now in the library of the Society for the Preservation of New England Antiquities) advertised sale of interior details and stone from the Old Hancock House at 4 p.m. on the premises, June 26, 1863.[1] Massachusetts mourned the day, wrote Franklin Webster Smith, when a narrow-minded legislature refused to buy and save the home of John Hancock for a gubernatorial mansion.[2]

Within these events lies an even more fascinating story—that of the staircase from the house, which was preserved and re-used along with numerous other bits and pieces of the fabric, now widely scat-

1. Marshall Davidson, *American Heritage History of Colonial Antiques* (New York, 1967), p. 153. Here the information on the Hancock House is entitled "Lost Landmarks."

2. Franklin Webster Smith, *Designs, Plans and Suggestions for the Aggrandizement of Washington* (Washington, 1900, Senate Document No. 209), pp. 37–39. Here Smith, in advocating retention of the White House as the executive mansion, uses the obvious earlier example of the Hancock House demolition.

tered.[3] Measured drawings made of this staircase, and in fact of the entire building prior to its demolition, are now in the collections of the Society for the Preservation of New England Antiquities, being the first known full set of measured drawings to have been made of an American house.

The seven known drawings of the Hancock House, executed by the young architect John Hubbard Sturgis (1834–1888) just prior to its demolition in 1863, may well have been part of a larger series. Scaled at $\frac{1}{4}''$ to a foot are all four elevations (Figs. 25–28) and the full ground and chamber floor plans (Figs. 29 and 30). A final drawing at $1\frac{1}{2}''$ to a foot, the only one of the interior, shows details of the staircase and hall window (Fig. 31). Measured drawings are an essential process in historic preservation.[4] In the case of the Hancock House, these staircase drawings were a specific legacy to later houses of the Colonial Revival period of the late nineteenth century.

One of the most extensively documented of all Colonial buildings, the stone mansion of Thomas Hancock, wealthy Boston merchant, had been painstakingly constructed beginning in 1736. Many parts of the house were imported from England: the caps for four pilasters, glass for the windows, wallpaper, and many of the furnishings.

Arthur Gilman of Bryant and Gilman (largest architectural firm in the city) went through the documents concerning the house and wrote up its history for the *Atlantic Monthly* in 1863.[5] By this time

3. Walter Kendall Watkins, "The Hancock House and Its Builder," *Old-Time New England*, XVII (1926–1927), 3–19. Among these are the following: staircase in Greeley Curtis House, Manchester-by-the-Sea; balusters, one from stair and one from roof, two carved capitals in Essex Institute, Salem; larger carved pilaster cap from "Loer Rume" at National Museum, Independence Hall, Philadelphia; modillion from cornice at Massachusetts Historical Society; pendant from staircase, pilaster caps, and additional modillions at SPNEA; front door at the Bostonian Society; balcony at John Hancock Insurance Company, Boston; carved corbel at Martine Cottage, Portsmouth, New Hampshire, home of R. Clipston Sturgis; stone steps at Pinebank, Jamaica Plain, a house designed by John Sturgis in 1869. Many other elements survive as well.

4. For example, architectural measured drawings were the subject of a symposium on November 16, 1973, celebrating the fortieth anniversary of the Historic American Buildings Survey (HABS), which was established in 1933 using measured drawings as a prime documentary tool.

5. Arthur Gilman, "The Hancock House and Its Founder," *Atlantic Monthly*, XI

24.   Residence of John Hancock, Boston, Mass. Woodcut from *Sears Pictorial History of the United States* (1848).

the outstanding architectural merits of the building were reinforced by its patriotic and historic associations and its antiquity.

[The house] was thought to be a very grand and famous affair in the infant metropolis of New England in the year 1737 . . . [but] it is now the sole relic of the family mansions of the *old* Town of Boston, as in many respects it has long been the most notable and interesting of them all. . . . We enter the close front-gate from the sunny and bustling promenade of Beacon Street, pass up the worn gray terrace of steps, and in a moment more closes behind us the door that seems to shut us out from the whirl and turmoil and strife of the present, and, almost mysteriously, to trans-

(1863), 692–707. One of the most important architects in Boston, Gilman (1821–1882) had designed the Arlington Street Church in Boston (1859) and laid out the plan for the Back Bay. With his partner J. F. Gridley Bryant he had just designed the Boston City Hall (1862). He left Boston for New York and Washington in 1867.

port us to the grave shadows and the dignified silence of the past of American history.[6]

The central block of the house was a rectangle fifty-six feet in length and thirty-eight feet deep. The walls were of squared granite ashlar from Medford with rusticated quoins and window dressings of Connecticut brownstone ornamenting the symmetrical facade.[7] Two large wings, a ballroom to the east and kitchen and offices to the west, were gone by 1863. The date of these wings (Fig. 32) is unknown, but construction took place between 1737 and July of 1789, when Hill illustrated them in an engraving in the *Massachusetts Magazine*. Stur-

6. Ibid., pp. 692, 694, 706. This sort of poetic approach to old architecture is not without parallel. See, for example, Nathaniel Hawthorne's *The House of the Seven Gables* (1851), Chapter I.

7. Gilman, "The Hancock House and Its Founder." Descriptions of the house used in this article are based on Gilman unless otherwise noted.

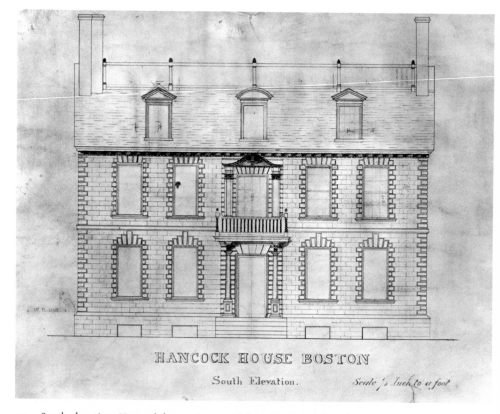

HANCOCK HOUSE BOSTON

South Elevation.   Scale ½ Inch to a foot

25.   South elevation, Hancock house. Measured drawing (1863) by John Hubbard Sturgis. Courtesy Society for the Preservation of New England Antiquities.

gis' measured drawings strongly suggest that these wings were not structurally original to the house. The thickness of the end walls (Fig. 27) indicates that they must have been intended as part of the exterior fabric, while the belt course between stories and at the eaves continues uninterrupted across the east and west elevations (Figs. 29 and 30). The east wing was removed in 1818 and both by 1848 (Fig. 24).

The double pitched gambrel roof had carved modillions at the cornice, a railing at the top, and three pedimented dormer windows, the central one arched in fine Baroque form. Below, the entrance was approached by a flight of stone steps. Rusticated from sill to eaves, it boasted ornate engaged columns, an ornamented door head with an elaborate balcony and a large window above, complete with broken scroll pediment (Fig. 25).

The plan of the interior was a typical one for a great mid-century

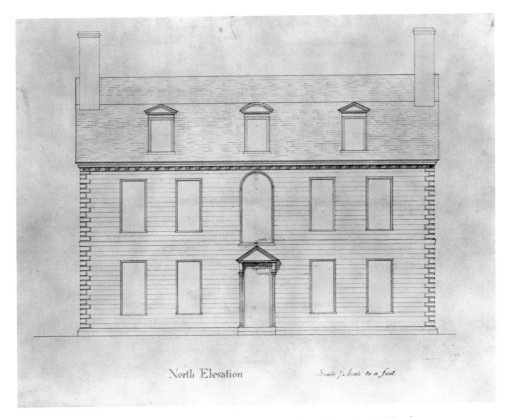

North Elevation   Scale 1/4 Inch to a foot.

26. North elevation, Hancock house. Measured drawing (1863) by John Hubbard Sturgis. Courtesy Society for the Preservation of New England Antiquities.

house, dominated by a staircase hall bisecting the building from front to back on both floors (Fig. 33). Above the landing was an arched window with deep reveals flanked by classical pilasters. The staircase itself had variously carved and twisted balusters and newel (Fig. 31). The Washington bedroom, 17'7" x 21'10", was located at the southeastern corner of the second floor, facing on Beacon Street (Fig. 34). The elaborate chimney breast, which jutted into the room from the east, was adorned with fluted Corinthian pilasters, more ornate than those on the stair landing. The great room was richly furnished and architecturally advanced for 1737, with panelling from floor to ceiling.[8]

8. Watkins, "The Hancock House and Its Builder," p. 19. Here it is specified that the east wing, or ballroom, was removed to Allen Street in Boston's West End by 1818. Its exact date of construction is not documented but may well have been shortly after John Hancock inherited the house from his uncle (who died in 1764) just prior

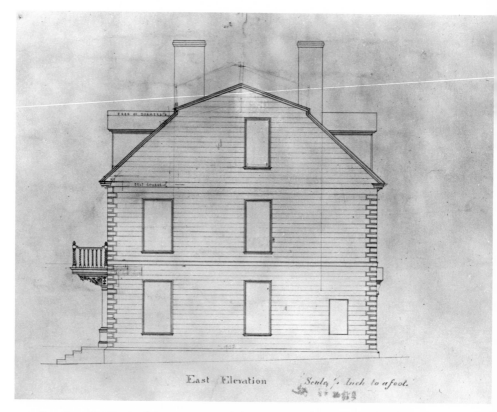

27.   East elevation, Hancock house. Measured drawing (1863) by John Hubbard Sturgis. Courtesy Society for the Preservation of New England Antiquities.

Following the death of Thomas Hancock in 1764, the property (which included much of the south slope of Beacon Hill) was inherited by his nephew John, first signer of the Declaration of Independence, who lived there as the first governor of Massachusetts. With his death in 1793, financial difficulties concerning the house began. For, despite his popularity and eminence, John Hancock was notorious (particularly to those in contact with him during his tenure as treasurer of Harvard College) as incompetent and inattentive, if not totally dishonest, in financial matters.[9] In 1795 the Common-

---

to the Revolution. Figure 1 showing the house without wings is a lithograph published in 1848 after a drawing of the house by A. J. Davis, the New York architect, who may have executed it as early as 1827–1828 on his well-known sketching trip to Boston.

9. "Surely I Did Not Run Away with the Property of the College," *Harvard Bulletin*, x (June 1973), 72.

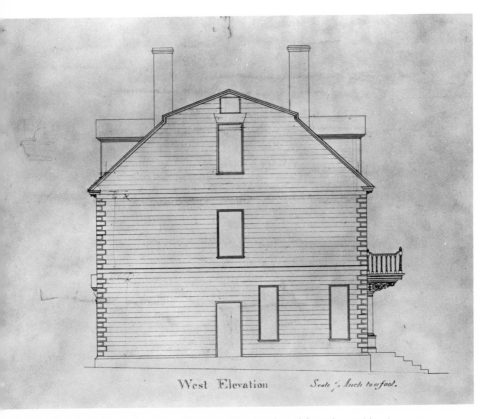

West Elevation   Scale ½ Inch to a foot.

3.   West elevation, Hancock house. Measured drawing (1863) by John Hubbard Sturgis. Courtesy Society for the Preservation of New England Antiquities.

wealth of Massachusetts purchased the pasture just to the east of the house for the site of Charles Bulfinch's new State House, further reducing the acreage, and by 1863 the estate had fallen onto hard times and taxes were overdue. Plans to extend Hancock Street south from Cambridge Street to Beacon, directly through the site of the house, strongly suggested to many the demolition of the building. Speaking in favor of saving (or relocating) the Hancock House, Arthur Gilman may also have recommended that measured drawings be made when demolition was inescapable. He may well have suggested his young associate John Sturgis for the job.[10]

Sturgis made measured drawings of the house and at the auction purchased the staircase. His plans for using it were uncertain, and it was put into storage in Boston. It was still there when in 1866 he

10. John Sturgis was in partnership with Bryant and Gilman in Boston 1861–1866. He was also designing independently during this period.

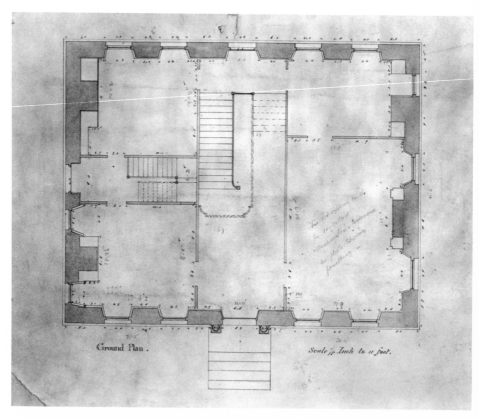

29.   Ground plan, Hancock house. Measured drawing (1863) by John Hubbard Sturgis. Courtesy Society for the Preservation of New England Antiquities.

sailed for England to remain for four years, leaving his young partner Charles Brigham in charge of his Boston architectural office. But on April 5, 1869, Brigham wrote to England:

Hancock staircase—I have advertised it for sale but I cannot answer your question as to its worth inasmuch as it would fetch but little, but for its value historically. Mr. Poland will have to move from his shop on the 15th to make way for the new P. O. Building (which by the way Bryant has to superintend) and we shall have to remove the staircase unless I get a purchaser previous—I shall demand $150—please write me at once of your approval if you think it right—I enclose a drawing of plan of it.[11]

11. Charles Brigham to John Hubbard Sturgis, Letters to England, April 5, 1869, and April 18, 1870, Sturgis Papers, The Boston Athenæum. The Hancock staircase was stored in the shop of one Poland, a Boston mason who did considerable other work for Sturgis and his partner Charles Brigham (1841–1925). One of these jobs was "Pinebank" in Jamaica Plain (1869), where the stone steps from the Hancock House are now located. This suggests Sturgis may also have purchased the steps. The Post

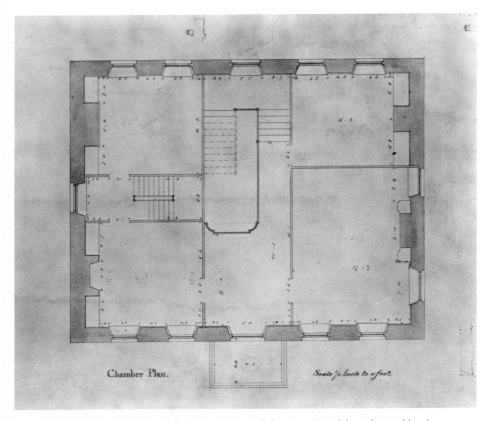

Chamber Plan.   Scale ⅛ Inch to a foot.

30. Chamber floor plan, Hancock house. Measured drawing (1863) by John Hubbard Sturgis. Courtesy Society for the Preservation of New England Antiquities.

Not hearing from his partner, however, Brigham made the decision to sell the staircase, writing again on May 26:

I did not have time to mention the subject of the Hancock staircase but as the deed was done and could not be retracted I deferred till now to reply to your regrets or rather expressions of fear that I had sold it. I did understand that you would like to dispose of it but had there been time to have received more definite instructions from you I should have delayed any actions till then. As I intimated in my letter of April 5th the shop where it was stored was not torn down until about May 1st and I waited till the last moment. I had had an offer from Mr. Greeley Curtis of $50 and of

Office building referred to here (destroyed in the fire of 1872) was designed by Arthur B. Mullett, then architect of government building. Arthur Gilman collaborated with Mullett on the design of the State War and Navy Building in Washington 1871–1875.

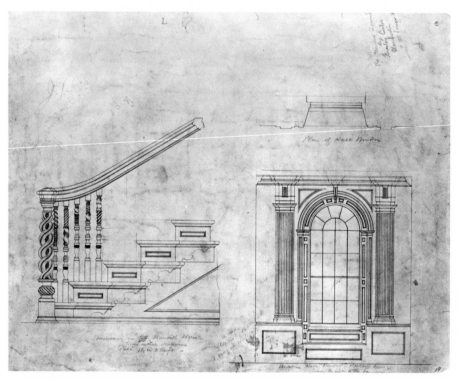

31.   Interior details, staircase and window, Hancock house. Measured drawing (1863) by John Hubbard Sturgis. Courtesy Society for the Preservation of New England Antiquities.

course refused it. I had gone so far as to have sent a portion of it down to Broad Street where your furniture is stored and was in search of a place to store the more bulky parts which could not be got up to the attic on account of their weight and size when I received a note from him saying that he would give $125 which I at once accepted. If I could have stored it all together I should have let it remain till further news from you, but the only place where I could find a shelter for it was under an open shed. The carpenters are driven to small quarters and I feared that the cost of storage would be too much. I regret to have misunderstood you, but I think it has gone into the possession of those who will appreciate it. Mr Curtis is having it put up in his house at Manchester now building. He

32. Hancock house. Detail of fireboard painting of Park Street Church, Boston (c. 1812). Oil on panel 35¾″ × 49½″. Painted for Joseph Allen. Courtesy Bostonian Society.

could probably have been induced to give more for it but that he had already got his stairs half built before he knew this was for sale which excuses his first paltry offer.[12]

A picture thus emerges of Sturgis, whatever his reasons, being reluctant to part with the unused staircase. Had he known its location,

12. John Sturgis was visiting with his father Russell Sturgis of Boston, who had settled permanently in London as senior partner of Baring's Bank. The enterprising Brigham was from Watertown, Massachusetts, where he continued to live all his life. Capital for the architectural partnership, which lasted 1866–1886, was provided by Sturgis.

33. Front hall and staircase in the Hancock house. Wood engraving from *Ballou's Pictorial Drawing-Room Companion* (March 26, 1859). Courtesy Bostonian Society.

he would have been even less enthused, for the great house at Man-chester-by-the-Sea, of stone, with Flemish gables, was designed by Greeley Curtis (an enthusiastic amateur architect) and Henry Van Brunt of the Boston firm of Ware and Van Brunt.[13] Spectacular in siting, high above the ocean, and with an impressive exterior, the house was constricted and fragmented on the interior during the first building campaign of 1869. Because the staircase in the house was already half built, that from the Hancock House was badly cut up and reversed in run in order to fit the existing space (Fig. 33).[14] Brig-ham himself could hardly have been pleased, for he had unwittingly disposed of his senior partner's property, and worse, Van Brunt (no friend of Brigham's) would have the credit for utilizing the staircase, no matter how he had botched the job of installation![15]

So the Hancock House was demolished and the staircase saved, but more important even than its preservation were the measured draw-ings which Sturgis made from the staircase in situ. Recently it has been suggested that measured drawings should in fact be termed measuring drawings, for they differ from designs or plans which an architect makes for a projected new building in that they are created after the fact of the edifice.[16] A measured drawing is done to scale from an existing structure and requires a rather complex set of cal-culations with tedious attention to detail. The central point of con-sideration for any measured drawing is why it is needed in the first place. In the case of the Hancock House, the demolition controversy and historical importance of the structure provided the impetus which had heretofore been missing in America, a young and growing country with few ancient buildings to measure. So until the mid-

13. For information on Van Brunt, a pupil of Richard Morris Hunt, see William A. Coles, ed., *Architecture and Society, The Selected Essays of Henry Van Brunt* (Cam-bridge, 1969).

14. Bainbridge Bunting, "The Greeley Curtis House," in *Architecture of H. H. Rich-ardson and His Contemporaries in Boston and Vicinity* (Philadelphia, 1972), pp. 46–47.

15. See Sturgis Papers. Brigham's letters make clear that Henry Van Brunt's aca-demic orientation annoyed him.

16. Adolf Placzek, Librarian, Avery Architectural Library, Paper delivered at HABS Symposium on Architectural Measured Drawings (Washington, D.C., No-vember 1973).

34. The Washington Room in the Hancock house. Wood engraving from *Ballou's Pictorial Drawing-Room Companion* (March 26, 1859). Courtesy Bostonian Society.

nineteenth century when a new consciousness of the importance of our Colonial architecture began to become apparent, measured drawings had not really been needed.

Some idea of the state of the art emerges if we consider the number of architects travelling up and down the east coast sketching Colonial buildings during the 1870's[17] and the numerous books on Colonial architecture published following the 1876 Centennial Exhibition in Philadelphia. Sketches like those of Arthur Little, *New England Interiors* (Boston, 1878), or Edwin Whitefield, *The Homes of Our Forefathers in Boston, Old England and Boston, New England* (Boston, 1889),

17. Vincent Scully, *The Shingle Style* (New Haven, 1955), pp. 19–33.

were picturesque endeavors but not measured drawings from which specific details could be reproduced.

Therefore, in 1863, since few American architects were familiar with the process of measured drawings, John Sturgis, who had been trained in England during the 1850's, was an obvious choice to make those of the Hancock House. He had been the pupil of James K. Colling, renowned as one of England's finest draughtsmen, who had published numbers of books of measured drawings.[18] Although measured drawings were uncommon in America, such was not the case in England. There, within the heightening fever of the Gothic Revival, numerous architects, armed with sketch pads and yardsticks, were examining the moldering ruins of countless country churches and Gothic halls, sadly in need of restoration.[19] The middle decades of the nineteenth century had brought a realization of the condition of the national architectural heritage in England, leading ultimately to the founding of the Society for the Protection of Ancient Buildings in 1876 by William Morris.[20]

A product of this tradition, John Sturgis had returned to Boston only in 1861, less than two years before the demolition of the Hancock House. During the next two decades he was to continue as the prime purveyor of English architectural taste in Boston.[21] He imported not only theory and design but specific elements of buildings: terra cotta, tile, wrought iron, and woodwork from London to build

18. James K. Colling Sketchbooks (London, RIBA Drawings Collection). Also see James K. Colling to Russell Sturgis, London, March 6, 1867 (Sturgis Papers). Here Colling discusses making measured drawings of Russell Sturgis' home Mount Felix in Surrey (1838) by Sir Charles Barry at John Sturgis' request.

19. See, for example: Edmund Sharpe, *The Rise and Progress of Decorated Window Tracery* (London, 1849) or *The Seven Periods of Gothic Architecture* (London, 1851); Samuel Carter Hall, *The Baronial Halls and Picturesque Edifices of England*, 2 vols. (London, 1848).

20. Asa Briggs, *William Morris: Selected Writings and Designs* (Baltimore, 1962), pp. 13–26. Concern for architectural preservation in England was well advanced by 1877, and Morris, artist, designer, Pre-Raphaelite, poet, and novelist, first formalized the movement.

21. Margaret Henderson Floyd, "A Terra Cotta Cornerstone for Copley Square: Museum of Fine Arts, Boston, 1870–1876, by Sturgis and Brigham," *Journal of the Society of Architectural Historians*, XXXII (1973), 83–103. Here is further information on Sturgis' training and on J. K. Colling.

great houses for the Boston aristocracy of the late nineteenth century, much as Thomas Hancock had done for his own house over a century before.

By the autumn of 1870, when John Sturgis again returned to Boston to win the competition for the Museum of Fine Arts on Copley Square, the Hancock House staircase was installed at Manchester-by-the-Sea. But Sturgis' measured drawings remained in his papers. Of special interest is his drawing of the staircase (Fig. 31), which he later would use as the basis for stairs in two houses in Cambridge—early examples of Colonial Revival design.

An overall relationship to the Hancock House is apparent in the exteriors of both the Edward W. Hooper house (1872) at 25 Reservoir Street (Fig. 35) and the Arthur Astor Carey house (1882) at 28 Fayerweather Street (Fig. 37), only a block away.[22] Like their model, both houses have gambrel roofs, are essentially rectangular, and are bisected by a central hall with staircase (Figs. 36, 38). In each case, however, the architect has subdivided the hall (which no longer completely bisects the depth of the house), has moved the stair from its position opposite the entrance to one adjacent to it on the main facade, and has added a fireplace to create a Queen Anne Revival living hall.[23] The Hooper House, which is earlier by ten years, reflects much exterior detail reminiscent of the 1870's, freely combined with elements borrowed from the Hancock House. For example, the two over two windows, shed dormers, and mansarded wing suggest its date. Revealed construction with a band of stickwork forms the belt course between the floors and continues uninterrupted across the two-story bay window. The ornate wooden parapets are identical to those in stone then being used by the architect in several other houses

22. Edward W. Hooper was Treasurer of Harvard College and brother-in-law of Henry Adams. Arthur Astor Carey was a grandson of John Jacob Astor and an instructor of English at Harvard. Both men were on the Committee for the Foundation of the Museum of Fine Arts, Copley Square, for which Sturgis was architect. The Cambridge Historical Commission has kindly shared its research with the author on these points.

23. Scully, *The Shingle Style*, passim. Here the nineteenth-century evolution of the living hall with both staircase and fireplace is extensively documented and the early Colonial Revival discussed.

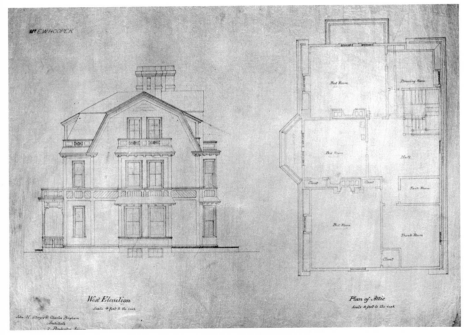

35. West elevation and plan of attic, E. W. Hooper house (1872), 25 Reservoir Street, Cambridge, by Sturgis and Brigham. Courtesy Mr. Charles Eliot.

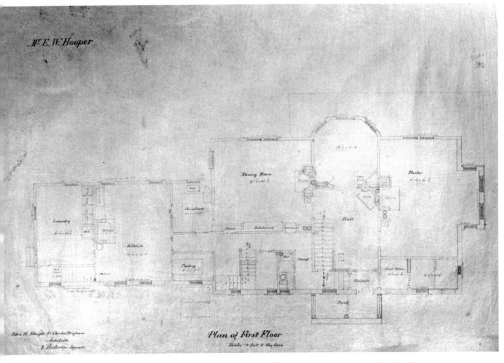

36. Plan of ground floor, E. W. Hooper house (1872), 25 Reservoir Street, Cambridge, by Sturgis and Brigham. Courtesy Mr. Charles Eliot.

37.   A. A. Carey house (1882), 28 Fayerweather Street, Cambridge, by Sturgis and Brigham. Courtesy Society for the Preservation of New England Antiquities.

in the Back Bay.[24] Although the elevation is symmetrical and the appearance of the gambrel roof notable, the composition is treated freely and creatively, one of the most interesting characteristics of early Colonial Revival design.

The later Carey House (1882) is more classical in its ornament, much closer to the original Hancock House, but the architect now manipulates the frame of the building more freely (Fig. 37). The dormer windows, dentilled entrance bay with balcony on carved brackets, and the scrolled pediment above the central window are very specific ornamental components of the eighteenth-century model. To these Sturgis adds a round arched window derived from that on the Hancock House staircase, but now penetrating the main facade adjacent to the entrance. The two-story bay windows seen on the

24. Sturgis used a terra cotta parapet in a similar design on his Charles Joy house, 86 Marlborough Street, Boston (1872), and also on Pinebank, Jamaica Plain (1869).

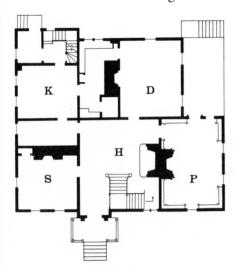

38.   Plan of A. A. Carey house (1882), 28 Fayer-weather Street, Cambridge, by Sturgis and Brigham. Measured drawing by Susan Maycock Vogel. Courtesy Cambridge Historical Commission.

Hooper House, characteristic elements of American post–Civil War design, do not appear in the later Carey House. Instead a studied "colonializing" of the frame has been introduced with a lean-to at the rear and an overhang in the end gable as well, both features associated with seventeenth-century design.

The interior detailing of both houses is creatively varied but also closely derived from the Hancock House drawings. Each house has a great panelled chimney breast in the parlor based on that in the Washington bedroom of the Hancock House (Figs. 34, 39, 40). The newel post of the Carey House stair (Fig. 41) is a near copy of its model (Fig. 31), while the panelled shutters in the bedroom are additional colonializing elements (Fig. 42).

Certainly, then, in the work of John Sturgis the measured drawings of the Hancock House can be said to have influenced the course of design for new construction in the first quarter-century after the demolition of that great Georgian mansion. But in fact, by 1888, the year of Sturgis' death, the momentum of influence of the Hancock House was just beginning to accelerate. In the last decade of the nineteenth century it was transformed into far more than a destroyed monument—it had become an institution, one which was to be copied over and over again with varying degrees of faithfulness to the original, and used not only as a model for houses but for public buildings as well.

Only in the years following the Centennial Exposition in Philadelphia in 1876 had the importance of American Colonial architecture begun to be generally recognized. Robert Swain Peabody (1845–1917), a contemporary of Sturgis, who had been born in New Bedford, had already surfaced as its spokesman, notwithstanding his training at the Ecole des Beaux-Arts in Paris in 1868, two years after graduating from Harvard College.[25] It was he who was to carry forward the Hancock House legend after Sturgis' death in 1888. In 1877,

25. Wheaton A. Holden, "The Peabody Touch: Peabody and Stearns of Boston, 1870–1917," *Journal of the Society of Architectural Historians*, XXXII (1973), 114–131.

39.   Chimney breast (1872), E. W. Hooper house. Photo, author.

writing in the *American Architect and Building News*, he stated his affinity for Colonial design:

There is no revival so little of an affectation on our soil, as that of the beautiful work of Colonial days. Its quiet dignity and quaintness, its cosiness and elegance, always attract us. It is our legitimate field for imitation, and we have much of it to study right in our own neighborhood. In fact, anyone who in summer drives over the ancient turnpike from Hingham to Plymouth will not only pass through a beautiful country full of old homesteads, but will find the sun-flowers still nodding behind the gambrel roofed houses that line the road through Queen Anne's corner.[26]

26. *American Architect and Building News*, II (1877), 133–134. Scully, *The Shingle Style*, p. 42. Peabody's comment was made famous within the context of Scully's landmark volume, where it is reproduced under discussion of the Colonial Revival.

40.   Chimney breast (1882), A. A. Carey house. Photo, author.

Twelve years later Peabody's admiration for the Hingham area was rewarded when he received the commission for a Parish House for the Old Ship Church (Fig. 43), even then a seventeenth-century sacred cow among Colonial structures. The resulting design, linked physically to the ancient meetinghouse on the opposite promontory through the umbilical cord of an underground heating system engineered to run under Main Street, seems to have served as an interim exercise in 1889 for the Massachusetts State Building which he was to erect in Chicago three years later. It was closely based on the features of both the Old Ship Church and the Hancock House

The first Parish House was necessarily a rectangle housing an oblong auditorium, but Peabody's perspective drawing, now in the collections of the Massachusetts Historical Society, appears centralized, reflecting the original seventeenth-century plan of the Old Ship Church. The elevation, dominated by two great intersecting gam-

41.   Staircase newel post (1882), A. A. Carey house. Photo, author.

42.   Bedroom shutters (1882), A. A. Carey house. Photo, author.

brel roofs, is marked at their crossing with a cupola. The double slope
of the roof system, the Palladian window, balconied porch, and classical detail clearly evoke the Hancock House, while the swelling profile and cupola echo the famed truss system of the meetinghouse. It
was a brilliant and typically free nineteenth-century version of a parish house to "match" the church and appears to have been directly
connected to the design which the architect produced three years
later for the World's Columbian Exposition in Chicago (Fig. 44).

    Discussing the Massachusetts State Building at the time of the
Chicago Exposition, Peabody is specific in expressing his debt to the
Hancock House:

Casting about for models that might fitly recall New England surround-
ings . . . the Old State House and the Hancock Mansion which once stood

on Beacon Hill, seemed to offer the best possible types. This Hancock house, with its terraced gardens, was the most picturesque as well as the most architectural of the two buildings. For these reasons it was selected as a model. . . . The valuable quality in the design of the original Hancock house was the air of aristocratic distinction and reserve and dignity that it bore, without losing a homelike and comfortable appearance.[27]

So by 1893 the Hancock House had moved from its role as a model for houses to a symbolic structure considered also appropriate for public buildings.

The saga of the Hancock House is thus prototypical in historic preservation. It would almost appear that circumstances conspired to maximize its stature after 1863. The immense controversy attending the demolition (not to mention the artifacts distributed through the

27. *Report of the Massachusetts Board of World's Fair Managers, World's Columbian Exposition, Chicago 1893* (Boston, 1894), pp. 31–33.

43.   Old Ship Church Parish House, Hingham, Mass. (1889), by Robert Swain Peabody. Courtesy Massachusetts Historical Society.

44. Massachusetts State Building (1893) by Peabody and Stearns, from *Report of the Massachusetts Board of World's Fair Managers, World's Columbian Exposition, Chicago, 1893.*

auction) and the publicity naturally associated with the fame of the owners gained initial attention. The prominent location on Beacon Street adjacent to Bulfinch's State House (now memorialized with a bronze plaque) kept the site continually in the public eye, and the unique circumstance of Sturgis' measured drawings and their utilization in his own work drew continuing attention to the design. But those elements were only a prelude to the selection of the Hancock House as model for Peabody's Massachusetts State Building at the World's Columbian Exposition in Chicago in 1893, for this later structure, seen repeatedly by visitors from all over the world, was more responsible than any other factor for making it the sine qua non as a model for late nineteenth-century buildings in America: the archetype of Colonial Revival design.

Massachusetts and Its First Period Houses:
A Statistical Survey

I N 1956, in connection with a documentary history of the Parson Thomas Barnard House in North Andover, formerly known as the Anne Bradstreet House, the writer published certain statistics having to do with the First Period dwellings of Massachusetts, those structures erected between 1620 and 1725. The tabular figures were concerned fundamentally with demonstrating the fact that from the nineteenth century onwards the average lay person and many historians as well had tended to assign earlier dates than were justified to a significantly large number of houses built during the first century of Massachusetts' settlement in a homogeneous style consistent with what the English scholar defines as post-medieval. Fiske Kimball, writing early in this century, was sufficiently concerned with the problem to confine his study of the period to only a small group of firmly documented buildings, and to warn his readers further against acceptance of dates found in the documents which prove little more than that there was a dwelling house on a given site in the early years. Any dates prior to 1650, he concluded, "must be advanced with extreme caution. Thus in the case of the Fairbanks house at Dedham . . . it is rash to maintain the very year of Jonathan Fairbanks's admission as a townsman, 1636–7, as the date of the building of the central part of the existing house."[1] His choice of this example to prove a thoroughly justifiable point was a poor one, for the traditional date of the Fairbanks House has recently been confirmed

---

1. Fiske Kimball, *Domestic Architecture of the American Colonies and of the Early Republic* (New York: Charles Scribner's Sons, 1922), p. 35.

through structural and dendrochronological examination, and this celebrated landmark now ranks as the earliest in the State. It is assuredly our oldest building in point of style.

Nevertheless, there are a surprisingly large number of houses in Massachusetts which have been advertised as earlier than they actually are, and the statistical analysis to which we have referred reveals an interesting correlation. Material for the table is taken from the 1937 Federal Writers' guide to Massachusetts which lists extensively the historic houses in the Commonwealth whether open to the public or privately owned. The dates given are based mostly on unverified tradition and include a number of structures which are not of our period at all. Yet because of this the figures reflect even more critically the popular desire to make the house as old as possible. Dividing the century between 1620 and 1725 into four quarters and grouping the number of structures accordingly a curious graph line develops:

1620–1649	twenty-seven
1650–1674	forty-three
1675–1699	fifty-three
1700–1725	thirty-eight

There was clearly a mystique in the 1930's and even now associated with a construction date in the more romantic-sounding 1600's. Nor had it been sufficiently appreciated that houses of the first quarter of the eighteenth century belong, generically, to that style period which we have too loosely labelled "seventeenth century." Thus, a good many later houses (like the Parson Barnard House) had long masqueraded under much earlier dates.

No amount of argument, it seems, can disabuse proud houseowners of the fond conviction that theirs is the first or second oldest in town. This kind of pride, in fact, is indulged in by whole communities. One village north of Boston has boasted in connection with an "open house" day that ten seventeenth-century houses would be on view when actually there is but a single structure remaining within its corporate limits which *may* have been erected before 1700.[2]

2. *Boston Sunday Herald,* July 31, 1949, p. 12.

Even the most authoritative documentation has seldom succeeded in changing many minds. A significant cross section of the public continues to side with the mid-nineteenth-century newspaper editor in Plymouth who, having learned that because of the calendar reform of 1752 the town had been observing the first landing of the Pilgrims for nearly a century on the wrong day, stoutly resisted a local movement to change the date of celebration, declaring that "we much prefer established error to novel truth."[3]

In 1922 Fiske Kimball was limited by the "rigorously established" system for dating which he had accepted to some ten houses in Essex County (not all of which even then were correctly authenticated).[4] This fundamental group of documented buildings has been considerably enlarged through more recent scholarship, including new methods by which one can make defensible assumptions about the date of a building. Contemporary documents, especially those relating to the title, remain when carefully considered one of the principal sources of verification, but tend to be less effective for the earlier years of the seventeenth century where the danger becomes intensified that we may be confusing a valid First Period structure with an older house described in the records as occupying the same site. More recently a dendrochronological study in eastern Massachusetts, initiated in 1968, has produced sufficient correlation with documentary evidence to suggest the validity for this area of dates based upon tree-ring analysis.[5] And further, through structural comparison of vernacular buildings erected in old and New England during the seventeenth century and carpenters' joints in particular, it is now possible to suggest some chronological relationships at least for many of the houses which have hitherto lacked adequate evidence as to the time of erection.

Much of this enlarged historical data as it relates particularly to

3. George F. Willison, *Saints and Strangers* (New York: Reynal & Hitchcock, ᶜ1945), p. 425.

4. Kimball, *Domestic Architecture*, p. 14.

5. Frank A. Demers, "Progress Report No. 1, Chronological Identification of 17th Century New England Oak Timbers through Tree-Ring Analysis" (August 21, 1968), MS, Society for the Preservation of New England Antiquities.

Massachusetts Bay has been summarized in the Appendix and will have the additional advantage of shedding some light on the dimensions of the writer's forthcoming study of the framed houses of that area built during the first century of settlement. For the purposes of the present study, however, all domestic structures of framed and masonry construction between 1620 and 1725 and for all counties of the Commonwealth have been included.

We begin then with the raw statistics themselves, divided into four chronological categories: First, those houses which can be accepted without reservation as having been erected before 1660. The cutoff date may seem somewhat arbitrary, but there are good reasons, architecturally speaking, for establishing a boundary marker here, and it is interesting to note that several recent scholars, concerned more with seventeenth-century social and political history, have acknowledged a turning point more or less at this moment in time when the first immigrant generation of preponderantly younger settlers had come to full maturity.

Our second category includes houses erected between 1660 and 1700, at the close of which period there are discernible evolutionary developments in terms of style which lead directly into the third category, those houses built in the final quarter of the First Period between 1701 and 1725. In the case of some buildings, however, authentication has not been possible, for which reason a fourth category has been established. Here will be found all those houses which, because an insufficient amount of the original structure is exposed for inspection, or because the documentary evidence is equivocal (or for the moment unexamined) and the building looks both forwards and backwards in style, have been lumped together under the heading "Circa 1700."

The revised statistics, therefore, are as follows:

10 extant houses in Massachusetts were built before 1660 as structural evidence clearly indicates; of these, 6 have been firmly documented and only 2 might conceivably be any later.

61 extant houses in Massachusetts were built between 1660 and 1700, and here it should be added parenthetically, only one

structure in this category has given any pause: What does one do with the Hart House in Ipswich? Of genuine early date, the house was restored just after 1900 by Ralph Burnham, at which time molded sheathing from another seventeenth-century Ipswich house was introduced. Then, in the mid-1930's the oldest room and its chamber were completely dismantled, the parlor to be reassembled in the American Wing of the Metropolitan Museum of Art in New York City and the chamber at the Henry Francis du Pont Winterthur Museum in Delaware. This left only a portion of the old house in situ, to which a modern replica of the missing elements was attached! Query: Is the Hart House extant or is it not?

In a more serious vein, it should be noted here that nonexisting houses, of which portions survive in museums, have been counted nevertheless as no longer extant, and these structures are caught up in another set of statistics altogether.

Proceeding then to our third category:

    103 houses in Massachusetts survive from the period 1701 to 1725 of which a few at least may conceivably be retardatory First Period houses whose date of construction is somewhat later than 1725.

Finally, in the fourth category:

    83 as yet undocumented houses in Massachusetts can be accepted on the basis of style, and for the reasons mentioned earlier, as having been built either just before or just after 1700, with the larger percentage falling probably in the latter classification.

Thus the graph line becomes entirely predictable for the three major subdivisions: 10 – 61 – 103, which together with category four gives us a total of 257 known First Period houses now surviving in the Commonwealth, a claim which it is unlikely that any other state in the Nation could make.

Now for some further refinements of these figures. What, for example, is the record of individual counties? Essex County leads by a generous margin with a total of 151 among all houses erected be-

tween 1620 and 1725. The exact breakdown by chronological category is as follows:

Before 1660	5
1660–1700	39
1701–1725	53
Circa 1700	54

Ipswich, in Essex County, has always claimed the highest density of
seventeenth-century houses, and the statistics readily bear this out,
especially when we include all houses of the First Period. It is clear,
however, that in categories 1 and 2 alone, Salem trails very closely
behind:

Houses erected before 1701	
Ipswich	12
Salem	9

Middlesex County is second to Essex with a total of forty-three extant houses. Then follow in order Suffolk County (as originally de-
fined, including the more recent Norfolk County taken out of it and
portions of the modern Plymouth County) with a total of twenty-
nine existing houses; Plymouth, Bristol, and Barnstable Counties
(the Old Colony) with twenty-two; the Island of Nantucket with
nine; and the original counties of Hamden and Hampshire with three.

At which point one might well ask, are these data complete and
definitive, and the answer is, of course, negative. The writer cannot
claim to have blanketed the entire area. On the other hand, he has
examined most of the town histories and published historical society
records for the older communities of Massachusetts (where the earliest houses erected by the settlers are almost always a subject of discussion), and he has persistently inspected in person as many so-called
First Period houses as have been brought to his attention. Here, we
have recently seen a significant improvement in terms of quantitative
analysis as more and more communities have undertaken professional
inventories of their historic architectural assets. Beverly is an excellent
case in point where a large area, both urban and rural, has been thoroughly canvassed by a well-informed Historical Commission, and
virtually every early house flushed out.

In light of these intensified surveys, will there be any unusual surprises, and if so, where? The figures for Middlesex County, with a present known total of forty-three First Period houses, will probably be subject to greater revision than those of any other county. Despite the efforts of the late Harriette M. Forbes, who sought to inventory all the county's seventeenth-century houses in the 1920's and 1930's, the area has been neglected by students until very recently, and the writer's own investigations here have lagged somewhat behind those for the other historic counties which constituted the original Massachusetts Bay Colony.

For that always exciting possibility, the discovery of an early house buried within the frame of a later structure, the outlook is certainly less sanguine than seems to be the case in England where buildings which reflect outwardly the prosperity of Queen Elizabeth's reign and even later periods are continually being found to have earlier, medieval cores. Americans on the whole seem to have been more prone to replace their earliest dwellings. Dramatic discoveries will certainly continue to be made, two of the more interesting in recent years being the uncovering within the shell of the late eighteenth- or early nineteenth-century-appearing house at 250 Sandwich Street in Plymouth of a story-and-a-half seventeenth-century planked frame with crossed summer beams, and in Salem, at the corner of Charter and Liberty Streets, within the envelope of a nondescript tenement with late Mansard roof, a structure dating to about 1680 with carved posts as handsome as any yet discovered in the Salem area and rare evidence for a fireplace having a Tudor-like four-centered arch. These hitherto unsuspected rarities had gone totally unnoticed as far as recorded history is concerned.

Up to this point we have been dealing entirely with the subject of houses which are standing. It is important, however, that some effort at least be made to document the sad and not so gradual loss of First Period houses in Massachusetts since the development of photography in the mid-nineteenth century. For this purpose an entirely new set of data has been compiled, and one need hardly add that the figures are more tentative than those we have advanced for extant houses. The reason, of course, is simple: It is difficult, if not largely impossible, to assess the precise age of a house which is known only from a photograph or written description. The figures presented, therefore, are conservative. Included only, in fact, are nonexisting houses for which a date before 1726 has been determined by personal observation, either on the writer's part or that of a trustworthy architectural historian, or houses for which the photographs reveal at least some unmistakable evidence of an early date. The figures, arranged roughly by each quarter-century, are as follows:

Before 1875
    (and following the introduction of photography)   9
1876–1900   22
1901–1925   18
1926–1950   9
1951–1977   14

It is not surprising that the destruction of more First Period houses cannot be documented before 1876 when the Centennial at Philadelphia focused attention upon our past glories, and made the passing of an ancient landmark henceforward a more noteworthy matter. Otherwise, and particularly in light of the overall small sampling, only one significant fact emerges from our table, namely, that between 1926 and 1950, during which period the Nation experienced a major depression and was deeply involved in World War II, fewer early houses were demolished, on the one hand because the demolisher could not afford to build anew, and on the other presumably because of wartime preoccupations. It is further typical of conditions in this period that at least one of the nine houses rotted down through neglect and decay during the 1930's.

Aside from this one-quarter-century interval, it might appear that the loss of First Period houses had progressed at a relatively stable rate. One could argue also from the table that a heightened awareness of the rarity of structures erected during the first century of our country's settlement has had only modest impact upon contemporary thinking in light of the figures for 1951 to the present. Of the fourteen houses lost during this period, however, twelve, representing the majority, went down before 1964, which makes the record of the past ten or fifteen years look much better (no more than two First

Period houses demolished)! Thus it might be safe to say that the process of erosion has been checked for the moment, and as suggested earlier, to the local historical commissions belongs much of the credit for an increased blanket of surveillance.

Among the total of seventy-two unquestioned First Period structures in Massachusetts, for which the cause of destruction since the introduction of photography is known, fifteen have been lost through fire and only four by neglect and decay. Of the balance, forty-seven, or nearly 70%, have been demolished for street widenings, for school playgrounds, for replacement with more up-to-date structures—in short, for those many reasons which have always grouped themselves around the banner of Progress.

To recapitulate, then, there remain standing today in the Commonwealth of Massachusetts some two hundred fifty structures or more built before 1726. At least seventy-two houses of the same age have been lost since the middle of the nineteenth century, though this figure represents only a modest fraction of the real losses which can never be accurately estimated.

And finally, a word about Boston, the leading seaport and urban center among our thirteen original colonies throughout the seventeenth century. As the twentieth century dawned, there still remained on the old Shawmut Peninsula, wholly or in part, at least ten structures of First Period vintage, four of them wooden buildings dating to the seventeenth century. Today, three-quarters of a century later, we have but a single wooden seventeenth-century structure left, the Paul Revere House, and three early eighteenth-century brick houses which together with portions of a fourth give us a bare total of five First Period buildings, or just one-half of what had survived into the twentieth century. Among these, and here in conclusion let me emphasize as strongly as possible what raw statistics can never show, is to be numbered the Province House, built originally in 1679, and by the 1920's little more than a remnant of its former glory. However, those who will take the time to examine the photographs published in a recent issue of *Old-Time New England*, exposed when the house was demolished, may judge for themselves the startling importance of this imposing seventeenth-century mansion, and ponder whether or not its loss was indeed to be reckoned first among all the others.

APPENDICES

Summary abstracts of the structural history of a significant sampling of First Period Houses at Massachusetts Bay

By Abbott Lowell Cummings

NOTE: All dates throughout Appendices I and II are consistent with the modern calendar which acknowledges January 1 as the beginning of the year. Where there is any question as to whether the date is according to the current system or Old Style (i.e., one which recognized March 25 as the beginning of the year) the uncertainty has been expressed with a double date, for example: February 15, 1685/6.

ANDOVER: ABBOT HOUSE, 9 Andover Street   after 1700

The house has descended in the family of Benjamin Abbot of Andover, married in 1685.[1] Style and construction of original right-hand portion of single-room plan with chimney bay would suggest a date in all likelihood after 1700, and for the addition to the left of another unit of single-room plan a date just before or about 1725. It will presumably have been at the time of the latter addition that both chambers, old and new, received their present molded and applied trim. (Right-hand chamber frame had previously been exposed and whitewashed.) Leanto at the rear has been added, possibly in two stages. House acquired July 28, 1933, by Arthur Stone Dewing[2] who carried out a partial restoration. Property purchased on July 1, 1974, by Frank A. Demers who has furthered the work of restoration.[3] Privately owned.

1. *Historic Houses in Andover, Massachusetts*, Compiled for the Tercentenary Celebration, 1946, house no. 23-II.
2. Essex County Deeds (North District), Lawrence, Mass., vol. 572, p. 242.
3. Ibid., vol. 1244, p. 313.

BEVERLY: BALCH HOUSE,
    448 Cabot Street   of undetermined 17th-cent. date

Original right-hand portion of single room, story-and-a-half form
(now minus its chimney bay), stands on land granted by the Town of
Salem to John Balch in January 1636.[1] There is some surviving structural
evidence (despite Norman Isham's sketches in 1916; see Fig. 45) that first-
story joists were housed in the summer beam with butt cog joints, which
would preclude a date before the 1660's. Inasmuch as the frame has under-
gone two major overhauls in the twentieth century the question may remain unresolved. Later two-story block of single-room plan with chimney bay to the left is just before or after 1700 in character, and the original
story-and-a-half house was probably pulled up to this frame and attached,
at which time the earlier building was raised to a full two stories. Enlargements at the rear of the original structure, including a new and
higher roof, are later still. House acquired by the Balch Family Association
June 8, 1916,[2] and restored in 1921–1922 with William Sumner Appleton
and Norman Isham as consultants. Property conveyed to the Beverly
Historical Society March 30, 1932.[3] House further restored in 1961–1962
by the restoration contractor Roy W. Baker.

    1. Alice G. Lapham, *The Old Planters of Beverly in Massachusetts* . . . (Cambridge,
Mass.: The Riverside Press, 1930), p. 12.
    2. Essex County Registered Land, Doc. no. 4235 (Certif. of Title, no. 2070).
    3. Ibid., Doc. no. 26323 (Certif. of Title, no. 9473).

BEVERLY: REV. JOHN CHIPMAN HOUSE,
    634 Cabot Street   after 1715

Research by Sidney Perley indicates that there was a house here, erected
probably by Exercise Conant, in 1695 and perhaps as early as the 1660's.[1]
The present structure, however, of two-room, central-chimney plan as
originally built, is assuredly after 1700 in style. Perley shows that the
property was acquired on September 6, 1715, by the Rev. John Chipman,
pastor of the new North Beverly Church, and in light of the ambitious
character of the pine frame it will undoubtedly have been he who built the
house and, since he lived here until his death on March 23, 1775, altered it
before the middle of the century, judging again from style.[2] By these
alterations the fine pedimented frontispiece and paneled trim throughout
the house were introduced and the central chimney removed and replaced
with two stacks along the rear wall, one for each of the two principal files

of rooms. Kitchen ell dates apparently to the same mid-century period. House privately owned.

1. Sidney Perley, "Beverly in 1700, No. 1," *Essex Institute Historical Collections*, LV (1919), 88.
2. Ibid.

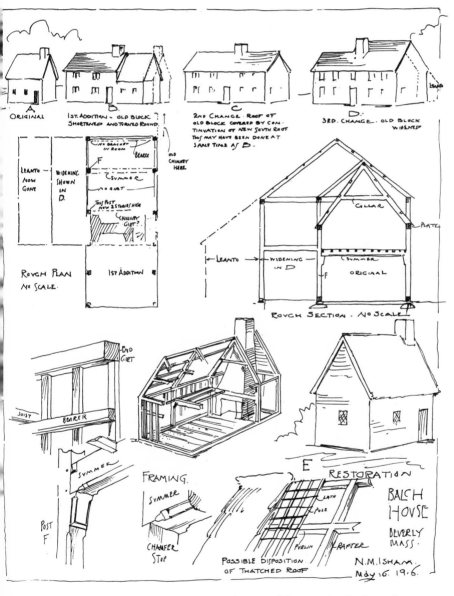

45.   Balch house, Beverly, Mass. Schematic evolution and framing details, drawn by Norman M. Isham, May 16, 1916. Courtesy Society for the Preservation of New England Antiquities.

BEVERLY: HALE HOUSE, 39 Hale Street   1694

On July 25, 1694, the Town voted that "yᵉ reverand Mʳ John Hale minister of yᵉ Gosple amongst us hath Liberty to cut so much Timber on yᵉ
Towne common as will Build halfe of yᵉ frame of the Dwelling House he
is now in building of[.]"[1] As constructed by Mr. Hale in 1694 the house
was of two-room, central-chimney plan. His grandson, Col. Robert Hale,
according to family tradition, built the gambrel-roofed wing towards the
street about 1745, a date consistent with its style. Improvements by the
family to convert the house to a summer residence, beginning about 1845
and continuing throughout the nineteenth century, included removal of
the original central chimney (c. 1848), addition of piazza, rearrangement
of interior partitions, etc.[2] The house, never having gone out of the family,
was conveyed by a descendant of the Rev. John Hale to the Beverly Historical Society on August 6, 1937.[3]

    1. Beverly Town Records, MS, City Clerk, Beverly, Mass., II (1685–1711), 68.
    2. Notes on the Hale House, Beverly, 1903, by Robert Hale Bancroft and Ellen
Bancroft, Archives, Hale House Committee, Beverly.
    3. Essex County Deeds, vol. 3117, p. 137.

BOSTON: MATTHEW BARNARD HOUSE,
23 North Square   c. 1680

Previously existing dwelling here, owned by Matthew Barnard, carpenter, was destroyed in the Boston Fire of November 27, 1676.[1] Barnard
rebuilt presumably soon after, the new structure nearly touching the left-
hand gable end of the adjacent Paul Revere House. Built probably as a
house of two-room, central-chimney plan with possible original extensions at the rear, the left-hand portion retained its two-and-a-half-story
character as late as 1798 when the Direct Tax was levied. The right-hand
portion was then described as having three stories.[2] By 1872 when the only
known view was executed the whole house was a full three stories in
height.[3] A permit for its demolition was issued October 16, 1876.[4]

    1. Suffolk County Deeds, IV, 313; M. Halsey Thomas, ed., *The Diary of Samuel Se-
wall, 1674–1729* (New York: Farrar, Straus and Giroux, ᶜ1973), I, 28.
    2. *A Report of the Record Commissioners of the City of Boston, Containing the Statistics
of the United States' Direct Tax of 1798, as assessed on Boston* . . . (Boston, Mass., 1890),
pp. 188 (Gibbs Atkins) and 199 (Eliza Phillis).
    3. Samuel Adams Drake, *Old Landmarks and Historic Personages of Boston* (Boston:
Little, Brown & Co., 1906), opp. p. 158.
    4. Boston Building Department Records, City Hall, Boston, Mass., Permit no. 127
(J. G. Carlson).

BOSTON: BRIDGHAM HOUSE (JULIEN'S),
  Milk and Congress Streets   1670–1671

Henry Bridgham, tanner, of Boston provided by will dated November
8, 1670, that "the new house that I have raised & proceed in the building
of itt . . . be finished [and] made habitable. . . ."[1] The house, fronting
southerly on Milk Street, was acquired in July 1794 by Jean Baptiste Gilbert Payplat dis Julien, "Restorator," who conducted a celebrated eating
establishment here.[2] Following his death in 1805 it continued as a restaurant, and was demolished July 1824.[3]

  1. Suffolk County Probate Records, VII, 115.
  2. Suffolk County Deeds, vol. 178, p. 220.
  3. Caleb H. Snow, *A History of Boston* . . . (Boston, 1825), p. 244. See also, Nathaniel B. Shurtleff, *A Topographical and Historical Description of Boston* (Boston, Mass.,
1871), pp. 649–662.

BOSTON: CLOUGH-VERNON HOUSE
        (CHARTER HOUSE), Charter Street   1697–1698
        CLOUGH(?)-HOW HOUSE, Vernon Place   prob. 1697–1700

William Clough, bricklayer, purchased an unimproved tract of land
here December 22, 1696.[1] On July 16, 1698, he subdivided, selling a house
which fronted on Charter Street, presumably the Charter House, so called,
with brick ends, demolished in 1931.[2] October 28, 1700, Clough sold the
rear portion of the tract with a "Tennement" in his own occupation to
Nathaniel Goodwin, bricklayer. The property was conveyed September
22, 1707, to James How, housewright.[3] In March 1714 How sold this tract
in two parcels, each with its own house.[4] That which stood at the extreme
rear of the property has been long gone, and nothing is known of its character. The framed house at the forward end of the rear lot which survived
until 1931 is assumed (though with no absolute assurance) to be that built
by Clough between 1697 and 1700. A corner cupboard from this house
was given about 1887 to the Bostonian Society. Portions of frame salvaged
and preserved by the Society for the Preservation of New England Antiquities.

  1. Suffolk County Deeds, XVII, 341.
  2. Ibid., XXI, 270; *The Boston Globe*, Oct. 28, 1931.
  3. Suffolk County Deeds, XX, 544; XXIV, 109.
  4. Ibid., XXXII, 46; XXVIII, 102.

BOSTON: PAUL REVERE HOUSE, 19 North Square   c. 1680

This site, on which stood the home of the Rev. Increase Mather, was swept by fire November 27, 1676.[1] A new house of two-room plan, the second room incorporated in a rear ell, had been erected by November 2, 1681, when conveyed to Robert Howard, merchant.[2] The property was purchased by Paul Revere, "Goldsmith," on February 15, 1770,[3] and was owned by him until October 7, 1800.[4] Having acquired a third story just before or during its ownership by Revere (and in any event before the Direct Tax was levied in 1798),[5] this historic building was sold to the Paul Revere Memorial Association on May 1, 1907, and restored by Joseph Everett Chandler during 1907–1908.[6] (See pages 3–21 of the text.)

1. M. Halsey Thomas, ed., *The Diary of Samuel Sewall, 1674–1729* (New York: Farrar, Straus and Giroux, c1973), I, 28.

2. Suffolk County Deeds, XIII, 86.

3. Ibid., vol. 116, p. 128.

4. Ibid., vol. 196, p. 291.

5. *A Report of the Record Commissioners of the City of Boston, Containing the Statistics of the United States' Direct Tax of 1798, as assessed on Boston* . . . (Boston, Mass., 1890), p. 201.

6. Suffolk County Deeds, vol. 3221, p. 172. See also, *Handbook of the Paul Revere Memorial Association* (Boston, Mass.: Printed for the Assoc., 1954), pp. 17–25.

46. Stanbury house (The Old Feather Store), Dock Square, Boston, Mass. Detail of gable ends from a stereographic view, 1860. Courtesy Society for the Preservation of New England Antiquities.

BOSTON: STANBURY HOUSE (THE OLD FEATHER STORE),
North Street and Market Square   1680

A former building on this site, owned by Thomas and Susanna Stanbury, shopkeepers, was destroyed by fire in August 1679.[1] The house newly built by the Stanburys bore the date of 1680 impressed in the roughcast surface of one gable end. Daniel Pomroy and John K. Simpson were listed as early as 1810 as proprietors of a "feather store" here.[2] Structure demolished July 1860.[3]

   1. Thomas Hutchinson, *The History of the Colony of Massachusetts-Bay* . . . (Boston, Mass., 1764–1828), I, 349n.
   2. Boston city directories.
   3. *Daily Evening Traveller* (Boston, Mass.), July 10, 11, 1860. See also Abbott Lowell Cummings, "The Old Feather Store in Boston," *Old-Time New England*, ser. no. 172 (Apr.–June 1958), pp. 85–104.

BRAINTREE: GEN. SYLVANUS THAYER BIRTHPLACE,
1505 Washington Street [now 786 Washington Street]   c. 1720

The traditional date of about 1720 seems consistent with the style and character of construction of this house of two-room, central-chimney plan with soon added leanto at the rear. Acquired by the Braintree Historical Society, moved to its present site in October 1958, and restored during 1958–1960 under the direction of the Society's president, Gilbert L. Bean.

CAMBRIDGE: COOPER-FROST-AUSTIN HOUSE,
21 Linnaean Street   c. 1689

The site was owned in 1657 by Dea. John Cooper.[1] The earliest, right-hand portion of "half-house" plan with chimney bay and integral leanto was erected presumably by his son, Samuel Cooper, who by November 29, 1689, had "Built & settled" in Cambridge according to the contemporary record.[2] At Samuel Cooper's death in 1718 an inventory mentions only the rooms in the original house.[3] The fireplace in the leanto kitchen is later than the original chimney. Addition at left of single-room plan with leanto was made probably soon after Samuel's death by his son Walter Cooper who married June 7, 1722. The projecting one-story porch, stairs and other Federal trim are presumably the work of Thomas Austin who lived here from 1807 to 1816. House conveyed to the Society for the Preservation of New England Antiquities May 16, 1912,[4] and partially restored by Joseph Everett Chandler during the same year.[5] Chamber fire-places restored in 1962.

1. Middlesex County Deeds, II, 152.
2. *The Register Book of the Lands and Houses in the "New Towne"* . . . (Cambridge Mass., 1896), p. 167.
3. Middlesex County Probate Records, first ser., docket no. 5172.
4. Middlesex County Deeds, vol. 3694, pp. 333, 335 and 338.
5. See "The Repairs on the Cooper-Austin House," *Old-Time New England*, ser. no. 8 (Feb. 1913), pp. 12–18.

CHELMSFORD: OLD GARRISON (so-called),
   Garrison Road   early 18th cent.

This house of two-room, central-chimney plan would appear to date to the early eighteenth century, perhaps as late as about 1725, on the basis of style and character of construction. Acquired by the "Old Chelmsford" Garrison House Association, Inc., and restored 1961.'[1]

1. Middlesex County Registered Land (North District), Lowell, Mass., Land Registration Book, LXIV, 215 (Certif. of Title, no. 12308).

DANVERS: DARLING-PRINCE HOUSE,
   177 Hobart Street   probably after 1700

Early reminiscences which include an eyewitness account of moving this house with oxen from the foot of Hathorne Hill to the present site in 1845 have been published.[1] On grounds of style and construction it would appear to have been erected probably soon after 1700. Originally of two-room, central-chimney plan, the building has been added to at the left-hand end and at the rear with a later, higher roof raised over the entire structure. House purchased on August 15, 1975, by Richard C. Dabrowski[2] who initiated a restoration drawing upon the services of the Society for the Preservation of New England Antiquities. Privately owned.

1. "Some Reminiscences of Elizabeth (Prince) Peabody," *The Historical Collections of the Danvers Historical Society*, XXV (1937), 37–38.
2. Essex County Deeds, vol. 6173, p. 29.

DANVERS: JOHN HOLTEN HOUSE,
   27 Centre Street   probably c. 1700

According to research by the historian Sidney Perley there was a house on this lot by January 21, 1692, which, if not much earlier in date, may

47. Cooper–Frost–Austin house, Cambridge, Mass. Detail of front slope of roof showing cut in original boarding for facade gable. Photo, Richard Merrill, 1968, courtesy Society for the Preservation of New England Antiquities.

possibly be the original left-hand portion of the present structure of single-room plan with narrow chimney bay.[1] The house has been enlarged through the addition of another room to the right and has been moved (though remaining on the same lot). Principal interest, however, attaches to the early nineteenth-century owners who between 1801 and 1818 were housewrights[2] and were probably responsible for the unusual way in which the original narrow chimney bay has been widened and the original room reduced in size during this period. House privately owned.

1. Sidney Perley, "Center of Salem Village in 1700," *The Historical Collections of the Danvers Historical Society*, VII (1919), 46.
2. Ibid., p. 47.

DANVERS: REBECCA NURSE HOUSE (so-called),
    149 Pine Street   probably after 1700

On this property stood the home of Rebecca Nurse, who was hanged as a witch in 1692. The present dwelling, however, originally of "half-house" plan with integral leanto, is almost certainly after 1700 in terms of style and construction, and was probably erected by Rebecca's son, Samuel Nurse. The left-hand unit of single-room plan and leanto at the rear are later additions. Acquired by the Rebecca Nurse Memorial Association April 30, 1908,[1] and restored by Joseph Everett Chandler in 1909. Conveyed to the Society for the Preservation of New England Antiquities June 25, 1928.[2]

1. Essex County Deeds, vol. 1915, p. 180.
2. Ibid., vol. 2779, p. 410.

DANVERS: PORTER-BRADSTREET HOUSE,
    487 Locust Street   probably c. 1700

Sidney Perley's research shows that the property was still unimproved on January 2, 1664, when acquired by Joseph Porter who presumably erected a house here.[1] The present structure of two-room, central-chimney plan with added leanto, while considerably modified through the years, reveals no evidence of such an early period, and is probably closer to 1700 in date. Privately owned.

1. Sidney Perley, "The Plains: Part of Salem in 1700," *The Historical Collections of the Danvers Historical Society*, VII (1919), 120.

DANVERS: REA-PUTNAM-FOWLER HOUSE,
111 Locust Street   c. 1700

Sidney Perley's research would indicate that the Reas had owned this site from the late 1630's and were surely living here by 1662.[1] In that year Daniel Rea devised the property in tail to his son, Joshua, and to his grandson, Daniel, though it is clear from the character of construction that the original left-hand portion of the present dwelling, of "half-house" plan with integral leanto, was not erected until about 1700. The son, Joshua, died in the autumn of 1710 and his son, Daniel, in the winter of 1714–1715, whereupon Daniel's son, Zerubabel, received that portion of the farm with buildings in a division of March 8, 1715.[2] In all likelihood it will have been Zerubabel Rea who added the right-hand "half" of the house with pine frame and also of integral leanto plan, between 1715 and 1725. The original chimney was removed in the nineteenth century. House privately owned.

1. Sidney Perley, "The Plains: Part of Salem in 1700," *The Historical Collections of the Danvers Historical Society*, VII (1919), 113.
2. Ibid.

DEDHAM: FAIRBANKS HOUSE, 511 East Street   c. 1637

Jonathan Fairbanke was accepted a townsman March 23, 1637, and received an allotment of twelve acres about the same time.[1] The original house of two-room, central-chimney plan, probably with an appendage at the left, was erected presumably soon thereafter, the date of c. 1637 being confirmed by a provisional reading of tree-rings. At Jonathan Fairbanke's death in 1668 an inventory mentions "the Roome called the new house" and "Chamber in the new house,"[2] possibly the present rear leanto which is consistent with that date in terms of construction. Extension of the parlor to the right with a longer, chamfered summer beam may well have been projected at an early date, and has settled uniformly with the original frame of the main house. Western gambrel-roofed ell was in existence (recently to judge from the style) by February 15, 1764, when its rooms are mentioned in a partition of the property.[3] Eastern ell at the right (originally with pitched roof), also eighteenth century in style, is a separate building, moved up and attached to the earlier house, perhaps, as tradition asserts, at the time of the American Revolution. Its roof was then or later given a gambrel profile, at which time the enclosed porch was probably constructed in the angle of the parlor extension and eastern ell. The house, conveyed June 16, 1904, to The Fairbanks Family in America, Inc.,[4] has never been restored, though there have been extensive repairs in 1912,

48. Fairbanks house, Dedham, Mass. Rear wall of leanto added probably before 1668, showing original chamfered posts and studs and extent of structural repairs undertaken in 1975–1976. Photo, Richard Cheek, courtesy Society for the Preservation of New England Antiquities.

1953–1954, 1964, 1967 and in 1974–1976, the latter under the direction of the Society for the Preservation of New England Antiquities.

1. Don Gleason Hill, ed., *The Early Records of the Town of Dedham, Massachusetts, 1636–1659* . . . (Dedham, Mass., 1892), p. 28; *A Plan of Dedham Village, Mass., 1636–1876*, published by the Dedham Historical Society (Dedham, Mass., 1883), pp. 3, 4 and 13.

2. Suffolk County Probate Records, v, 112.

3. Suffolk County Deeds, vol. 103, p. 8, and vol. 104, p. 73.

4. Norfolk County Deeds, vol. 975, pp. 602 ff.

DORCHESTER: BLAKE HOUSE,
150 East Cottage Street (rear) [now Edward Everett Square]   c. 1650

The original house of two-room, central-chimney plan was built traditionally for James Blake at about the time of his marriage at mid-century,[1] a date which is amply confirmed by the style and character of construction. The building is first mentioned December 6, 1669, when the Town voted to erect a parsonage, "such an house as James Blaks house is, namly 38 foot in lenth and 20 foote wid," dimensions which correspond exactly with the existing structure.[2] The extension to the left was in existence by 1748,[3] and that to the right according to a contemporary account was added between 1825 and 1857[4] (both shown in early photographs). These later additions were shorn away when the house was acquired by the Dorchester Historical Society, moved to its present site and partially restored in 1895–1896. (See pages 61–74 of the text.)

1. Alvin Lincoln Jones, *Under Colonial Roofs* (Boston, Mass., c1894), p. 234.

2. *Fourth Report of the Record Commissioners of the City of Boston, 1880, Dorchester Town Records*, 2nd ed. (Boston, Mass., 1883), p. 162.

3. Plot dated Apr. 22, 1748, MS, Collections, Dorchester Historical Society.

4. Samuel Blake, *Blake Family* . . . (Boston, Mass., 1857), pp. 15–16.

DORCHESTER: CAPEN HOUSE, 523 Washington Street (opposite Melville Avenue) [now 427 Hillside Street, Milton]   before 1658 (?)

The title for this unarguably early house which descended in the Capen family of Dorchester has not been perfected. The building is similar to the Pierce House of c. 1650 in all major respects except the wider spacing of floor joists, suggesting, perhaps, a slightly later date. In any event, John Whipple, carpenter, to whom the Pierce House has been attributed, left Dorchester in 1658, and we have dated the house provisionally before his departure. As originally built the structure was of one-room plan with chimney bay. The principal rooms upstairs and down may have been subdivided from the outset. Evidence for a partition remains in the first story, and an existing partition in the second story is composed of seventeenth-century molded sheathing. The addition of single-room plan at the right dates to the eighteenth century. The leanto represents a separate build. The house was taken down and re-erected in Milton on its present site in May 1909 by Kenneth Webster. Privately owned.

DORCHESTER: PIERCE HOUSE, 24 Oakton Avenue   c. 1650

According to an unrecorded deed (privately owned), the faded date of which appears to be 1652, John Smith of Dorchester conveyed six acres to Robert Pierce in the Great Lots, "upon w^{ch} . . . the said Robt Pearse haue since the verball agrem^t between them erected a howse & [is] in possession. . . ." The latest reference to Pierce's former house "on the pyne necke" is 1644.[1] The house consisted originally of the middle portion of (probable) single-room plan with chimney bay. The single room with chamber was added at the left probably by Robert's son, Thomas, who died in 1706. At the death of Thomas' son, John, in 1744, the chamber in the original house had apparently been subdivided for the inventory mentions "West Chamber," "East Chamber" and "Middle Chamber."[2] When John's son, Samuel, drew his will November 11, 1767, he refers to the "Back Lintall" (a separate addition) and that portion of the structure "from the partition of the House & Cellar lately built by my Son [Col.] Samuel Pierce" who was a carpenter.[3] References to construction in Col. Samuel's diary (privately owned) extend from March to October 1765, and thus date more precisely this enlargement at the east end of the original house with the addition of paneled trim here and in the earlier rooms. House conveyed by the Pierce family to the Society for the Preservation of New England Antiquities May 29, 1968.[4]

1. *Fourth Report of the Record Commissioners of the City of Boston, 1880, Dorchester Town Records*, 2nd ed. (Boston, Mass., 1883), p. 58.
2. Suffolk County Probate Records, XXXVII, 162.
3. Ibid., LXVII, 176 and 174.
4. Suffolk County Deeds, vol. 8205, p. 204.

ESSEX: BURNHAM HOUSE (THE HEARTHSIDE),
Eastern Avenue   c. 1685–1695

The date of erection for this house is based at present upon the character of style and construction which reveals that the left-hand portion of "half-house" plan with integral leanto is the earlier, built probably between 1685

49. Capen house, Dorchester, before removal to Milton, Mass. Photo, William H. Halliday Collection, c. 1900, courtesy Society for the Preservation of New England Antiquities.

and 1695. The right-hand unit with rooms at the front and rear was added apparently towards the end of the first quarter of the eighteenth century. The rear leanto wall was then or subsequently raised to a full two stories and the entire structure was re-roofed, wholly or in part. The house was conveyed to Marion A. Costello on November 19, 1947,[1] who performed a partial restoration, and by her to Royal Barry Wills on November 30, 1955.[2] Converted in the 1960's to a restaurant, the original building has been considerably added to for the same purposes by H. Clark Dexter, Jr., who purchased the property on May 8, 1973.[3] Privately owned.

1. Essex County Deeds, vol. 3577, p. 74.
2. Ibid., vol. 4235, p. 230.
3. Ibid., vol. 5972, p. 412.

ESSEX: GEORGE GIDDINGS HOUSE (so-called),
   Choate Street   late 17th cent.

The house stands presumably upon the early farmstead of George Giddings who was possessed of a dwelling at his death in 1676.[1] The present
structure, however, of two-room, central-chimney plan, is later in terms
of style, and will more reasonably have been erected towards the end of
the seventeenth century. The original roof was apparently replaced during
the eighteenth century, and at any event before the central chimney was
removed. Up to this time the house faced south. Early in the nineteenth
century, judging from the character of the new trim, the orientation was
altered and the building henceforth faced north with a new entrance and
staircase on that side. The two new stacks which replaced the original
chimney, one in each of the principal rooms, were located (contrary to
normal practice) along what was to become the new front wall at the
north. The house was purchased on August 2, 1965, by Alvan L. Doane
and partially restored.[2] Title was conveyed on February 14, 1975, to Dr.
David W. Sauer[3] who has furthered the work of restoration, drawing
upon the services of the restoration contractor Harold C. Dexter. Privately
owned.

   1. George Francis Dow, ed., *The Probate Records of Essex County, Massachusetts* (Salem, Mass.: The Essex Institute, 1916–1920), III, 63.
   2. Essex County Deeds, vol. 5290, p. 327.
   3. Ibid., vol. 6128, p. 363.

ESSEX: STORY HOUSE, Story Street   c. 1684

William Story, carpenter, began to acquire land in this vicinity in 1649[1]
which he conveyed to his son, Seth, also a carpenter, on March 31, 1693,
together with "housing."[2] On March 27, 1712, the Town of Ipswich sold
Seth Story about an acre next to his own land[3] which Seth conveyed to
his son, Zachariah, on March 22, 1714, "with ye New house Standing
upon it together with ye old house and ye Oarchard adjoyning to it. . . ."[4]
The "old house" is presumably the structure of single-room plan with
chimney bay which formed the nucleus of the building which survived
here, and is assumed on the basis of style and construction alone to have
been erected upon the original William Story tract about 1684 when Seth
was married. When Zachariah Story executed his will in 1761 he mentions
both "the Eastern End" and "the western End of my Dwelling House,"
the latter, containing a hall and two service rooms with chambers above,
having been added about 1725 or later on grounds of style.[5] The house

was taken down in May–June 1957. The lower room in the earliest portion has been installed in the Henry Francis du Pont Winterthur Museum and its chamber has been re-erected in the galleries of the National Museum of History and Technology in Washington, D.C.

1. Essex County Deeds, I (Ipswich), 240.
2. Ibid., V (Ipswich), 596.
3. Ipswich Town Records, MS, Town Hall, Ipswich, Mass., III (1696–1720), 221.
4. Essex County Deeds, XXXIII, 64.
5. Essex County Probate Records, vol. 350, p. 156.

50.   Story house, Essex, Mass. Detail of plaster cove over first-story fireplace lintel and remnants of original vertical sheathing which formed fireplace recess, shown immediately following the removal of later trim. Photo, Peter Zaharis, 1957, courtesy Society for the Preservation of New England Antiquities.

GLOUCESTER: WHITE-ELLERY HOUSE,
Washington Street   after 1703

John J. Babson, the historian, writes that the Rev. John White, ordained pastor of the church in Gloucester on April 21, 1703, received "soon after his settlement here, a grant of land, just below the plain on which his meeting-house stood; and undoubtedly built on that spot the house still standing. . . ."[1] Mr. White's first marriage occurred on June 9, 1703. The house, of central-chimney plan with integral leanto, was conveyed to William Ellery, merchant, on July 14, 1740,[2] and remained in the hands of his descendants. In order to avoid demolition when a traffic circle was constructed in connection with Rt. 128, the house was acquired from the Commonwealth of Massachusetts and moved a few yards in 1947 to a municipally owned site by the Cape Ann Scientific, Literary and Historical Association. Restoration (with much of the archeological evidence retained) was carried out under the direction of the antiquarian Alfred Mans-

51.   White-Ellery house, Gloucester, Mass. Detail of upper end of sawn vertical planks which formed rear partition wall of principal chambers. Photo, William W. Owens, Jr., 1974, reproduced by permission of the photographer.

field Brooks when the house was moved. Title to the new site was trans-
ferred to the Association by the City of Gloucester on December 21, 1949.[3]

1. John J. Babson, *History of the Town of Gloucester* . . . (Gloucester, Mass., 1860),
p. 230.
2. Essex County Deeds, LXXIX, 199.
3. Ibid., vol. 3714, p. 16.

HAMILTON: BROWN HOUSE, 76 Bridge Street   1662–1673

A recent title search by Catherine Lynn West has shown that there was
"Housing" here in 1673 when, on December 22, John Brown, Sr., gave
the property to his son, Nathaniel, who had married Judith Perkins a few
days earlier on December 16.[1] The frame of the first-built portion at the
right, of single-room plan with chimney bay, appears to be earlier still on
the basis of a number of significant features. The time at which John Brown,
Sr., acquired the land, however, cannot be fixed precisely. William Hubbard conveyed a large farm of some 800 acres here to his son, Richard, of
Ipswich on June 24, 1662,[2] and Richard sold the fifteen-acre parcel upon
which the present house stands to Brown probably soon thereafter, the
deed for which was early lost and only confirmed in general terms by
Hubbard on January 6, 1679.[3] During the 1680's or 1690's, to judge from
the style and character of construction, an addition was made at the left-
hand end consisting of a principal room with its chamber and attic and a
room at the rear covered by a leanto roof which may have been extended
to provide a leanto at the rear of the earlier house as well. Both the gable
end of the addition and its leanto were finished with molded overhanging
girts at the first story. At the turn of the nineteenth century a pair of rooms
was added at the rear right end of the house and even later another room
was projected at the rear of these and all three rooms were raised to a full
two stories. The original chimney was removed in the mid-nineteenth century, at which time also, perhaps, newer rafters were superimposed upon the
originals to create overhanging eaves and a consequently lower roof pitch.
William Sumner Appleton writes in 1918 that the gable-end overhang "was
long concealed by the lower story having been built out flush with the upper.
In this case it happened that the same carpenter who boarded it in was
years later employed to uncover it. One of the drops was found in place
and the other, which was in the carpenter's possession, was returned. . . ."[4]
This will have occurred before 1912 when a dated photograph in the files
of the Society for the Preservation of New England Antiquities shows the
overhang restored. It may perhaps have been at the time of restoration
that the leanto was removed and its molded overhanging girt saved and

stored in the barn (where Mr. Appleton saw it in 1916).[5] Subsequently he secured both the girt and molded wall sheathing which had been stored in the attic for the architectural collections of the Society. The house was further restored, probably in the 1920's, at which time dormer windows in the front slope of the roof were removed, and a pilastered chimney was introduced together with stairs which copy those in the Parson Capen House in Topsfield and molded sheathing modeled on the original boards found in the attic. Privately owned.

1. Essex County Probate Records, docket no. 3747. (See will of Nathaniel Brown; deed referred to therein not on file.)
2. Essex County Deeds, III (Ipswich), 68–69.
3. Ibid., IV (Ipswich), 373–374.
4. William Sumner Appleton, "Annual Reports of the Corresponding Secretary . . . ," *Old-Time New England*, ser. no. 18 (Nov. 1918), p. 29.
5. Notes by William Sumner Appleton on the Brown House, Hamilton, Mass., Sept. 25, 1916, Corr. Files, Society for the Preservation of New England Antiquities.

HAMILTON: WHIPPLE-MATTHEWS HOUSE, Bay Road   1680–1683

The land without improvements was conveyed to Matthew Whipple by his father, Capt. John Whipple, on June 25, 1680.[1] The house, of central-chimney plan with integral leanto, was presumably erected soon thereafter, for Capt. John in his will dated August 2, 1683, confirms the conveyance and provides "that my son Matthew enjoyes yᵉ Lands [and] houses where he now lives," which can be identified with the present property. The inventory of Capt. John's estate, taken September 10, 1683, includes "Matthew's house & barn" appraised at £140.[2] House acquired by Nathan Matthews on June 1, 1912,[3] and restored by Norman Isham in 1914–1915. Privately owned.

1. Essex County Deeds, IV (Ipswich), 533.
2. Essex County Probate Records, vol. 304, pp. 10 and 14.
3. Essex County Deeds, vol. 2150, p. 327.

HINGHAM: ANDREWS HOUSE (THE OLD ORDINARY), 19 Lincoln Street   1685–1690

The will of Thomas Andrews, Sr., November 26, 1690, provides that his son, Thomas Andrews, Jr., yeoman, shall have "that dwelling house which I built for him with the land about it y^t was Edmond Pitts's y^t I bought of his son & Daughter Eastman. . . ."[1] Pitts' death had occurred by May 26, 1685.[2] The house was originally of one-room plan with a chimney bay at the east end. Addition of another room with chamber and roof of lower pitch at the *west* end is mid-eighteenth century in character. A file of rooms was added across the rear of the house probably before the end of the eighteenth century. Renovations including a new staircase and subdivision of the earliest rooms are Federal in style. House conveyed November 9, 1922, to the Hingham Historical Society.[3] Eastern end of original chamber restored in 1955 by the restoration contractor G. Holden Greene.

    1. Suffolk County Probate Records, VIII, 24.
    2. For correct identification of site with present house see Suffolk County Deeds, xv, 198, and vol. 148, p. 47, and Suffolk County Probate Records, xxv, 450.
    3. Plymouth County Deeds, vol. 1429, p. 18.

HINGHAM: CUSHING HOUSE, 210 East Street   1679

    Daniel Cushing, Sr., on June 19, 1675, acquired "severall small planting lotts and parcells of Land lying . . . in the ffeild there called the plain-neck" (the ancient name for that section of Hingham in which the house is situated).[1] In his will dated September 11, 1693, Daniel leaves these lots and an additional three and a half acres to his son, Peter, together with "the Dwelling house and Barne and all other Buildings standing thereupon. . . ."[2] The date of erection of the house, originally of two-room, central-chimney plan, one and a half stories high, is fixed by an entry in Daniel's diary (privately owned) on July 11, 1679: "my dwelling-house raised in the plaine neck." A room by room inventory taken November 25, 1783, would suggest that the house had by then been raised to a full two and a half stories and that the leanto had been added.[3] A "back new kitchen" is mentioned in 1803.[4] The house was partially restored by Joseph Everett Chandler in 1936, at which time eight feet were added to the rear of the leanto and the service sheds were relocated at the east end of the house. This homestead has come down in the male line and is now occupied by descendants in the ninth generation from Daniel Cushing, Sr.

    1. Suffolk County Deeds, x, 83.
    2. Suffolk County Probate Records, xiv, 294.
    3. Ibid., LXXXIII, 630–632.
    4. Ibid., docket no. 21875.

HINGHAM: CUSHING-ROBINSON HOUSE,
46 South Pleasant Street   c. 1725

The original left-hand portion of the house, of single-room plan with chimney bay, was built according to tradition by Abel Cushing, probably about 1725 in terms of style and character of construction. The right-hand unit of single-room plan was added later in the eighteenth century. There have been additions at the rear and construction of a later roof. The house was acquired in the fall of 1923 by Thomas P. Robinson, architect, who uncovered many of the original features during 1924–1925. Privately owned.

HINGHAM: WOODCOCK-LANGLEY HOUSE,
81 North Street   before 1687

The Rev. Peter Hobart of Hingham records the destruction by fire in March 1646 of John Otis, Sr.'s, house which stood upon this site,[1] and on May 23, 1655, Otis conveyed the houselot without mention of buildings to his son, John Otis, Jr.[2] Not until November 19, 1687, however, do the deeds refer to another house here when William Woodcock, "lately of Hingham," sold "his Dwelling House and Land . . . near to the Town Cove" which "was given to John Oatis Senior decd by the Town" to John Langley, called tavern-keeper at the time of his death in 1703.[3] As first built the house was apparently of four-room, central-chimney plan, a single story in height. Raising of the original structure to a full two and a half stories occurred probably in the eighteenth century. Privately owned.

1. C. Edward Egan, Jr., ed., "The Hobart Journal," *New England Historical and Genealogical Register*, 121 (1967), 18.
2. Suffolk County Deeds, II, 161.
3. Ibid., XXI, 341.

IPSWICH: BOWLES-SMITH HOUSE,[1]
26 High Street   c. 1675–1700

Philip Call, by will dated May 6, 1662, left a "House and Land" here valued at £40 to his wife, Mary, for life and then to his daughter of the same name[2] who married first a Bowles and then, on December 31, 1685, Nathaniel Lord. Following the death of Call's widow on January 12, 1708, Nathaniel Lord on March 29, 1710, conveyed to his "Son in Law" (i.e., step-son), Joseph Bowles, carpenter, of Ipswich, the Call property which by now consisted of land only, without a dwelling.[3] The present house of single-room plan (perhaps subdivided) and chimney bay as first built is earlier than 1710, dating rather on the basis of style to the last quarter of the seventeenth century, and the frame minus chimney was thus moved here from some undisclosed site following Bowles' acquisition of the land. It is described as his "House Lott or homestead" on March 5, 1722/3,[4] and later paneling in the chamber would seem consistent with this period. Bowles' descendants sold the property on April 25, 1798, to Ammi R. Smith of Ipswich, mariner.[5] A two-story ell with leanto roof at the west end, if not earlier, was presumably added by Smith. The finish trim is about 1800. Also during Smith family possession and about 1860–1870, to judge from the character, the ell was extended back in two-story form with a cellar kitchen. The name Abbie S. Smith and the date October 9, 1870, is scratched in a rear windowpane of the second story. The mid-century alterations included an extension of the main house to the west, creating a new entry with relocated stairs. The property was acquired July 11, 1966, by Paul J. McGinley,[6] and the house has been restored by him. Privately owned.

1. The title as recorded by Thomas F. Waters, *Ipswich in the Massachusetts Bay Colony* (Ipswich, Mass.: The Ipswich Historical Society, 1905–1917), I, 358 (Philip Call lot), is incomplete.
2. Essex County Probate Records, docket no. 4528.
3. Essex County Deeds, XXVI, 176.
4. Ibid., XLII, 79.
5. Ibid., vol. 163, p. 117.
6. Essex County Registered Land, Certif. of Title, no. 36484.

IPSWICH: CALDWELL HOUSE,
33 High Street   probably after 1709

Deeds mention a house on this site as early as August 31, 1654, when it was conveyed to John Caldwell for £26.[1] At Caldwell's death in 1692 the "house & lands at home" were appraised at £109, implying a major improvement, probably a new structure altogether.[2] The present house, however, of two-room, central-chimney plan with added leanto, appears on structural and stylistic analysis to be later still. Caldwell's widow conveyed the property to their son, Dillingham Caldwell, on January 19, 1709, reserving one end for her own use,[3] and the present house may possibly have been erected by the son following this transfer, or, more likely, after the widow's death on January 26, 1722, the key being the early and probably original interior finish trim which cannot be much earlier than the latter date. House acquired August 17, 1956, by Charles Woolley and restored,[4] at which time the later leanto was entirely reconstructed. Privately owned.

1. Essex County Deeds, II (Ipswich), 128.
2. Essex County Probate Records, vol. 303, pp. 84–85 and 154.
3. [Thomas F. Waters], "Thomas Dudley and Simon and Ann Bradstreet," *Publications of the Ipswich Historical Society*, XII (1903), 15.
4. Essex County Deeds, vol. 4298, p. 52.

IPSWICH: COLLINS-LORD HOUSE,
   High Street [next left of No. 33]   probably 1675–1700

Abraham Perkins sold to Robert Lord, Sr., on April 11, 1682, "my dwelling house . . . which I Lately purchased of Robert Collins. . . ."[1] On the grounds of style and construction the old house of two-room, central-chimney plan which long stood here cannot have been much earlier in date. As seen in early photographs the house stood with its gable-end to the street, but a deed of April 23, 1784, notes that a line of division began "at the highway opposite the middle of the chimney . . . [and ran through] the middle of said Chimney. . . ."[2] The house had thus apparently been turned at a right angle, and indeed, the local historian Daniel S. Wendel felt that it was not on its original foundation. Dismantled in March 1938 and the frame re-erected as an ell of the relocated Ross Tavern at 52 Jeffrey's Neck Road in Ipswich (q.v.).

1. Essex County Deeds, XV, 115.
2. Ibid., vol. 137, p. 212.

IPSWICH: GIDDINGS-BURNHAM HOUSE,
   37 Argilla Road   c. 1680–1690

Thomas Franklin Waters, the Ipswich historian, reports from his study of the town records that George Giddings, yeoman, had a grant of 100 acres here in 1635.[1] On June 3, 1667, Giddings conveyed to Thomas Burnham, carpenter, a "dwelling house wherein the said Thomas now dwelleth" together with twelve acres of land.[2] A widely chamfered summer beam and large joists laid flatwise have been salvaged from an older house, probably that mentioned in the 1667 deed, for re-use in the framing of the ground-story floor, and these features may easily date to the earliest years of the town. The main body of the present structure, however, of two-room, central-chimney plan, appears on the basis of style and character of construction to date to the 1680's or 1690's, and almost certainly before the death in 1694 of Thomas Burnham, the carpenter and presumed builder. He was aged about sixty-two in 1680 which may account for the conservative use of wattle and daub fill in the walls. The house was owned by generations of Burnhams until acquired about 1880 by Mrs. Charlotte Lord. A drawing by Edwin Whitefield in the collections of the Society for the Preservation of New England Antiquities dated that year shows a central pilastered chimney, overhangs at the front and in both stories of the gable end, and a one-story gambrel-roofed ell at the rear. The changes which followed Mrs. Lord's purchase could not have been made all at once. A photo published in 1884[3] shows the chimney with, however, the front and east end overhang at the first story boxed in and the ell raised to a full two stories with a pitched roof. Later, and before 1900, the central chimney and much early interior trim were removed and a small chimney stack erected at the rear of each of the principal rooms. In the ell on the ground floor William Sumner Appleton discovered in 1914 a wainscot door of oak in a re-used position which he secured for the collections of SPNEA.[4] The house was thoroughly restored about 1935, and a wing at the left-hand end to accommodate modern conveniences was added in 1977. Privately owned.

1. Thomas F. Waters, "A History of the Old Argilla Road . . . ," *Publications of the Ipswich Historical Society*, IX (1900), 17.
2. Essex County Deeds, XI, 216.
3. *The Celebration of the Two Hundred and Fiftieth Anniversary . . . of the Town of Ipswich* . . . (Boston, 1884), next to frontispiece.
4. Notes by William Sumner Appleton on the Thomas Burnham house, Ipswich, Mass., Sept. 17, 1914, Corr. Files, Society for the Preservation of New England Antiquities.

IPSWICH: HART HOUSE, 51 Linebrook Road   1675–1700

The house was built according to tradition by Thomas Hart of Ipswich who was settled here before the middle of the seventeenth century and who died in 1674. Style and construction of the original left-hand portion of single-room plan with chimney bay, however, would suggest a date within the last quarter of the century. The portion to the right of single-room plan and of one-story height, owing to the terrain, would appear to have been added about 1725 or later. There have been periodic enlargements at the rear and right-hand side, particularly after 1902 to adapt the property to the purposes of a guest house. Title passed to the Lord-Kimball family in the mid-eighteenth century and was conveyed by Philip Kimball to Ralph W. Burnham of Ipswich, the antiques dealer, on June 30, 1902.[1] Burnham undertook a partial restoration concerning which two important facts should be noted: (1) the tea-room with its guest chamber which he attached to the Hart House was made up of the timbers of the Saltonstall-Merrifield House, so-called, on Country Road near the South Cemetery, torn down in May 1907;[2] (2) the sheathing with its creased moldings and denticulated lintel cover board in the left-hand lower room may have come from the Saltonstall-Merrifield House also (Thomas F. Waters writes of the latter's demolition, "Portions of a wooden partition, with the same rude tooling that occurs in the Whipple House, were found, but not in their original place"[3]); in any event, one of the masons who worked on Burnham's restoration reported that the sheathing was imported from another old house in Ipswich,[4] and it is interesting to note, in light of Mr. Waters' statement, that the profiles of the Whipple and Hart House moldings are identical. On October 2, 1920, Burnham conveyed the property to Martha Lucy Murray[5] who sold the lower left-hand room and its chamber to the Metropolitan Museum of Art in New York City (MMA purchase authorized April 20, 1936; sale of the chamber to Henry Francis du Pont authorized December 21, 1936).[6] The left-hand half of the frame was thereupon dismantled and the lower room with its molded sheathing installed in the American Wing of the Metropolitan Museum of Art while the chamber was installed in the galleries of the Henry Francis du Pont Winterthur Museum (then privately owned). A replica of these portions of the house was fabricated on the original site. The Hart House as it now stands is privately owned.

1. Essex County Deeds, vol. 1678, p. 438; see also vol. 1682, p. 515.
2. *Ye Olde Burnham House . . . kept by Martha Lucy Murrary* (promotional pamphlet, no publisher, no date), unpaged; see also, Thomas F. Waters, "The Old Bay Road . . . ," *Publications of the Ipswich Historical Society*, xv (1907), 2n.
3. Ibid.
4. Ralph Ladd to author, Feb. 27, 1954, Corr. Files, American Wing, Metropolitan Museum of Art, New York City.
5. Essex County Deeds, vol. 2466, p. 256.
6. Secretary's Files, Metropolitan Museum of Art, New York City.

IPSWICH: GEORGE HART HOUSE,
16 Elm Street   probably c. 1698

George Hart, cooper, purchased a house and two acres here on April 16, 1696.[1] The deeds suggest that he built a new house on the property, perhaps at the time of his marriage May 5, 1698,[2] and on the basis of style alone this newer house may well be the structure consisting of a room with its chamber and attic (and only a fraction of the original chimney bay) which was moved up and attached as a kitchen ell to the central-chimney structure erected facing Elm Street before George Hart executed his will on December 7, 1752.[3] Following demolition in 1963 the frame was re-erected as an exhibition in the galleries of the National Museum of History and Technology in Washington, D.C.

1. Essex County Deeds, XI, 92.
2. Ibid., XXIII, 76; XLI, 265, and LXXIX, 185.
3. Essex County Probate Records, vol. 331, p. 136.

IPSWICH: HOVEY-BOARDMAN HOUSE,
47 Turkey Shore Road   c. 1710–1720

On July 14, 1744, Stephen Boardman conveyed to Benjamin Wheeler six and a half acres with buildings "y[t] I the Grantor purchased of Tho[s] Hovey. . . ."[1] The lot, granted originally to Stephen Jordan, had been owned by Daniel and then Thomas Hovey, according to Thomas F. Waters. Title passed apparently from one generation to the next through the probate court, and we have little knowledge of how early there was a dwelling here, though Mr. Waters surmises correctly that the present house was built "probably early in the eighteenth century," a date consistent with its style.[2] Of two-room, central-chimney plan, the structure was still basically of this form and had retained its original pilastered chimney when acquired by the restoration contractor Philip W. Ross on September 27, 1965.[3] Restoration carried out by Mr. Ross in 1965–1966 included re-creation of the plaster cove cornice for which evidence was discovered under the eaves. Privately owned.

1. Essex County Deeds, LXXXV, 229.
2. Thomas F. Waters, *Ipswich in the Massachusetts Bay Colony* (Ipswich, Mass.: The Ipswich Historical Society, 1905–1917), I, 482.
3. Essex County Deeds, vol. 5307, p. 173.

IPSWICH: WILLIAM HOWARD HOUSE,
41 Turkey Shore Road   late 17th cent.

William Howard, feltmaker, by means unrecorded acquired part of John Dane's original houselot here (*not* the Emerson-Wardwell lot, as Waters claims).[1] The whole tract is described as "the dwelling house & land of John Dane" as early as 1648,[2] and the house may have been that which stood on a portion of the land conveyed by Dane in 1683 to a son.[3]

It is the latter conveyance which informs us that Howard was then in possession of the balance of the lot at the corner of the present Turkey Shore Road and Wood's Lane. Style and character of construction of the original left-hand portion of the existing house of single-room plan with chimney bay suggests a date towards the end of the seventeenth century when the builder was already middle-aged. William Howard by will executed July 23, 1709, leaves to his son John "yᵉ New End of my House which is not yett Fully Finished with one half yᵉ Stack of Chimnye built in sd New End," and to his son Samuel "my Old Mansion House And also one half of yᵉ Stack of Chemnye built in sd New house. . . ."[4] The property was acquired in 1902 by the Ipswich artist/antiquarian Arthur W. Dow,[5] and conveyed by his widow December 16, 1929, to the Society for the Preservation of New England Antiquities.[6] The present chimney dates probably to about 1800. The older half of the house was restored in 1943–1944 by William Sumner Appleton and Frank Chouteau Brown.

1. Thomas F. Waters, *Ipswich in the Massachusetts Bay Colony* (Ipswich, Mass.: The Ipswich Historical Society, 1905–1917), I, 481.
2. Essex County Deeds, I (Ipswich), 169.
3. Ibid., IV (Ipswich), 501.
4. Essex County Probate Records, docket no. 14024.
5. Essex County Deeds, vol. 1682, pp. 241–242.
6. Ibid., vol. 2857, p. 369.

IPSWICH: KNOWLTON HOUSE, 25 Summer Street   c. 1700

On December 5, 1688, Dea. Thomas Knowlton, Sr., cordwainer, conveyed to his nephew, Nathaniel Knowlton, also a cordwainer, two acres with "A Certaine Dwelling house" in which Thomas then lived.[1] Subsequent deeds, however, make clear that this house was located farther down on Summer Street than the present structure, which was in existence at the corner of Summer and County Streets by May 5, 1725, when it is described in a deed as the "upper" of the two dwellings.[2] The house appears to have been of two-room, central-chimney plan from the outset and was erected probably about 1700 on the evidence of several late features, including the frame of the left-hand lower room which seems to have been cased from the start. The house was purchased on August 27, 1962, by Ernest A. Crocetti[3] and partially restored. Privately owned.

1. Essex County Deeds, V, 338.
2. Ibid., XLIV, 218.
3. Ibid., vol. 4974, p. 196.

IPSWICH: AUSTIN LORD HOUSE (so-called),
  97–99 High Street   before 1653

The present structure consists of two very early story-and-a-half houses, later joined, raised to a full two stories, and enlarged at the rear in all likelihood during the eighteenth century with an extended roof covering the whole. Although there is a gap in the beginning years of the title chain, the critical portion of the property can probably be identified with a half-acre houselot granted by the Town to William Simmons on August 30, 1638.[1] Simmons sold this lot to William Whitred "together with one Dwelling house built by the sayd William Symmons," and Whitred in turn conveyed the house and land to Thomas Smith of Ipswich on June 4, 1639.[2] Theophilus Shatswell was later in possession and on March 29, 1653, sold to William Merchant, husbandman, a parcel of land here and a "dwelling house in which said William now lives. . . ."[3] The complete frame of single-room plan with chimney bay at the left is presumably the Merchant house, and physical evidence suggests that it may have been raised to two stories before the junction of the two buildings occurred. The other (right-hand) frame, a pre-existing single room with loft, was apparently moved up minus its chimney bay from another site. Merchant died in 1668 and the property passed ultimately to his son-in-law, Henry Osborn, who on April 20, 1694, conveyed to his son, John, "ye dwelling house yt was formerly Sd William Merchants. . . ."[4] The character of construction and a comparison of values as revealed in the land and probate records would indicate that the bringing together of the two early cottages and erection of the present central chimney stack occurred following a transfer of title on November 29, 1705, to James Lord of Ipswich, cordwainer, who henceforth made this his home.[5] The house was acquired by Ian F. Forman on June 20, 1967, and has been partially restored.[6] Privately owned.

1. George A. Schofield, ed., *The Ancient Records of the Town of Ipswich. . .* (Ipswich, Mass., 1899), unpaged.
2. Ibid.
3. George Francis Dow, ed., *Records and Files of the Quarterly Courts of Essex County, Massachusetts* (Salem, Mass.: The Essex Institute, 1911–1975), I, 308.
4. Essex County Deeds, XI, 147.
5. Ibid., XXI, 188.
6. Ibid., vol. 5451, p. 705.

IPSWICH: NATHANIEL LORD HOUSE,[1] High Street   after 1683

This portion of a larger houselot was unimproved as late as September 13, 1683, when it was appraised as "a parsell of land" worth £14 in the inventory of the estate of Robert Lord, Sr.[2] Robert's son, Nathaniel Lord, carpenter, inherited and presumably erected the earliest left-hand portion of single-room plan with chimney bay. The addition of a single room to the right may have been made about 1725 (and if so, probably by Nathaniel Lord, Jr., housewright), for this date would seem right for the casement frame with transom found blocked up in the second story of the gable end wall. The stairs in the original portion of the house dated seemingly to the same period, c. 1725. A final addition of single-room plan with a chimney of its own (laid in clay) which concealed the casement window was made about 1750, to judge from the character of construction. The whole house, which measured about sixty feet on High Street and had also been widened at the rear, was demolished in February 1955.

1. The title of this house is confused by Thomas F. Waters, *Ipswich in the Massachusetts Bay Colony* (Ipswich, Mass.: The Ipswich Historical Society, 1905–1917), I, 358 (Cartwright lot).

2. Essex County Probate Records, docket no. 17017.

Ipswich: Lummus-Low House, 45 High Street   after 1712

Thomas Franklin Waters' research reveals that this lot is a portion of Gov. Thomas Dudley's original grant of nine acres on which, according to the Town records, he had built a house by October 1635.[1] The property was conveyed to Jonathan Lummus, Sr., June 18, 1712.[2] On grounds of style and construction the present house of two-room, central-chimney plan with added leanto can be no earlier and was erected presumably either by Lummus after his purchase or even later by the next generation following his death on August 10, 1728. Mr. Waters writes in 1903: "The house has lately been remodelled."[3] It was acquired by the restoration contractor Philip W. Ross March 17, 1964, and restored by him the same year.[4] Privately owned.

1. [Thomas F. Waters], "Thomas Dudley and Simon and Ann Bradstreet," *Publications of the Ipswich Historical Society*, XII (1903), 5 and 8.

2. Essex County Deeds, XXIV, 236.

3. [Waters], *op. cit.*, p. 10.

4. Essex County Deeds, vol. 5156, p. 235.

Ipswich: Manning House,[1] High Street   probably 1692–1693

There was a dwelling on this lot in 1672,[2] but the Manning House (so-called) of central-chimney plan could not have been that early because of its integral leanto construction, and was almost certainly built by William

Stewart, merchant, who acquired the land with its dwelling house on March 5, 1692, for £65 in silver and £20 in pork.[3] At his premature death a year later on August 5, 1693, the property was appraised at £300,[4] a jump in value which implies a major improvement. The house, having been altered to a full two stories throughout and with its main entrance reoriented to open west onto Manning Street instead of towards the east as originally designed, was razed in 1925. The frame of its principal, right-hand (northern) chamber was subsequently installed in the galleries of the Museum of Fine Arts in Boston.

1. Incorrectly identified by Thomas F. Waters as having been built by Job Harris before 1751; *Ipswich in the Massachusetts Bay Colony* (Ipswich, Mass.: The Ipswich Historical Society, 1905–1917), I, 355.
2. Essex County Deeds, IV (Ipswich), 74.
3. Ibid., V (Ipswich), 492.
4. Essex County Probate Records, docket no. 26839.

IPSWICH: PAINE-DODGE HOUSE (so-called),
   53 Jeffrey's Neck Road   after 1700

Robert Paine, Sr., conveyed a farm here on February 12, 1689, to his son, Robert, Jr., described as then living upon the premises.[1] The present house, however, of central-chimney plan with integral leanto, is later in terms of style and character of construction, and was built almost certainly some few years following the marriage of Daniel Smith, husbandman, to the younger Paine's daughter, Elizabeth, on June 29, 1702, and conveyance from Paine to Smith on January 19, 1703, of the entire farm.[2] The property was acquired on June 30, 1916,[3] by Robert G. Dodge of Boston whose wife restored the principal room to the right of the entrance about 1930. Privately owned.

1. Essex County Deeds, V (Ipswich), 590.
2. Ibid., XVII, 21.
3. Ibid., vol. 2334, p. 585.

IPSWICH: CAPT. MATTHEW PERKINS HOUSE
(formerly the Norton-Cobbett House), 8 East Street   1701–1709

The land without improvements was acquired October 11, 1701, by Matthew Perkins, weaver.[1] The house of central-chimney plan with integral leanto was probably in existence by May 25, 1709, because Perkins then conveyed to a son another house in town "which I formerly Lived in. . . ."[2] The chimney top was incorrectly rebuilt in the 1940's, but the house was otherwise unrestored when conveyed to the Society for the Preservation of New England Antiquities on August 12, 1966.[3]

1. Essex County Deeds, XVII, 108.
2. Ibid., XXXV, 104–105. See also, Thomas F. Waters, *Ipswich in the Massachusetts Bay Colony* (Ipswich, Mass.: The Ipswich Historical Society, 1905–1917), I, 389–390.
3. Essex County Deeds, vol. 5384, p. 592.

IPSWICH: PERKINS-SUTTON HOUSE,
   East Street [now (in part) grounds of
   the Concord Antiquarian Society]   probably c. 1700

This house of two-room, central-chimney plan can apparently be identified with the "buildings" which William Sutton of Peabody acquired as part of a fifty-acre tract on October 24, 1870.[1] In his examination of the title Thomas F. Waters suggests that it was the house conveyed by Capt. Matthew Perkins in 1709 to his son, Matthew, Jr., after the Captain had built a finer house on East Street nearer the town (q.v.). It cannot, in any event, have been much earlier than 1700 in terms of construction and style. Mr. Waters reports further that Gen. Sutton "made extensive repairs and enlargement of the ancient dwelling, and it attained such a modern look that its venerable age would never be suspected."[2] Known locally as the Gen. Sutton House, it was dismantled about 1934 and roughly half of the frame, including the chimney bay, was re-erected during the summer of 1939 at the Concord Antiquarian Society, with some juggling of the individual units.[3] Molded sheathing was then introduced which had been acquired from Ralph W. Burnham, the Ipswich antiques dealer. The sheathing may have come originally from the Wilson-Appleton House in Ipswich (q.v.).[4] The boards themselves were seen about this time in a pile at the latter house when it was owned by Burnham.[5]

1. Essex County Deeds, vol. 809, p. 196.
2. Thomas F. Waters, "Jeffrey's Neck and the way leading thereto . . . ," *Publications of the Ipswich Historical Society*, XVIII (1912), 4–5, 8–11.
3. See Russell H. Kettell, "The Reconstruction of the Captain Matthew Perkins House . . . ," Scrapbook, Society for the Preservation of New England Antiquities.
4. Ibid.
5. Daniel S. Wendel, in conversation with the author.

IPSWICH: ROSS TAVERN, South Main Street
   [now 52 Jeffrey's Neck Road]   late 17th cent.

The early history of this important house is obscure. It stood until recent years upon a small tract which formed one corner of the Wilson-Appleton houselot (q.v.), originally owned by John Proctor. The site was unimproved when acquired on September 20, 1734, by Isaac Fitts, hatter.[1] Two years later on April 5, 1736, when Fitts sold this thirty-rod corner lot next the "Southerly Abuttment" of Choate Bridge, it then contained a "House and barn. . . ."[2] The present structure, originally of single-room plan with chimney bay and possibly a projecting two-story porch, is unarguably late seventeenth century in date, and must have been moved to this lot from some undisclosed earlier location between 1734 and 1736. The addition at the right of single-room plan was made in all likelihood at the time of relocation. There is evidence for the addition of a leanto in the 18th century as well. Jeremiah Ross, who acquired the property in 1809, "kept an inn in the old house, and it is still remembered as Ross's Tavern," writes Thomas F. Waters in 1905.[3] The property was purchased on December 24, 1923, by the antiques dealer Ralph W. Burnham who uncovered some of the early features.[4] Daniel S. Wendel in 1940 acquired the house which he dismantled, re-erected, and restored on its present site, adding at the rear the frame of the Collins-Lord House in Ipswich, taken down in March 1938 (q.v.). Privately owned.

1. Essex County Deeds, LXXI, 131.
2. Ibid., LXXII, 269.
3. Thomas F. Waters, *Ipswich in the Massachusetts Bay Colony* (Ipswich, Mass.: The Ipswich Historical Society, 1905–1917), I, 448.
4. Essex County Deeds, vol. 2583, p. 304.

IPSWICH: WHIPPLE HOUSE, 53 South Main Street   c. 1655

The site of this house, granted as a houselot in 1637, was in possession of John Whipple as early as 1642[1] (sale confirmed October 10, 1650[2]). The left-hand portion of single-room plan with chimney bay was built probably about 1655 as a provisional reading of the tree-ring evidence would suggest. Right-hand addition of single-room plan (perhaps subdivided) was in existence by 1683 when John Whipple's son and successor of the same name refers to the "one halfe" of the house in his will executed on August 2 of that year.[3] The leanto at the right may have been added at about the same time (was surely in existence by August 30, 1721, when mentioned in the will of the third John Whipple[4]), and was later raised to two stories and enlarged. House acquired by trustees for the Ipswich Historical Society May 12, 1898, and restored that year under the direction of Thomas F. Waters.[5] Moved across town to its present site in 1928 and further restored in 1953–1954 by the restoration contractor Roy W. Baker.

1. Thomas F. Waters, "The John Whipple House in Ipswich, Mass . . . ," *Publications of the Ipswich Historical Society*, xx (1915), 1–2.

2. Essex County Deeds, 1 (Ipswich), 89.

3. Essex County Probate Records, vol. 304, p. 10.

4. Ibid., vol. 313, p. 458.

5. Essex County Deeds, vol. 1549, p. 6, and vol. 1561, p. 534.

52.   Whipple house, Ipswich, Mass. End wall of earliest portion shown during repairs in 1953–1954 which revealed the original frame of two-story studs and restoration features of 1898, including the introduction of window sash with diamond panes of glass set in wooden muntins. Photo, Peter Zaharis, courtesy Ipswich Historical Society.

53. Whipple house, Ipswich, Mass. Detail of molded post and end girts of the later over-hanging second story, showing repairs made during the restoration of 1898. Photo, Peter Zaharis, 1954, courtesy Ipswich Historical Society.

IPSWICH: WILSON-APPLETON HOUSE,
4 South Main Street   after 1672

At least three features associated with the frame of the original house, the joist spacing, the roof of principal and common rafters and wall fill of clay and chopped straw, when taken together, suggest an early date. The question depends upon the title, which is clear and unarguable, and upon what the seventeenth-century surveyor interpreted as a measuring point for a frontage of "seaven rods or poles" from "the banke of the River" when Shoreborn Wilson, cooper, purchased an unimproved lot here "neare the Bridge" on October 10, 1672.[1] Seven rods measured from the present water channel at spring tide fails by as much as ten feet to encompass the southern end of the house, which strictly interpreted would preclude a construction date until after April 3, 1685, when Wilson acquired the land (also unimproved) to the south.[2] The site is described on February 28, 1693, as the "homestead" of Shoreborn Wilson,[3] and both house and land were acquired December 17, 1702, by Samuel Appleton[4] (who had earlier built the Appleton-Taylor-Mansfield House in Saugus, q.v.). The house then, and as first built, was of two-room, central-chimney plan as principal purlin mortises in a single remaining original rafter on the north side of the chimney bay reveal. It was undoubtedly Appleton who added the higher-studded frame of single-room plan at the left, demolishing the existing left-hand portion of the house in the process. The walls of the remaining right-hand "half" with its chimney bay were raised by two feet or more and the entire structure was roofed with a new set of rafters. Those at the rear extended back in single lengths to cover a leanto (integral at the northern and added at the southern end of the house). Appleton's will, dated December 21, 1718, mentions "the Southerly End of the House I now Live in, that is the Parlor and Chamber over it and Garrotts, the Seller under itt & ye Lento behind itt,"[5] the latter raised still later to a full two stories. The house was purchased on January 2, 1929, by the antiques dealer Ralph W. Burnham and partially restored by him.[6] Privately owned.

1. Essex County Deeds, III (Ipswich), 285.
2. Ibid., v (Ipswich), 182.
3. Ibid., IX, 287.
4. Ibid., XV, 109.
5. Essex County Probate Records, vol. 315, p. 307.
6. Essex County Deeds, vol. 2793, p. 246.

LINCOLN: WHITTEMORE-SMITH HOUSE,
North Great Road   after 1693

Title research by the antiquarian Harriette M. Forbes has revealed that the site of this house was unimproved in 1693 when conveyed to Benjamin Whittemore.[1] The house as erected presumably soon thereafter was of two-room, central-chimney plan. The leanto is a later addition. The property was acquired November 8, 1770, by Catharine Louisa Salmon who married Capt. William Smith of Revolutionary War fame. The original central chimney was removed probably before 1900. House conveyed to the United States of America by deed recorded May 29, 1975, to be administered as a historic site by the National Park Service.[2]

1. Harriette M. Forbes, "Some Seventeenth-Century Houses of Middlesex County, Massachusetts," *Old-Time New England*, ser. no. 95 (Jan. 1939), pp. 97–99.
2. Middlesex County Deeds, vol. 12800, p. 721.

MARBLEHEAD: AMBROSE GALE HOUSE,
17 Franklin Street   probably c. 1663

Research by Robert Booth has revealed reference in a deed of December 16, 1663, to a dwelling house in this immediate vicinity belonging to Ambrose Gale,[1] called fisherman and shoreman in the early records and prominent in town affairs. The date is consistent with the character of the earliest, left-hand portion of the house of single-room plan and chimney bay. As first built the frame of the principal room was furnished with crossed summer beams. The bridging agents were removed later in the seventeenth century, perhaps at the same time that the right-hand unit of single-room plan was added. This addition is seventeenth century in character and may have been made when Gale married for the second time in August 1695. The original chimney has been removed (probably in the 19th century) and there has been partial restoration in the twentieth century. Privately owned.

1. Essex County Deeds, II, 92.

MARBLEHEAD: NORDEN HOUSE, 15 Glover Street   c. 1680–1687

The present structure of "half-house" plan with integral leanto cannot, because of the latter feature, have been built before the early 1680's. In light of the high style quality of the frame it can probably be identified with a conveyance of February 21, 1687, whereby Christopher Lattimer, vintner, deeded to his well-to-do son-in-law, Nathaniel Norden, mariner, both of Marblehead, a small "tract of Land [about 165 by 124 feet] . . . whereon the Dwelling howse of yᵉ sᵈ Norden now stands partly, And part of itt the land house & orchard wᶜʰ sometimes since was yᵉ estate of, & Occupied by my ffather Wᵐ Pitt, (decᵈ). . . ."[1] At Norden's death an inventory of April 5, 1728, valued "The mansion House with gardens ware-houses Small dwelling House & barn" at £1,550.[2] In further support of this identification with the existing structure at the head of Glover Street Sidney Perley writes of his researches in the neighborhood that Glover Street was "laid out about 1720, being called, at first, the lane that leads down from Captain Norden's house to ye great harbor . . . [and] the highway leading to Nathaniel Norden's mansion house in 1722. . . ."[3] The property was purchased on July 27, 1920, by Philip W. von Saltza,[4] described by William Sumner Appleton as "a Swedish artist working in Marblehead, who uncovered the old woodwork and did more or less restoration."[5] It may well have been he who introduced the early staircase with twisted balusters and vine carving of as yet uncertain provenance which overlies paneled trim of a period later than the stairs themselves. House privately owned.

1. Essex County Deeds, IX, 3.
2. Essex County Probate Records, vol. 319, p. 31.
3. Sidney Perley, "Marblehead in the Year 1700, No. 5," *Essex Institute Historical Collections*, XLVII (1911), 68.
4. Essex County Deeds, vol. 2461, p. 585.
5. "Re: House 15 Glover Street, Marblehead," undated notes by William Sumner Appleton, Corr. Files, Society for the Preservation of New England Antiquities.

MARBLEHEAD: PARKER-ORNE HOUSE, 47 Orne Street   c. 1711

David Parker, bricklayer, purchased an unimproved lot here on December 19, 1710.[1] The original house of single-room plan with chimney bay was erected presumably soon thereafter and forms the central portion of the present structure. Within ten or twenty years, to judge from the style and construction, an addition of single-room plan was made at the northern or left-hand end of the building, and was probably without fireplaces at the outset. Later, about 1800, another unit of single-room plan was projected at the opposite southern end. A separate chimney was constructed along the rear wall of this added bay, and a new staircase with partitions was introduced in what had been the lower end bay of the principal room of the original house which is furnished with transverse summer beams on posts. A cooking fireplace exists in the rear face of the later chimney as though a kitchen ell at right angles had been planned as part of the latest addition. It is blocked by the present rear wall, however, and shows no signs of ever having been used. A bay window at the front is late nineteenth century. Privately owned.

1. Essex County Deeds, XXII, 210.

MEDFIELD: PEAK HOUSE, 347 Main Street   late 17th cent.

The existing foundation is eighteenth rather than seventeenth century in character which confirms a well-authenticated local tradition that the frame, of single-room plan, a story and a half high, has been moved to this site. It is of further significance that there is no chimney bay in the conventional sense, nor any evidence for its former presence. We may be dealing, therefore, with a portion only of an early house. If erected in the immediate vicinity the builder was probably Benjamin Clark who owned the land and whose original dwelling here was burned when Medfield was

54. Peak house, Medfield, Mass. Early woodcut from John Warner Barber's *Massachusetts Historical Collections* . . . (Worcester, Mass., 1839), p. 472.

fired by the Indians on February 21, 1676. The house was acquired by the Medfield Historical Society on October 13, 1924,[1] and restored during 1924–1925 with William Sumner Appleton as consultant. A new chimney stack with fireplace was constructed at this time, utilizing the eighteenth-century arched foundation which had survived in the cellar.

1. Norfolk County Deeds, vol. 1604, p. 301.

MEDFORD: BLANCHARD-WELLINGTON HOUSE, 14 Bradbury Avenue   c. 1720

There was a dwelling being erected on this property in August 1657,[1] although the house of two-room, central-chimney plan with added leanto which survived here until its demolition in 1968 was clearly much later. A date towards the end of the first quarter of the eighteenth century was indicated by the style and character of construction. When demolished the original staircase and an early corner cupboard (the latter having been introduced into the house c. 1900 from another old house, perhaps in Concord) were salvaged by the Society for the Preservation of New England Antiquities. Major portions of the frame were also salvaged and are now privately owned.

1. John H. Hooper, "Some Old Medford Houses . . . ," *Medford Historical Register*, VII (1904), 49.

NEWBURY: COFFIN HOUSE, 16 High Road   c. 1654

The early history of the site is obscure. Joshua Coffin, the historian, tells us in 1845 that Tristram Coffin, Jr., "about 1654 erected the house, in which the compiler of this work now resides,"[1] a date confirmed by the character of construction and a provisional reading of the tree-ring evidence. Tristram, Jr., married in March 1653 Judith, widow of Henry Somerby. The original portion of the house facing south, of single-room plan with chimney bay, forms an ell at the rear, extended to the east probably about 1700. This addition was subsequently engulfed by the main block of the house with central passage erected apparently during or before the mid-eighteenth century (though considerably altered in finish detail in the late eighteenth and early nineteenth centuries). All major elements of the present structure are included in a probate division of February 28, 1785,[2] except for an enlargement of the room at the northwest corner (beside the original ell) which dates to 1799 according to family account books.[3] Conveyed February 20, 1929, to the Society for the Preservation of New England Antiquities.[4] Partially restored.

1. Joshua Coffin, *A Sketch of the History of Newbury* [Massachusetts] . . . (Boston, Mass., 1845), p. 391.
2. See James W. Spring, "The Coffin House in Newbury, Massachusetts . . . ," *Old-Time New England*, ser. no. 57 (July 1929), pp. 16–18.
3. Ms Collections, Society for the Preservation of New England Antiquities.
4. Essex County Deeds, vol. 2798, p. 446.

NEWBURY: DOLE-LITTLE HOUSE, 289 High Road   c. 1715–1725

The present house of two-room, central-chimney plan was erected late in the first quarter of the eighteenth century, as style and construction would suggest, making copious use of building materials from an earlier structure. The leanto is a later addition, preceded by a small original kitchen addition about twelve feet wide at the rear, as structural evidence has revealed. Having been owned for many years by the Dole and other New-

bury families, the house was acquired by Florence Evans Bushee of Newbury on August 17, 1954,[1] and restored by the restoration contractor Roy
W. Baker in 1955 to reflect an earlier period in time. Early if not original
paneling from the left-hand chamber has been installed as an exhibition
room in the galleries of the National Museum of History and Technology
in Washington, and stair balusters, also presumably original, were removed (and are now preserved in the house). Title passed to the Society
for the Preservation of New England Antiquities under a pre-existing
agreement at Mrs. Bushee's death on November 21, 1975.

1. Essex County Deeds, vol. 4094, p. 504.

NEWBURY: NOYES HOUSE,
    7 Parker Street   of undetermined 17th-cent. date

Joshua Coffin tells us in 1845 that "Mr. Noyes [the minister] built a
house on what is now called Parker street," and he refers to it as "one of
the oldest houses in Newbury."[1] The frame of the original front portion
of two-room, central-chimney plan is almost entirely concealed by later
trim, and while the chamfered roof frame is mid-seventeenth century in
character the joist spacing would indicate a date of construction later in
the century. The rear ell is an addition or separate building altogether,
butted up, and has been extended in length in 1977. Privately owned.

1. Joshua Coffin, *A Sketch of the History of Newbury* [Massachusetts] . . . (Boston,
Mass., 1845), p. 375.

NEWBURY: SWETT-ILSLEY HOUSE, 4–6 High Road   c. 1670

On March 12, 1670, in a conveyance of land, Stephen Swett reserved
for himself a small tract here which when sold by Swett to Hugh March,
Jr., on November 16, 1691, contained a "dwelling house. . . ."[1] While the
cellar evidence is not entirely conclusive, the first-built portion of the present structure, of single-room plan with chimney bay, appears, nevertheless, to stand on its original foundation, and is presumably that erected by
Swett about 1670, judging from the style and character of construction.
This house faced south, with the land falling away at the left-hand end.
The first addition, therefore, was projected at the rear, but not in the usual
form. Rather, a unit of single-room plan, nearly twelve feet wide and two
and a half stories high, was attached to the existing carcass and a new roof

was raised over both portions with the ridge now running north-south instead of east-west. The original chimney must have been retained, though the new roof (which re-uses the earlier rafters) would have required some modification of the stack above the attic floor level. There is little change in the monetary value of the house and its small plot between 1694 and the death of the then owner, Isaac Noyes, in 1718,[2] and in terms of structural characteristics the alteration just described will probably have occurred about 1720. The next major change was made before or shortly after a sale of the property by Isaac Noyes' heirs on February 26, 1739,[3] and in any event during the second quarter of the eighteenth century, to judge from the style. The addition at the north was extended in the same direction twelve feet along the front wall and fourteen along the rear, these unequal measurements being dictated, obviously, by the constricted boundaries of the narrow houselot. At the same time, the first-story end girt of the first extension was removed and a new girt, seated on one-story posts, was introduced to create a chimney bay. The original chimney was then presumably demolished and the present central chimney constructed, at which time also two summer beams or bridging agents were inserted between the newly introduced chimney girt and the new northern end girt. Additional land was purchased at the north end of the property on March 20, 1756,[4] which made possible during the ensuing years a final extension to the north of single-room plan with stair-hall, separate chimney (later replaced with a smaller stack[5]) and rooms behind covered by a leanto roof which projected towards the south to provide rooms across the entire length of the house at the rear. This latest addition at the north end was reportedly utilitarian at first and then finished off, probably about 1820, with the present domestic trim.[6] A one-story projecting porch, seen in mid-nineteenth-century photos, is mentioned in a deed of May 25, 1802.[7] The house was acquired by the Society for the Preservation of New England Antiquities on June 24, 1911,[8] and the older rooms were restored during 1915.[9]

1. Essex County Deeds, III (Ipswich), 215, and X, 17.

2. See ibid., XVIII, 48; XXXI, 61; and XXXVIII, 18; and Essex County Probate Records, docket no. 19766 (inventory).

3. Essex County Deeds, XCV, 192.

4. Ibid., vol. 104, p. 10.

5. William Sumner Appleton, "The Ilsley House," Old-Time New England, ser. no. 4 (Aug. 1911), p. 10.

6. John J. Currier, "Ould Newbury" . . . (Boston, Mass., 1896), pp. 196–197.

7. Essex County Deeds, vol. 194, p. 233.

8. Ibid., vol. 2088, pp. 301 and 306.

9. William Sumner Appleton, "Annual Report of the Corresponding Secretary," Old-Time New England, ser. no. 14 (May 1916), pp. 5–9.

NEWBURYPORT: BENAIAH TITCOMB HOUSE, 4 Green Street
[now 189 John Wise Avenue, Essex]   probably after 1700

John J. Currier, the historian, states that the house was built on a half-acre lot acquired by Benaiah Titcomb, mariner, from Richard Dole in 1695.[1] This land, however, the only conveyance from Dole to Titcomb on record,[2] was still without improvements on February 8, 1729, when the latter devised to his son, Benaiah, Jr., "about half an acre of Land that I formerly bought of M[r] Richard Dole...."[3] Rather, the house was erected on an unimproved tract of one and a quarter acres which Titcomb purchased earlier on October 9, 1678, from Anthony Morse.[4] The structure itself, of two-room, central-chimney plan as originally built, would appear to date to the period just after 1700 on grounds of style. The rear leanto is an addition. The property was purchased by Moses Brown of Newburyport, merchant, on January 23, 1801,[5] and remained in that family until taken by the City as a site for a new police station. The old house was then in 1911 acquired by the antiques dealer Ralph W. Burnham, dismantled, stored in Ipswich, and re-erected on its present site in Essex in 1917.[6] Privately owned.

1. John J. Currier, *History of Newburyport, Mass., 1764–1909* (Newburyport, Mass.: Printed for the Author, 1909), II, 54.
2. Essex County Deeds, XIV, 108.
3. Essex County Probate Records, vol. 316, p. 289.
4. Essex County Deeds, XIV, 107. See also, John J. Currier, *"Ould Newbury"* . . . (Boston, Mass., 1896), pp. 119 and 142.
5. Essex County Deeds, vol. 167, p. 306.
6. "The Benaiah Titcomb House," *Old-Time New England*, ser. no. 4 (Aug. 1911), pp. 15–18; William Sumner Appleton, "Annual Report of the Corresponding Secretary," *Old-Time New England*, ser. no. 7 (July 1912), p. 16, and "Annual Reports of the Corresponding Secretary . . . ," *Old-Time New England*, ser. no. 18 (Nov. 1918), p. 29.

NORTH ANDOVER: PARSON BARNARD HOUSE (formerly the
Anne Bradstreet House), 179 Osgood Street   c. 1715

The land without improvements was acquired March 12, 1714, by the Rev. Thomas Barnard, third minister of the original north parish of Andover.[1] At his death on October 13, 1718, the lot contained a "New house,"[2] the present dwelling of central-chimney plan with integral leanto. Further extension of the leanto at the rear is nineteenth century in character and appears in a photo taken about 1866. The property was conveyed October 20, 1950, to the North Andover Historical Society.[3] The chimney top above the roof level was rebuilt about 1920 along its original lines.

The house was restored in 1956–1957 with most of the later architectural features retained.[4]

1. Essex County Deeds, xxix, 94.
2. Essex County Probate Records, docket no. 1788.
3. Essex County Deeds (North District), Lawrence, Mass., vol. 742, p. 359.
4. See Abbott Lowell Cummings, "The Parson Barnard House," *Old-Time New England*, ser. no. 166 (Oct.–Dec. 1956), pp. 29–40.

QUINCY: BASS HOUSE,
70 Granite Street   probably early 18th cent.

The house was much altered in the early nineteenth century and moved in 1903 a short distance. The original portion was perhaps that house described as "new" in the will of John Bass in 1712. Destroyed in 1959.[1] Documentation and photographs taken at the time of demolition are on file at the Quincy Historical Society.

1. See *Quincy Patriot Ledger*, Oct. 22, 1959, p. 14.

QUINCY: BAXTER HOUSE,
Spear and Canal Streets   probably early 18th cent.

The house as originally constructed was of two-room, central-chimney plan. The leanto was added later. The overall proportions and projection of the tie-beams over the front plate would suggest a date no earlier than about 1700. Demolished in July 1960. Documentation and photographs taken at the time of demolition are on file at the Quincy Historical Society.

QUINCY: QUINCY HOMESTEAD, 34 Butler Road   probably c. 1686

The house as it stands reveals a complicated pattern of evolution. The rear right-hand Coddington kitchen, so-called, is the oldest portion, of single-room plan with chimney bay, and was in all likelihood (when compared with other components) pulled up to the present site. If constructed originally on this tract of land, early owned by the Quincy family, it can probably be identified with the building described by Samuel Sewall on March 22, 1686, as "Unkle [Edmund] Quinsey's new House,"[1] a date entirely consistent with its style. The second earliest portion is the single vertical file of rooms with chimney bay in front at the left, erected in 1706 for Edmund Quincy of the following generation on the present foundation, as we learn from the diary of John Marshall who performed the mason's work and assisted in the raising of the frame on June 14 of that year.[2] The next set of changes occurred apparently in the middle of the eighteenth century. It was at this time, presumably, that the seventeenth-century "kitchen" was pulled up and the front right rooms infilled to achieve first an L-shaped plan and then, with the further addition of the rear left rooms, the roughly four-square, central-passage plan which now exists. Two stages of growth for the present roof covering all elements can be traced in the structure. A single-bay, two-story projection at the left is problematical in date, but appears in any event in a watercolor view of 1822. There have been nineteenth-century modifications and partial restoration by Joseph Everett Chandler at the time the house was acquired in 1906 by the Metropolitan Park Commission (now Metropolitan District Commission). The property is administered by the National Society of Colonial Dames of America in the Commonwealth of Massachusetts.

1. M. Halsey Thomas, ed., *The Diary of Samuel Sewall, 1674–1729* (New York: Farrar, Straus and Giroux, c1973), I, 101.
2. John Marshall, Diary, MS, The Massachusetts Historical Society.

READING: PARKER TAVERN, 103 Washington Street   c. 1725

Abraham Bryant, Jr., acquired the land on October 22, 1693.[1] His taxes in 1695 show a major increase, suggesting improvements, and he was certainly living here in 1700 as a deed of that year would indicate.[2] The present house, however, of central-chimney, integral leanto plan, appears on the basis of style and construction to be later still, and may well have been built soon after Abraham Bryant, Jr.'s, son and heir sold the property on April 28, 1724, to a brother-in-law, Nathaniel Stow, blacksmith.[3] The Town of Reading voted to purchase the house for museum purposes on March 27, 1916, and in 1923 conveyed it to the Reading Antiquarian Society, which inaugurated the work of restoration that year under the direction of Winthrop D. Parker, architect, and Eugene Dow of Topsfield, carpenter (although the restoration was not completed until 1930).[4]

1. Middlesex County Deeds, XIII, 162.
2. *The Parker Tavern* . . . , pamphlet, printed by the Reading Antiquarian Society, 1930, pp. 9–10.
3. Middlesex County Deeds, XXIII, 259.
4. See the Reading *Chronicle*, June 27, 1930.

ROCKPORT: WITCH HOUSE or OLD GARRISON HOUSE
(so-called), 188 Granite Street   c. 1700

Allen Chamberlain, the historian, having examined the Gloucester town records and land titles for this area, writes: "On February 27, 1687/8 a town meeting voted that every householder, and every male native of the town twenty-one years of age and upward, should be granted six acres of land 'upon the Cape,' that being the term used by Gloucestermen of those days to describe the northern and northeastern shores, including the Pigeon Cove section of what is now Rockport."[1] Francis Norwood, Sr., had acquired several of these lots before 1700, including apparently the site of the present structure, and an inventory taken following his death on March 4, 1709, credits the estate with sixty-six acres " 'leying neare pidgeon cove so called on the Cape and on which land Joshua Norwood [a son of Francis] now dwells.' "[2] Whether erected by Francis or Joshua Norwood (who was married in September 1704), the existing log house of two-room, central-chimney plan would appear to date to c. 1700 on the basis of style and character of construction. The eighteenth-century addition which created an L-shaped plan and resulted in the rebuilding of the roof was undoubtedly made by Moses Wheeler who lived here from 1778 to 1824. The original chimney was radically altered, probably at the same time, and bay windows were added in the second half of the nineteenth century. The house was acquired Nov. 8, 1925, by Oliver E. Williams of Boston[3] who carried out an extensive restoration, including the introduction of a new period fireplace in the left-hand room and early sheathing, doors, etc., from other sources. Privately owned.

1. Allen Chamberlain and Thomas Williams, *The Old Castle* . . . (Pigeon Cove, Mass.: Village Improvement Soc., 1939), p. 8.
2. Ibid., p. 9.
3. Essex County Deeds, vol. 2663, p. 125.

SALEM: COL. WILLIAM BROWNE HOUSE (SUN TAVERN),
Essex Street   after 1664

William Browne, Jr., of Salem, merchant, acquired a parcel of land here on August 3, 1664, and the house was erected presumably soon thereafter.[1] Sidney Perley's research reveals that the property was conveyed to the Union Marine Insurance Co. of Salem in 1805, upon which the dwelling became the Sun Tavern. On November 15, 1824, the estate was purchased by William Manning who took down the old structure and erected the "Bowker block" on its site in 1830.[2] A section of the original ornamental rough-cast covering is preserved in the collections of the Essex Institute.

1. Essex County Deeds, II, 83.
2. Sidney Perley, "Salem in 1700, No. 16," *The Essex Antiquarian*, VIII (1904), 114–116.

SALEM: CORWIN HOUSE (WITCH HOUSE),
310½ Essex Street   c. 1675

The administrators of the estate of Capt. Richard Davenport of Boston conveyed to Jonathan Corwin of Salem, merchant, on February 11, 1675, this houselot and other lands in Salem together with "all houses, edifices, buildings," etc.[1] On the 19th of that same month Corwin contracted with Daniel Andrews, mason, for a "parcell of worke . . . to be bestowed in filling, plaistering & finishing a Certaine Dwellinghouse bought by the said owner of Capt. Nath.^ll Dauenport of Boston" (see page 217).[2] Early efforts to identify this house with that owned before 1636 by the celebrated Roger Williams have been refuted.[3] The Corwin/Andrews contract implies, moreover, that Capt. Richard Davenport's son, Capt. Nathaniel, had nearly finished a house here which he apparently sold to Corwin independently of the 1675 land transaction, as style and construction confirm. As completed by Corwin the house was of central-chimney plan with a contemporary leanto at the rear and a projecting two-story porch. Corwin's grandson, George, died in 1746, and his inventory suggests that the house retained then more or less its original form.[4] George Corwin's widow, Mrs. Sarah Corwin, enlarged the house according to a well-substantiated word of mouth tradition in the family,[5] at which time the facade gables and porch were removed, two chambers built over the leanto and a gambrel roof constructed which covered the entire frame. A mid-nineteenth-century photograph of the house in this state reveals that a separate central chimney stack existed at the rear of the house as well,[6] which according to the mason's contract of 1675 may have been an original feature. The property was conveyed June 3, 1856, to George Pickman Farrington, druggist,[7] who between this date and his death in 1885 appended a drug store to the eastern side of the front which projected out towards the street. The house was acquired April 9, 1945, by Historic Salem, Inc.,[8] moved back a few feet and thoroughly restored in 1945–1946, drawing upon the services of Frank Chouteau Brown as consultant. Title was conveyed by Historic Salem, Inc., to the City of Salem on January 28, 1948.[9]

1. Essex County Deeds, IV, 103.

2. Corwin Family MSS, American Antiquarian Society.

3. See Sidney Perley, "Where Roger Williams lived in Salem," *Essex Institute Historical Collections*, LII (1916), 97–111.

4. Essex County Probate Records, docket no. 6946.

5. William P. Upham, "An Account of the Dwelling-Houses of Francis Higginson, Samuel Skelton, Roger Williams, and Hugh Peters," *Essex Institute Historical Collections*, VIII (1866), 258.

6. Collections, Society for the Preservation of New England Antiquities.

7. Essex County Deeds, vol. 537, p. 45.

8. Ibid., vol. 3400, p. 437.

9. Ibid., vol. 3585, p. 340.

SALEM: DOWNING-BRADSTREET HOUSE,
Essex Street   of undetermined 17th-cent. date

Knowledge of this high-style house, which stood where the present Essex Institute buildings are located, is based almost entirely on the sketch executed c. 1820 by Samuel Bartoll who was born about 1765, *after* the structure had been demolished. His source has never been identified. By June 8, 1640, the property, which included a "Mansion house," was in possession of Emanuel Downing who had settled in Salem in 1638 with his wife, Lucy, sister of Gov. Winthrop.[1] Both Emanuel Downing and his celebrated son, George, for whom Downing Street in London was named, returned ultimately to England, and the property was conveyed to Joseph Gardner in 1656, described as "his dowry & mariage porcõn wᵗʰ Ann yᵉ daughter of yᵉ sd Emanuell & Luce Downing...."[2] Capt. Joseph Gardner died in 1675; his widow, Ann, married Gov. Simon Bradstreet, and he lived here until his death in 1697. Following Mrs. Bradstreet's death a few years later the house was owned by successive generations of the Ropes family, and operated for some time as a public house "by yᵉ Name of yᵉ Globe Tavern," as recorded in 1716.[3] Probate records in 1717 refer to the "great Entry," and a division of 1728 suggests that the house may have measured fifty-eight feet along Essex Street.[4] Land records indicate that demolition occurred in 1758.[5]

1. Suffolk County Deeds, I, 56.
2. Essex County Deeds, I, 31.
3. Ibid., xxxi, 95.
4. Essex County Probate Records, docket no. 24147.
5. Essex County Deeds, vol. 104, p. 164, and vol. 105, pp. 36 and 57.

SALEM: PHILIP ENGLISH HOUSE,
Essex and English Streets   c. 1690

Philip English of Salem, mariner, acquired half a house here on January 3, 1683.[1] The Rev. William Bentley states on April 14, 1791, that the house which bore the Philip English name and which stood upon the northeast corner of Essex and English Streets "was built as says his G. daughter in 1690. It was the largest in Town...."[2] On April 15, 1791, the diarist wrote:

The Cellars are compleatly finished. The Stone wall is built of as large stones as are now in use which contradicts the opinion that they generally built of small stones of choice, at that age. There is an hearth, very large oven, & all conveniences. The Rooms are the largest in

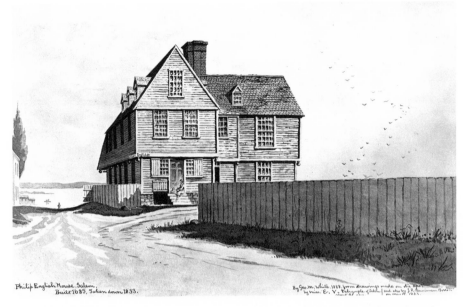

55. Philip English house, Salem, Mass. From a drawing by Miss E. W. Dalrymple and J. R. Penniman, 1823, courtesy The Essex Institute.

Town. The floors are laid in plank, & are sound at this day, the sweep at the hearth where they are worn down having a curious appearance. The upper part of the house among the Peeks have curious partitions and very much Room. Even the Cellars are plastered.[3]

On May 21, 1793, he wrote again:

The Mansion house now standing & most compleatly finished for the times, having cellars, stoned at bottom, lathed & plastered over head upon the floors above, divided for all purposes, furnished with fire places, & ovens, laid in lime, floors which are good now after one hundred years, pantries, counting house, shop, & various apartments, halls, was more splendid in that day. Two gable ends in the west part, & another in the east have been taken down, a plank floor was laid upon the top, & an entire balustrade around it, extending to the peeks, upon which were erected ornaments rising two feet. At the southern door was an open fence, with a Gate & Knocker. Over the Shop door was a Balcony with seats, and a door communicating with the southern chamber, & the dial was over the door.[4]

Sidney Perley writes that when the house passed by will in 1785 there is mention of the "great porch" and "porch chamber" at the west end.[5] It is not known whether the house as shown in later nineteenth-century views was of one or more build. The Boston *American Traveller* reported on Friday, May 10, 1833, that the house had been demolished during the preceding week.

1. Sidney Perley, "Salem in 1700, No. 21," *The Essex Antiquarian*, IX (1905), 168.
2. *The Diary of William Bentley, D.D.* . . . (Gloucester, Mass.: Peter Smith, 1962), I, 248.
3. Ibid.
4. Ibid., II, 25–26.
5. Sidney Perley, "Salem in 1700, No. 21," *The Essex Antiquarian*, IX (1905), 169.

SALEM: GEDNEY HOUSE, 21 High Street   c. 1665

The land without improvements was acquired April 20, 1664, by Eleazer Gedney, shipwright.[1] The house erected thereafter (Gedney married in June 1665) consisted originally of the left-hand room with its chamber, garret and chimney bay and a smaller room at the right covered by a leanto roof at right angles. Long-gone extensions at the rear (where some structural evidence survives) were probably original. They were surely in existence by Eleazer's death in 1683 when an estate inventory mentions the hall, hall chamber, "parlour or lento," "lento chamb^r," and "Kitchin[,] Loft over it & litle Leantoo."[2] After the widow's death in 1716 their daughter, Martha Gedney, who had married November 6, 1712, inherited.[3] Before or about this time the right-hand parlor was raised to a full two stories with framed overhang at the first story on the street. A two-story leanto at the rear with separate chimney replaced c. 1800 whatever preceded it. The building was acquired July 5, 1962, by Fred Winter of Marblehead[4] who removed the (later) central chimney and stripped the frame within. House conveyed to the Society for the Preservation of New England Antiquities March 23, 1967,[5] and is maintained as an architectural exhibit.

1. Essex County Deeds, II, 96–97.
2. Essex County Probate Records, vol. 302, pp. 125–126.
3. Ibid., vol. 312, p. 9.
4. Essex County Deeds, vol. 4943, p. 46.
5. Ibid., vol. 5431, p. 291.

SALEM: HOOPER-HATHAWAY HOUSE, 23 Washington Street
[now grounds of the House of Seven Gables]   c. 1682

The land without improvements (originally part of the Gov. Endicott field, so-called) was acquired by Benjamin Hooper, cordwainer, October

56.   Gedney house, Salem, Mass. Photo, John Robinson, 1886, courtesy The Essex Institute.

27, 1682.[1] The house erected thereafter was originally of single-room plan with chimney bay. Before 1784, when they are mentioned in a division of the estate, an addition of single-room plan had been made at the right and a leanto attached to the rear.[2] As seen in early photos this leanto was, or had subsequently become, a full two stories in height. The house was purchased by Miss Caroline O. Emmerton in June 1911, moved to the grounds of the House of Seven Gables and restored by Joseph Everett Chandler. (For more complete history and arguments that the building incorporates timbers from Gov. Endicott's dwelling house built originally for the Dorchester Co. at Cape Ann, about which eighty-year-old Richard Brackenbury of Beverly deposed January 20, 1680/1, that he with others had been sent to Cape Ann about 1628 "to pull downe yᵉ sd house for Mr. Endecotts use" [Essex County Deeds, v, 107], see C. M. Endicott, "The Old Planters' House," *Essex Institute Historical Collections*, II (1860), 39–42; Sidney Perley, "Salem in 1700, No. 14," *The Essex Antiquarian*, VIII [1904], 32–35; Frank C. Brown, "Salem, Massachusetts," *Pencil Points* [May 1937], pp. 307–308; Caroline O. Emmerton, *The Chronicles of Three Old Houses* [Boston, Mass.: Thomas Todd Co., Printers, 1935], pp. 40–47; and Alexander Young, *Chronicles of the First Planters of the Colony of Massachusetts Bay . . .* [Boston, Mass., 1846], p. 258n.)

1. Essex County Deeds, XXXIII, 245.
2. Essex County Probate Records, vol. 357, p. 366.

SALEM: LEWIS HUNT HOUSE,
   Washington and Lynde Streets   c. 1698

The land without improvements was acquired by Lewis Hunt, mariner, September 15, 1698.[1] The house was erected probably soon thereafter. Demolished August 1863.

1. Essex County Deeds, XIII, 54. See also, *The Essex Antiquarian*, II (1898), 173.

SALEM: NARBONNE HOUSE, 71 Essex Street   c. 1672

The land upon which the house stands was owned first by Timothy Laskin and then in 1669 by Paul Mansfield[1] (who sold at least three other contiguous houselots here without improvements). Thomas Ives, slaughterer, was in possession of this houselot by January 6, 1676,[2] and from the style and character of construction it is assumed that he was the builder, perhaps at the time of his marriage on April 1, 1672. The original appearance and subsequent structural history are not entirely clear. The house as built consisted of a room with chamber and garret and chimney bay (left-hand portion) and an original leanto with a fireplace of unusual size and character. The wall to the right of the chimney is studded up as an end wall with falling braces, but there is a large original fireplace here and some other structural evidence as well to suggest that the house extended to the right at the outset. Thomas Ives' inventory in 1695 mentions the northern (left) room and chamber, southern room and chamber, kitchen and kitchen chamber (presumably in the leanto) and shop (a separate building).[3] The present story-and-a-half gambrel-roofed ell at the right (which is made up of earlier, re-used timber) is a separate structure altogether butted up against the original house. Its style would suggest a date in the second quarter of the eighteenth century. Capt. Joseph Hodges, who acquired the house in halves in 1750 and 1757 for something more than £82,[4] sold in 1780 for £200 lawful money,[5] implying a major improvement, and recent archeological investigation of the site would confirm a mid-eighteenth-century date for the moving up and addition of the gambrel-roofed ell, replacing whatever had previously existed. The central portion of the present leanto may have been added at the same time, also replacing earlier construction. The northern and southern ends of the leanto are later still. House acquired September 10, 1964, by the United States of America to be administered as a historic site by the National Park Service.[6]

1. Essex County Deeds, III, 55.
2. Ibid., IV, 152.
3. Essex County Probate Records, docket no. 14656.
4. Essex County Deeds, XCIV, 248; XCVI, 22; and vol. 103, p. 236.
5. Ibid., vol. 137, p. 177.
6. Ibid., vol. 5221, p. 117.

SALEM: PARKMAN HOUSE, Essex and North Streets   c. 1670

Edmond Batter of Salem, on January 18, 1669, conveyed a lot without improvements here to his brother-in-law, Hilliard Veren, Sr., and the latter's daughters, Dorcas and Sarah.[1] Dorcas was married on February 21, 1672, to Timothy Hicks of Salem, shipwright, who may well have erected the house which he sold together with one half of the lot a year later on August 6, 1673,[2] to Deliverance Parkman of Salem, shipwright, who married Dorcas' sister, Sarah Veren, a few months later on December 9, 1673. An early sketch at the Essex Institute, executed c. 1830, reveals that there had been additions projected at the front of the house, then of two-room,

57. Parkman house, Salem, Mass. From an early sketch, c. 1830, courtesy The Essex Institute.

central-chimney plan. Sidney Perley reports that it was taken down about 1841.[3]

1. Essex County Deeds, VI, 76.
2. Ibid., p. 82.
3. Sidney Perley, *The History of Salem, Massachusetts* (Salem, Mass.: Sidney Perley, 1924–1928), III, 65–66.

SALEM: PICKERING HOUSE, 18 Broad Street   c. 1651

John Pickering, carpenter, first of the name in Salem, was in possession of land here before mid-century.[1] Recent research in the title by Robert Booth, Curator of the Pickering House, would indicate that the present structure stands on the western portion of the homestead rather than upon the unimproved lot to the east, which was sold to John and Jonathan Pickering in 1659, as Sidney Perley suggests.[2] Consequently one has only the statement of Col. Timothy Pickering as authority for dating. Referring in 1828 to repairs and alterations made in 1751 he writes: "I remember hearing my father [born 1703] say, that when he made the alterations and repairs above mentioned, the Eastern end of the house was one hundred years old, and the western end eighty years old."[3] The original right-hand portion of single-room plan with entry bay may thus have been erected by John Pickering, Sr., before his death in 1657. The addition of single-room plan to the left was made by the second John Pickering who, at his death in May 1694, willed to his wife, Alice, "ye Eastern End of my now dwelling house (to [w]it) the Chamber Garrett & Low room & halfe the Cellar with the use of the oven & well during her naturall life. . . ."[4] The house as originally constructed had acquired a leanto at the rear which was altered to two stories in 1751. Col. Timothy, born in 1745, writes further in 1828: "I well remember that when I went to the woman's school being then only six years old, my father raised the roof of the northern side of the present house, and so made room for three chambers. . . . The roof according [to] the fashion of the time, running down, on the northern side so as to leave but one upright story."[5] The exterior was Gothicized in 1841, and the carpenter's bills[6] suggest that the facade gables, hitherto thought to be original, formed a part of this transformation. A passage way cut through the central chimney on the first and second floors and the present form of the chimney stack above the roof date apparently to the same period of alterations. A two-story ell was added at the rear in 1904, and some interior restoration work was carried out in 1948 under the direction of the Boston architect Gordon Robb. The house has descended in the male line and is now occupied by the tenth John Pickering.

1. Sidney Perley, "Part of Salem in 1700, No. 5," *The Essex Antiquarian*, IV (1900), 169.
2. Essex County Deeds, II, 75.
3. Pickering Family papers, Pickering House, Salem.
4. Essex County Probate Records, vol. 303, p. 208.
5. Pickering Family papers.
6. Ibid.

SALEM: SAMUEL PICKMAN HOUSE, Charter Street   before 1681

Samuel Pickman, mariner, acquired the unimproved site for £5-10-0 in 1657[1] and land contiguous to the west with a dwelling for £24 on June 12, 1660.[2] He died not long before February 15, 1681,[3] and an inventory of his estate taken on May 9, 1687, values the house and half acre at £180, implying a major improvement.[4] That this had occurred prior to Pickman's death is confirmed by a deed of February 28, 1706, which refers to "that dwelling house that was the Said M[r] Samuel Pickmans. . . ."[5] The structure consisted originally of the large right-hand room with its chamber, attic and chimney bay. The room at the left with leanto roof at right angles may have existed at the outset, and was later raised to a full two stories about 1725. A new chimney was then constructed. The fireplace trim in the left-hand chamber is of this period. The one-story projecting porch dates to about 1800, while a Mansard roof and new stairs were introduced in the late nineteenth century. The house was acquired by Historic Salem, Inc., October 16, 1964,[6] and conveyed November 12, 1969, to Philip A. Budrose by whom it was restored.[7]

1. Essex County Deeds, I, 35.
2. Ibid., II, 55.
3. Essex County Probate Records, docket no. 22069.
4. Ibid., vol. 302, p. 27.
5. Essex County Deeds, XVIII, 162.
6. Ibid., vol. 5215, p. 421.
7. Ibid., vol. 5649, p. 629.

SALEM: TODD HOUSE (so-called),
39 Summer Street   late 17th cent.

Sidney Perley's research into the title of this property[1] does little to illuminate a possible date of construction for the house itself of two-room, central-chimney plan which had lost its original chimney and had been enlarged at some time in the eighteenth century to a full three stories. When demolished in December 1957 the frame revealed that the first-built portion was late seventeenth century in character, though one or two features (including some surviving trim preserved in the collections of the Society for the Preservation of New England Antiquities) might be interpreted as implying a date early in the eighteenth century.

1. Sidney Perley, "Part of Salem in 1700, No. 3," *The Essex Antiquarian*, IV (1900), 22 (Capt. Manasseh Marston House).

SALEM: TURNER HOUSE, (HOUSE OF THE SEVEN GABLES),
Turner Street   c. 1668

John Turner, merchant, acquired the site with an "old dwelling house" August 17, 1668.[1] The structure erected thereafter on an unimproved portion of the lot was of two-room, central-chimney plan (central core of the present building). The parlor wing (at the south) of single-room plan with separate chimney and the projecting two-story porch were added presumably before Turner's death in 1680 for they appear in an inventory of his estate taken later in 1693 which mentions all rooms in the existing house:

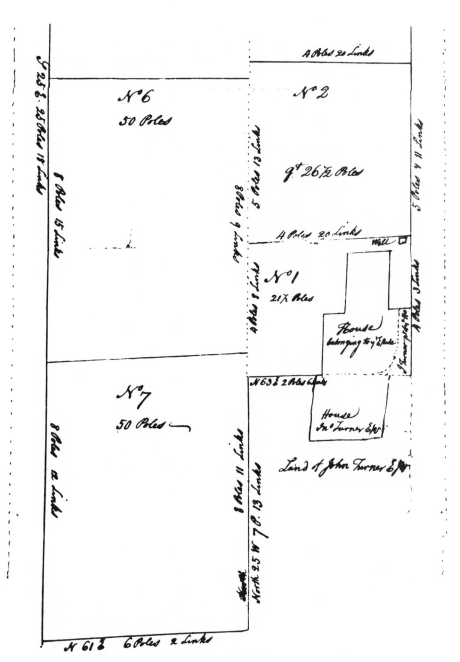

58. Probate division of Turner estate, Salem, Mass., 1769, showing schematic plan of the House of the Seven Gables. Essex County Probate Records.

59. Turner house, Salem, Mass. Photograph of south wing during the restoration of 1909 which revealed the original overhang and exterior molded wall sheathing (covered later by clapboards, some of which remain in place). Courtesy Society for the Preservation of New England Antiquities.

shop, shop chamber and garret, hall, hall chamber and garret, parlor, parlor chamber and porch chamber. In addition there was a "New Kitchen" and kitchen chamber,[2] no longer extant, probably in a centered rear ell shown in a plot of a probate division in 1769 (Fig. 58).[3] The "Kitchen & Leanter" are mentioned in an inventory of 1742,[4] and the Rev. William Bentley of Salem writes September 4, 1794, "The Old House of Col. Turner, back part taken away. . . ."[5] The present leanto and rear ell are twentieth century. John Turner, Jr., merchant, had inherited the estate from his father and introduced new stairs, paneling and up and down sash windows and boxed in the overhang of the parlor wing, probably about 1725. A later owner, Horace Conolly, after 1858, rebuilt the front porch entirely and added Victorian trim to the exterior. The house was acquired June 8, 1883, by Elizabeth A. Upton[6] whose husband, c. 1888, demolished the central chimney in the original portion. Caroline O. Emmerton purchased the house July 7, 1908, and restoration under Joseph Everett Chandler began in 1909.[7] Property conveyed to the House of Seven Gables Settlement Association December 30, 1936.[8]

1. Essex County Deeds, III, 49. See also, Sidney Perley, "Salem in 1700, No. 23," *The Essex Antiquarian*, X (1906), 62–65.

2. Essex County Probate Records, vol. 303, pp. 98–99.

3. Ibid., docket no. 28367.

4. Ibid., vol. 328, pp. 326–339.

5. *The Diary of William Bentley, D.D.* . . . (Gloucester, Mass.: Peter Smith, 1962), II, 463.

6. Essex County Deeds, vol. 1109, p. 288.

7. Ibid., vol. 1927, p. 225. See also, Caroline O. Emmerton, *The Chronicles of Three Old Houses* (Boston, Mass.: Thomas Todd Co., Printers, 1935), pp. 7–39.

8. Essex County Deeds, vol. 3098, p. 361.

SALEM: WARD HOUSE, 38 St. Peter Street
[now grounds of the Essex Institute]   after 1684

The land without improvements was acquired in December 1684 by John Ward, currier.[1] The house erected probably soon thereafter was of one-room plan with chimney bay (the present left-hand portion). The addition of single-room plan at the right and an added leanto were in existence when John Ward drew his will on June 19, 1732.[2] A wing at the right-hand end was added in the nineteenth century and taken away before 1905. The house was moved to the grounds of the Essex Institute in 1910 and restored during 1910–1912 by George Francis Dow.

1. Essex County Deeds, VII, 14. See also, Barbara M. and Gerald W. R. Ward, "The John Ward House . . . ," *Essex Institute Historical Collections*, 110 (1974), 3–32.

2. Essex County Probate Records, vol. 319, pp. 489–490.

SAUGUS: APPLETON-TAYLOR-MANSFIELD HOUSE
(formerly the Ironworks House), Saugus Ironworks   c. 1680

Thomas Dexter, yeoman, had a dwelling house in the immediate vicinity as early as 1639.[1] This he sold to the Undertakers of the Ironworks in New England in 1647, and they built a second house here before 1650.[2] Either or both structures may have still been standing by July 18, 1676, when three-quarters interest in the virtually defunct Ironworks was conveyed to Samuel Appleton, the Ipswich merchant, on behalf of his son, Samuel Appleton, Jr.,[3] who purchased the remaining one-quarter interest on May 26, 1682.[4] About this time the younger Appleton will have erected the present substantial house of central-chimney plan with projecting two-story porch. Characteristic of the 1680's in all structural and stylistic aspects, it was surely in existence by October 11, 1683, when described in a mortgage as Appleton's "mantion house."[5] The property was conveyed on February 15, 1688/9, to James Taylor, a Boston merchant,[6] whose estate inventory on August 28, 1716,[7] implies the presence of a leanto which, on the basis of the chimney construction and unused mortises found in the rear posts of the main house, was probably contemporary with original construction. The projecting porch is mentioned in the deeds for the last time in 1760,[8] and was gone by 1793,[9] at about which time also the earlier leanto was replaced with one of two stories. The house was acquired on March 2, 1915, by Wallace Nutting[10] who restored it that same year, removing the eastern half of the later leanto. Title was conveyed to the First Ironworks Association on December 30, 1944,[11] and by them on July 1, 1969, to the United States of America to be administered as a historic site by the National Park Service.[12]

1. Suffolk County Deeds, I, 69–71.
2. Essex County Deeds, XI, 240–241; George Francis Dow, ed., *Records and Files of the Quarterly Courts of Essex County, Massachusetts* (Salem, Mass.: The Essex Institute, 1911–1975), II, 89, and VIII, 201.
3. Massachusetts State Archives, 59/188.
4. Essex County Deeds, IV (Ipswich), 452.
5. Ibid., VI, 98.
6. Ibid., IX, 5.
7. Essex County Probate Records, docket no. 27301.
8. Essex County Deeds, vol. 118, p. 258.
9. Ibid., vol. 157, p. 117.
10. Ibid., vol. 2287, p. 364.
11. Ibid., vol. 3394, p. 535, and vol. 3382, p. 583.
12. Ibid., vol. 5693, p. 519.

SAUGUS: BOARDMAN HOUSE (formerly the
"Scotch"-Boardman House), 17 Howard Street   c. 1687

A house was erected here in 1651 for Scotch prisoners working at the Saugus Ironworks. The "Scotch house," as it is called in the records, was standing as late as 1678 to the rear and right of the present structure.[1] The latter was built unquestionably after conveyance of the property by absentee owners on February 4, 1687, to William Boardman, joiner,[2] a date confirmed by provisional reading of the tree-ring evidence. The house as constructed was of two-room, central-chimney plan. Boardman's inventory, May 25, 1696, indicates that the present added leanto was then in existence.[3] William Boardman, Jr., inherited[4] and introduced a new staircase about 1725. His grandson, Abijah Boardman, who succeeded to the title in 1800 and 1806, made the fireplaces smaller and added finish trim in the lower story.[5] The house was conveyed to the Society for the Preservation of New England Antiquities on May 1, 1914,[6] at which time the first-story fireplaces were restored, later partitions were removed and the chimney stack was rebuilt above the roof level (along its original lines).[7] Por-

60.   Boardman house, Saugus, Mass. Detail of overhang shown following removal of later exterior covering. While the pendant drop has been cut away there is a clear line of demarcation between the lower, weathered portion of the post and that (upper) portion protected from the outset by boarding. Photo, Richard Merrill, 1954, courtesy Society for the Preservation of New England Antiquities.

tions of the frame were renewed in 1954 by the restoration contractor Roy W. Baker.

1. *A Report of the Record Commissioners of the City of Boston, Containing the Boston Records from 1660 to 1701* (Boston, Mass., 1881), p. 120. See also, Abbott Lowell Cummings, "The 'Scotch'-Boardman House . . . Part I," *Old-Time New England*, ser. no. 151 (Jan.–Mar. 1953), pp. 57–73.

2. Suffolk County Deeds, XXIV, 21.

3. Suffolk County Probate Records, XI, 190.

4. Suffolk County Deeds, XXIV, 142–143.

5. Essex County Probate Records, vol. 368, p. 110; Suffolk County Deeds, vol. 218, p. 72.

6. Essex County Deeds, vol. 2258, p. 37.

7. See Abbott Lowell Cummings, "The 'Scotch'-Boardman House . . . Part II," *Old-Time New England*, ser. no. 152 (Apr.–June 1953), pp. 91–102.

STOW: HAPGOOD HOUSE, Treaty Elm Lane   c. 1726

The traditional date of this house coincides well with the style and character of construction and the report that Hezekiah Hapgood, married in 1724, settled here on the western half of his father's farm in 1726. As originally built the house was of two-room, central-chimney plan. The leanto is a later addition. The house was acquired on August 11, 1961, by Donald B. Rising by whom it has been restored.[1]

1. Middlesex County Deeds, vol. 9868, p. 367.

SWAMPSCOTT: JOSEPH BLANEY HOUSE, 280 Humphrey Street   c. 1700

On May 12, 1698, Joseph Blaney of Lynn, shipwright, purchased nearly sixty acres in that part of Lynn called Swampscott, including a houselot of one and a half acres bounded south "Upon ye Sea,"[1] and two years later, on September 20, 1700, acquired some forty-three acres adjoining which then contained "houses."[2] The structure which survived here, of central-chimney plan with integral leanto and cove cornice, could be no earlier than about 1700, and was almost certainly erected by Blaney soon after his purchase. The house, having long since lost its original chimney, was demolished in April 1914.[3]

1. Essex County Deeds, XIX, 148.

2. Ibid., XIX, 18.

3. Notes by William Sumner Appleton on the Blaney House, Swampscott, Apr. 21, 1914, Corr. Files, Society for the Preservation of New England Antiquities.

TOPSFIELD: PARSON CAPEN HOUSE, 1 Howlett Street   1683

The Rev. Joseph Capen received on February 28, 1683, as part of his settlement from the town, a grant of twelve acres "being Vpland and Swampe & medoe" which included the site of the present house of two-room, central-chimney plan.[1] Construction followed almost at once, and the contemporary date, 1683, was carved on the under surface of both summer beams in the left-hand room. The month in Roman capital letters is not entirely decipherable. The Rev. Donald Macdonald-Millar reports[2] that in one case at least the inscription read clearly "June," and was regrettably subjected to slight alterations with a sharp instrument in his presence. On September 27, 1814, the Rev. William Bentley of Salem writes, "This house of Mr. Capen is nearly in its primitive state. . . . The beams & joice are naked within. . . ."[3] House acquired by the Topsfield Historical Society on March 24, 1913, and restored by George Francis Dow during that year.[4]

1. George Francis Dow, ed., *Town Records of Topsfield, Massachusetts* (Topsfield, Mass.: The Topsfield Historical Society, 1917–1920), I, 44.
2. Donald Macdonald-Millar to Bertram K. Little, Dec. 6, 1958, Corr. Files, Society for the Preservation of New England Antiquities.
3. *The Diary of William Bentley, D.D.* . . . .(Gloucester, Mass.: Peter Smith, 1962), IV, 287.
4. Essex County Registered Land, Doc. no. 2266 (Certif. of Title, no. 1203).

TOPSFIELD: FRENCH-ANDREWS HOUSE (so-called),
86 Howlett Street   c. 1718

John French, Sr., had a dwelling here by 1693,[1] presumably the same conveyed with his farm to John French, Jr., on December 2, 1701, in return for support throughout the balance of the elder French's life.[2] An agreement among the latter's heirs on August 25, 1707, would suggest that the dwelling deeded in 1701 was still in existence.[3] That structure, however, as described in 1701, seems to have had but a single chamber, whereas the present house is of two-room, central-chimney plan and in terms of style and character of construction was probably not built until Joseph Andrews of Boxford bought the property from John French, Jr., on June 16, 1718.[4] The house was purchased on October 11, 1917, by Thomas Emerson Proctor[5] and restored in 1919 under the direction of George Francis Dow, at which time a modern leanto was added (although nineteenth-century photographs reveal the presence of an earlier leanto and a one-and-a-half-story ell at the west end) and a new chimney top constructed, modeled on that of the Parson Barnard House in North Andover.[6] Privately owned.

1. John H. Towne, "Topsfield Houses and Buildings," *The Historical Collections of the Topsfield Historical Society*, VIII (1902), 22.

2. Essex County Deeds, XV, 257.

3. Essex County Probate Records, docket no. 10156.

4. Essex County Deeds, XXXII, 289.

5. Ibid., vol. 2375, p. 370.

6. William Sumner Appleton, "Annual Report of the Corresponding Secretary," *Old-Time New England*, ser. no. 21 (July 1920), 21–22.

Topsfield: Stanley-Lake House, 95 River Road   c. 1680–1690

Matthew Stanley apparently owned this property during the last two or three decades of the seventeenth century, and deeds and depositions would indicate the presence of more than a single house in the vicinity.[1] The earliest left-hand portion of the existing structure, therefore, of single-room plan with chimney bay, is not easily documented, although style and construction would point to a date in the 1680's or 1690's. A frame of single-room plan with end overhang was added at the right quite soon, judging again from style and construction. Stanley's heirs conveyed some seventy acres here with "Buildings" to Eleazer Lake on February 28, 1718,[2] and a later deposition on September 24, 1733, refers to "Eleazer Lakes house that he bought of yͤ Stanleys. . . ."[3] The building was lengthened still further to the right with another bay of single-room plan with chimney by Eleazer Lake's son, Daniel, who was married November 30, 1749, and refers March 30, 1769, to "the Easterly End of yͤ Old Dwelling House and also the new end that I built at the Easterly end of that. . . ."[4] The property was acquired August 9, 1924, by Grace Blanchard who carried out some work of restoration.[5] Privately owned.

1. Essex County Deeds, LIV, 13, and LXI, 269.

2. Ibid., XXXIII, 139.

3. Ibid., LXIII, 262.

4. Ibid., vol. 122, p. 13.

5. Ibid., vol. 2609, p. 133.

Watertown: Browne House, 562 Main Street   1694–1701

Capt. Abraham Browne had acquired the unimproved site by January 22, 1694.[1] First mention of the house occurs in the Selectmen's records on

December 17, 1701,[2] and the physical evidence suggests a structure of single-room plan with chimney bay and leanto dependencies (probably original) both beyond the chimney and along the rear. Capt. Abraham conveyed to his son, Samuel, on March 11, 1727, "The Southerly or first Built Part of my now Dwelling House . . . and also The Shopp adjoyning thereunto. . . ."[3] The present northern ell, however, does not appear to be before 1727 in date. The ell to the south was added probably in the eighteenth century, consisting at first of one, later two stories. The present one-story leanto to the left of the chimney bay is nineteenth-century. The house was acquired for the Society for the Preservation of New England Antiquities on May 23, 1919,[4] and restored by William Sumner Appleton in 1919–1920, at which time the southern ell was removed.

1. Middlesex County Probate Records, first ser., docket no. 2941.
2. *Watertown Records* . . . , Prepared for publication by the Historical Society (Watertown, Mass., 1894–1900), II, 141. See also, Catharine W. Pierce, "The Brownes of Watertown and the date of the Abraham Browne House," *Old-Time New England*, ser. no. 98 (Oct. 1939), pp. 67–72.
3. Middlesex County Deeds, XXIX, 194.
4. Ibid., vol. 4259, p. 594.

WENHAM: CAPT. THOMAS FISKE HOUSE (formerly
Claflin-Richards House), 132 Main Street   c. 1698

Robert Claflin had a house on this site which the town acquired in 1673 for a parsonage.[1] Mr. Joseph Gerrish, the minister, conveyed this house May 24, 1692, to Thomas Fiske, Jr.,[2] and the latter presumably built the original portion of the existing structure (left-hand portion of single-room plan with projecting chimney bay), which cannot be considered on stylistic grounds as early as Claflin's house. On December 27, 1697, Fiske was granted "pine Timber for building his hous & for planke & board" (the present planked frame house is a mixture of pine and oak).[3] Thomas Fiske, Jr., died February 5, 1723. The addition of one-room plan at the right dates stylistically just before or after this time. Mention of "the back Lento" occurs in 1768.[4] The house was purchased November 18, 1921, by the Wenham Village Improvement Society, Inc.,[5] which took down and rebuilt the original chimney under the direction of George Francis Dow. The lower story of the earliest portion was restored between 1923 and 1926,[6] although the long-vanished two-story projecting porch and extension (probably original) covering at least one half of the rear wall were not reconstructed, and a three-part window opening for which there was no evidence was introduced into the rear wall. The right-hand (later) lower room was restored by the restoration contractor Roy W. Baker in 1954.

1. *Wenham Town Records* (Published by the Wenham [Mass.] Historical Society, 1930–1940), I, 39.
2. Essex County Deeds, XLI, 184.
3. *Wenham Town Records*, I, 157.
4. Essex County Deeds, vol. 125, p. 202.
5. Ibid., vol. 2501, p. 501.
6. See William Sumner Appleton, "A Description of Robert McClaflin's House," *Old-Time New England*, ser. no. 44 (Apr. 1926), pp. 157–167.

WENHAM: GOLDSMITH-PICKERING HOUSE, Larch Row c. 1700

The tract containing 160 acres was conveyed with housing April 4, 1695, to Joseph Fowler and Zaccheus Goldsmith, yeomen,[1] who divided the farm by an unrecorded agreement. Goldsmith received a timber grant January 8, 1700, "for a Dwelling hous of fourtey foott long and Twenty foott wide & Timber for boards & shingle & plank for finishing of it,"[2] somewhat unusual dimensions which coincide exactly with the original planked frame house consisting of two rooms on either side of a long-vanished central chimney, two full stories to the south and a single story covered with a leanto roof at the north. The eastern ell was added perhaps before 1729 as a deed of partition might suggest.[3] During the eighteenth century the northern half of the original house was raised to a full two stories. The two-story ell at the west was added probably in the 1780's or 1790's. The celebrated Timothy Pickering acquired the property in 1806.[4] Extensive improvements thereafter included removal of the original central chimney and introduction of two smaller stacks. The house was restored both before and after a near-disastrous fire March 2, 1963. Privately owned.

1. Essex County Deeds, XI, 205.
2. *Wenham Town Records* (Published by the Wenham [Mass.] Historical Society, 1930–1940), I, 178.
3. Essex County Deeds, LIV, 102.
4. Ibid., vol. 178, p. 242.

WEST GLOUCESTER: HASKELL HOUSE (so-called), Lincoln Street probably early 18th cent.

There was a house here, apparently, as early as 1652 when William Haskell acquired the property.[1] The present plank frame structure, however, of two-room, central-chimney plan, cannot be that old and would appear to date to the early eighteenth century on the basis of style and character of construction. The house was purchased on December 26, 1936, by Albert H. Atkins of Gloucester[2] who carried out a thorough restoration during 1937–1938 which included additions at the rear of the building at both ends to provide modern conveniences. Privately owned.

1. Frank Chouteau Brown, "The Interior Details and Furnishings of the William Haskell Dwelling . . . ," *Pencil Points*, xx (1939), 113–128.

2. Essex County Deeds, vol. 3098, pp. 389–391.

WINTHROP: DEANE WINTHROP HOUSE,
40 Shirley Street   c. 1638–1650

The house consists of a frame of single-room plan with chimney bay (the left-hand portion) to which an addition of single-room plan was made quite soon and perhaps by the same carpenter(s). The leanto is later still. It is uncertain from the foundation evidence whether the structure was originally erected on this spot or moved here at the time the existing chimney was constructed, probably in the mid-eighteenth century. The present site was granted in January 1638 to William Pierce, the celebrated mariner who piloted a number of the earliest settlers to New England.[1] Pierce's heirs conveyed "theire Messuage and Farme at Pullen point" to Deane Winthrop, youngest son of the Governor, in 1647 or 1648.[2] The title is clear and consistent, and the house appears to be about 1650 or earlier on the basis of style and construction. Is it the same dwelling (perhaps built by Pierce) referred to in 1720 as "the Farmhouse . . . late the Estate of Deane Winthrop . . ."?[3] We can say only that (1) a survey of an adjoining farm rendered in 1690 locates "Mr. Winthrop's" house here,[4] and (2) a later deed in 1864 describes the existing structure as "the old Winthrop Farm house. . . ."[5] Acquired by the Winthrop Improvement and Historical Association January 1, 1907.[6]

1. *Second Report of the Record Commissioners of the City of Boston, 1877* (Boston, Mass., 1877), p. 30.

2. Ibid., p. 168.

3. Suffolk County Deeds, xxxiv, 245.

4. Mellen Chamberlain, *A Documentary History of Chelsea . . .* (Boston, Mass.: Printed for the Massachusetts Historical Society, 1908), i, 193, and plan opposite.

5. Suffolk County Deeds, vol. 841, p. 87.

6. Ibid., vol. 3182, p. 590.

ADDENDUM

Since the foregoing Appendix went to press discovery of additional information has thrown important light on two houses we have discussed.

SALEM: PICKERING HOUSE, 18 Broad Street   c. 1660

Further investigation by Robert Booth leads to a revised conclusion that the house stands on the unimproved land purchased 1659 by John and Jonathan Pickering, sons of the first John.[1] Moreover, a deposition prior to 1722[2] reveals that the first John's dwelling, standing by February 11, 1642/3,[3] was moved away by oxen in 1663 or 1664. John Pickering II married Alice Bullock in 1657, and the eastern half of the present house was undoubtedly erected by him in 1659, or in any event before 1661 when the Salem Commoners' records, reciting the "Claimes" of John Pickering III, suggest that "his fathers house" was then in existence.[4] This date is reinforced by the fireback initialed I P A for John and Alice Pickering and dated 1660.[5] The western half, as noted, was added by John Pickering II whose unrecorded inventory May 30, 1694, mentions the parlor, hall, kitchen, hall chamber, porch chamber, parlor chamber, garrett, and cellar.[6] In contradiction of an 1841 date for changes in the chimney, George R. Curwen of Salem writes November 11, 1885, that that feature, laid in clay, had just been taken down. "The Fire Places in the rooms remain," he reports, but two new chimneys were built which "come together in one in the attic and the chimney on the outside . . . is an exact reproduction of the old one." The main staircase was then rebuilt, retaining some original balusters, apparently, and a chimney was added at the west end of the "Dining Room."[7]

1. Essex County Deeds, II, 75.
2. Harrison Ellery and Charles P. Bowditch, *The Pickering Genealogy* . . . (Cambridge, Mass., 1897), I, 22.
3. Essex County Deeds, vol. 144, p. 149.
4. George Francis Dow, ed., "Salem Commoners Records, 1713–1739," *Essex Institute Historical Collections*, XXXVI, 176.
5. Collections, The Essex Institute.
6. Pickering Family papers, Pickering House, Salem.
7. George R. Curwen to Henry FitzGilbert Waters, Oct. 26–Nov. 19, 1885, Waters Family papers: Henry FitzGilbert Waters (1833–1913), Corr. Box 2, Folder 3, The Essex Institute.

GLOUCESTER: WHITE-ELLERY HOUSE,
Washington Street   c. 1710

Recent research by Marshall W. S. Swan reveals that the Rev. John White requested of the Town March 7, 1710, "a smale parcell of land between the meeting house hill and the crick to sett a house upon. . . ." On March 13 a quarter of an acre was duly set out "on the south side of the meeting house," and the present structure was presumably erected soon thereafter.[1]

1. Gloucester Commoners' Books, MS, City Clerk, Gloucester, Mass., Bk. II.

Massachusetts Bay building documents, 1638–1726

Compiled by Abbott Lowell Cummings

NOTE: To preserve the accuracy and full flavor of the original documents the following transcriptions are literal in every respect, except that superfluous or misleading punctuation has been eliminated, and modern punctuation added in brackets where considered necessary. Dates are consistent with the modern calendar, as explained on page 125.

BEVERLY: PARSONAGE

Building contract, March 23, 1657.

the psents witneseth a bargan maid betweene John norman of manchester the one partie & Tho Lothrop & James patch the other ptyes for & in consideration of an house : that is to say[,] John norman is to build an house for them which is to be thirtie eyght foote longe[,] 17 foote wide & a leuen foote stodd with three Chimnies[,] towe below & one in the Chamber[.] he is also to finde boards & Clapboards for the finishing the same with a shingle couering [and] with a portch of eight foote square & Jetted ouer one foote ech way[;] to lay the floores booth below & a boue & one garret chamber & to make doores & windowes[,] foure below & foure aboue & one in the stodie[.] the said John is to make the the [sic] staires & to drawe the Clapboards & short their edges & also to smooth the boards of one of the Chamber flowres & he is to bring up the frame to the barre or the ferry att his owne charge & the saide John norman is to haue for his work fourtie fiue pounds to be paide in corne & cattell[,] the one halfe att or before the house be raised & the other halfe this next wheate haruist :[1]

---

1. Essex Quarterly Court Files, Office of the Clerk of the Superior Court for Essex County, Salem, Mass., V, 51.

BOSTON: HOUSE FOR WILLIAM RIX

Building contract, "ult. 6. 1640."

John Davys joyner is to build Willm Rix one framed house 16 foot long
& 14 foote wyde wth a chamber floare[;] finisht summer & ioysts[;] a celler floare wth ioysts finisht[;] the roofe & walles Clapboarded on the outsyde[;] the Chimney framed without dawbing to be done wth hewen
timber. Willm Rix is for this to pay to John Davis 21^l vz 4^l in hand 7^l
when it is finisht and the rest first of May 1641. wth one plott of ground
lying betweene John Davis & James Johnson.[1]

1. Edward Everett Hale, Jr., ed., *Note-Book kept by Thomas Lechford, Esq., Lawyer,
in Boston, Massachusetts Bay, from June 27, 1638, to July 29, 1641* (Cambridge, Mass.,
1885), pp. 302–303.

BOSTON: HOUSE FOR THOMAS BANISTER

Letters from Thomas Banister of Boston to Thomas Blettsoe in London.

[*Apr. 29, 1701.*] . . . The reason amoung^{ue} others that I am resolv'd to
sell [my English property] is I am now settling myself hear as long as it
pleases God to continue me in this world[.] for in order to own comfortable subsistence we are building a house at the South end of Boston[1]
and have bought allso a brick warehouse at the Dock of forty foot long:
it Lyeth next to Mr. Thomsons, so that I have now laid aside the thought
of coming to settle in England with my Family: My Eldest son is come
from Colledge in order to Settling to business of Merchandize. . . . S^r I
have seen at Boston some curious clear glass if I mistake not it is called
crown glass[.] it seems to me to be such as that put before the Diall plate
of Clocks. Mr. Eliakim Hutchinson hath glazed the front of his house with
it and it looks exceeding well[.] I have a great mind to have one room or
two glazed with that glass[.] Therefore would intreat you send me by the
first good ship about one hundred foot of S^d glass and if it be not very
dear send me 200 foot[.] I fancy it not very larg[,] about 6 Inches wide
and 8 inches long each square seems to be a very good size for I purpose
to set them in lead and not in wooden frames and to have Iron casements
for tho Sash windows are the newest Fashion I dont so well fancy them as
casements[.] I make my windows four foot broad and six feet long from
outside to outside. The place I build in is over against Capt Sam^{ll} Sewall[.]
I hope to be ready for the glasse by that time it can come[.] I have other
glass Enough for the back side of S^d house. . . . S^r having proceeded thus
far I gave my Letter to my son to Coppy who found fault with my direc-

tions about the above mentioned glass which caused a dispute and a reso-
lution to alter the above orders[.] we now resolve for sash windows: the
number as above to be four windows of four foot wide clear[,] that is
within side the frame[;] in Length or rather in depth [height] clear and
two narrow lights to stand in the closetts of the same depth and just half
the width[;] and for the upper storrie three windows of exactly four foot
square in the clear and one for the closet half so wide of the same depth
wch that you may understand fully I have Inclosed [a] crude draught of
my design drawn a quarter of one inch to every foot. I pray S^r as soon as
this advise comes to hand set workmen about it that it may if possible be
ready to send by the first ship that we may have it to put up the next fall.
For I hope to get ready by that time. The Cellar is near finished. . . .

By this Rough Draught you may see how all those windows mentioned
in my letter are to stand except two of the large wch are intended for our
best Low room behind the shop[.] Pray S^r let the glass be all made and set
in the Frames ready to put up[.] get a chest made of a fitt size to put it in.
One maine reason why I would have it sent ready fitted is that few if any
of our workmen know how to doe it[.] get good workmen and let it be
well done tho it cost something the more[.] I know you will be as good
an husband for me as you can[.] I have seen some set in wood and some
in Lead[.] I matter not wch way it is done[.] if it be sett in wood the putty
must be very good[;] if in Lead said Lead must be very thick and extraor-
dinarily well cimmented or by reason of the violence of our storms it will
not hold. . . .

[*June 19, 1701.*] . . . Since my letter of April 29 pr Capt Gilliam my window frames are made and in S^d frames my carpenter hath made a Rabbit
of 3 q^trs of an inch so that the sashes must be an inch and Half wider than
I advised for in my Former Letters[.] The above S^d Rabbit of 3 q^trs of one
Inch is only in the sides of each window and therefore makes no alteration
in the depth [height,] but in the width makes one inch and a half in Each
window[.] I pray that you would gett them sent by the first ship. . . .

[*August 12, 1701.*] Yours by Capt Mason S^r came to my hands as also the
goods according to invoice: wth being very Busie in fitting our new house
to get into if possible before winter I have not time to Examine your
acco^t: etc. . . .

[*October 16, 1701.*] Sr The goods by Wentworth came safe to my hands[.]
I give you thanks for your Care and Quick Dispatch[.] The Glass windows and other things are very well approved of[.] we are now finishing
to get into the new house if possible so that I have not time to Enlarge. . . .[2]

1. Minutes of the Council of Massachusetts Bay reveal that license was granted to
Thomas Banister on Mar. 20, 1701, "to erect a building of timber and brick" at the
south end of Boston. Cecil Headlam, ed., *Calendar of State Papers, Colonial Series,*

America and West Indies, 1701 (London: Published by His Majesty's Stationery Office, 1910), p. 138.

2. Charles F. Montgomery, "Thomas Banister on the New Sash Windows, Boston, 1701," *Journal of the Society of Architectural Historians,* XXIV (1965), 170.

BOSTON: HOUSE FOR JOHN BATEMAN

Building contract, August 20, 1679.

Articles of Agreement indented made and concluded . . . Betweene Robert Tafft of Brantery in New England housewright on the one part And John Bateman of Boston in New England afores^d Shopkeeper on the other part are as followeth

Imp^{rs} The s^d Robert Taft for himselfe his heires Exex^{rs} and Adm^{rs} doth hereby covenant promiss and grant to and with the s^d John Bateman his Exec^{rs} and assigns in manner and forme following (that is to Say) that the s^d Robert Taft his Exec^{rs} Assignes shall and will build erect set up and finish for the s^d John Bateman his Exec^{rs} or Assignes, the frame of a new Tenem^t or dwelling house to contain thirty foot in Length and twenty Seven foote or thereabout in breadth according to the dimentions of the Cellar fframe as it now stands; and to build the frame of the s^d house two Storey high besides the garrett, and each roome Seven foote high between the Sumer and floare, and to make the s^d house to jet at the first Storey in the front Eighteen inches and to make and place a fframe for the Cellar according to the present dimentions thereof and place the same, and to build three ffloares of Sumers and joice, and to make and place in the front of the s^d house two gable ends to range even with the Roofe of the s^d house, and also two gable ends on the backside to range as afores^d and to make and place in the front of ye Second Storey two large casement windows and two windows in the garett and in the end next the mill Creeke three windows Viz^t one large Casement window in the low[er] Roome, and one large casement window in the Second Storey, and one window in the garrett; and on the backside one large Casement window in the low[er] Roome, two large casement windows in the second Storey and two windows in the garrat, and to make & send to Boston the fframe of the Cellar within Six weekes next after the date hereof, and to rayse the same in place within one weeke then next following (provided the cills of the s^d Cellar be cleare) and to finish the frame of the s^d house on or before the first day of march next and rayse the same with all possible Speed after it is brought to Boston. In Consideration whereof the s^d John Bateman for himselfe his heires Executo^{rs} and Adm^{rs} doth hereby covenant promiss and grant to and with the s^d Robert Taft his Exec^{rs} and Assignes to pay for the transportation of the s^d fframe of the s^d Cellar and house from Brantery the place where it is to bee framed to Boston, and also to pay or cause to bee paid unto the s^d Robert Tafft his Exec^{rs} Adm^{rs} or Assignes the full and just Suñe of thirty pounds Viz^t one halfe part thereof in law-full money of New England, and the other halfe part thereof in English goods at money price; and to pay the same in manner and forme following (that is to Say) ffive pounds in money and five pounds in goods at the time of the Ensealing hereof and five pounds in money and five pounds in goods when the frame of the Cellar is laid down and the floare over the Cellar is laid and five pounds in money and five pounds in goods when the whole worke is compleated and in every respect finished in manner and forme afores^d And for the true performance hereof the s^d partys binde themselves their heires Exec^{rs} and Adm^{rs} each unto the other his Exec^{rs} and Assignes in the penall Suñe of ffifty pounds of lawfull money of new England well and truly to bee paid by virtue of these presents. . . .

Deposition of Giles Goddard, aged about 32, sworn in court April 28, 1680.

That about the beginning of march last I being in company with Robert Taft and John Bateman – some words past between them, and I did heare s^d Bateman say that hee would not take charge of the s^d house till s^d Taft had Done or finished, whereat s^d Taft did reply if any thing was remaining undone according to their Covenants, hee s^d Taft would do it[;] and about 4 or 5 dayes after I went with s^d Taft to the s^d house and there wee found that the s^d Bateman had taken possession thereof And had boarded a con-siderable part of s^d house[;] and then s^d Bateman found fault that there was a few joices wanting and s^d Bateman then said that hee would not come to a composition wth s^d Taft, and that hee knew not that hee owed s^d Taft any thing, and further this Deponent saith not

John Bateman's reasons for appeal from the verdict of the County Court, April 27, 1680, to the Court of Assistants, September 7, 1680 (received in court August 13, 1680).

1. It plainly appeareth by the Articles wch sd Taft produced in ye County Court that ye sd Taft was to build in ye sd house three floors of Summers and Joice, And it also as plainly appeareth by the Depositions of John Hay-ward, Ebenezer Ingoldsby, and James Browne, that in two of ye ffloors in sd house ther were places in each, of about Nine foot one way & Eight foot another, y^t wanted both Summers & Joice, & in one room of the ground floor ther was aplace of Eight foot one way & five foot another way wherin was neither Summer nor Joice, & in ye other ground room . . . [being] twenty four foot one way & Eleven foot the other way ther

were neither Summer nor Joice & that ther was noe window in the Gable
End [in the garret], all w^ch (yor Appellant humbly conseiveth) ought to
have been done according to ye Articles[.] This farther Appeareth by the
Testimony of Caleb Hobart, Testifieing that ye sd Taft told yor appellant
he thought (wch was but a thought) he had finished the said frame according to Covenant yet what appeared to be wanting (as the aforesd per-
ticulars doe) hee would doe it or else allow for it. . . .

Robert Taft's answers to John Bateman's reasons, presented in court
September 7, 1680.

1 It Apeers by Euidenc that ye sd frame was finished acording to Articuls
for which I Reseued a judgment att the County Court held att boston 27
apri 1680
2 As to the want of sumers and ioys that the sd batman mentioned twas
a place Left for his Chimnys: and now thay are built there is no Room
for sumer nor joys
3 As to the ground Roome at twenty four foote one way and Eleuen foot
the other way which ye s^d batman mentions was aplace wher there was
noe siller under it and therfore noe ned of sumer nor joys neither way if
acording to my Couenent as I Aprehended[;] yet not with standing I
brought timber for slepers which they haue disposed of:
4 As to the window in the gabell End which the sd batman mentioned it
was ther thow not put up as the others ware[,] for my Counent was to
put up only four windows in the frunt[.] I put up six more then my
Counant was which I hope your honers will understand by my Counant
5 As to the non performenc of the frame which the sd batman mentioned
I Aprehended it was done[.] I allso told ye sd batman before Caleb Hubord
[and] Gills Golerd [Goddard] of the saterday when I fineshed Raising the
frame that I would Come the Next munday or tusday following And if
any thing ware wantting of my Counent I would perform it[.] my tim
was not then out and when I Came upon the tusday foloing I found the
hous great part inclosed and found seuerall men att work about the said
hous: I hop thes with what euidences al Redy giuen your wisdom will find
the Articuls fullfilled: and the and the [sic] frame fineshed[.] the want of
my mony is to my great dameg which was eight pound eight shillings dew
to mee for the framing the hous and for the transporting of the the [sic]
frame which was to bee att the sd batmans Charge which Appers by
Counent three pound fortene shillings more[.] Thes together with the former euidences for this Case being seriously perused your Humbell Servent
doubteth not but this Honble Court will see Caus to grant my dameg with
Costs of Courts

John Bateman's reasons for the Chancery of the obligation in his covenant,
September 11, 1680.

Viz^t that he hath paid to Robert Taft Twelve pounds mony & Nine
pounds Twelve Shillings in goods in p^rt of the Summe of Thirty pounds
mentioned in the Coven^t wch by agreem^t was to be paid one halfe mony
and one halfe goods: also he hath paid to Sandors thirty Shillings for transportation of the frame of his house from Brant[ree] to Boston: So that
there remains due when the worke is finished Eight pounds Eight Shilling
Viz^t ffive pounds Eight shill in goods and Three pounds in mony and
Court Charges. And whereas there is a considerable pt of the worke left
unfinished by sd Tafft as appeares by Evidence in Court, he prays that the
honor^ble Court will allow for the Same Thirty Shillings. and Whereas
Taft demand[ed] Three pounds odd mony for carting my fframe to the
water side calling that transportation[,] now transportation properly Sig-
nifies the Carrying of a thing or passing by water from one port to another
wch is all the transportation that was ever intended by me or mentioned
to the Scriven^r that drew the Articles as may Appeare by his Testimony:
and there was never any word of Carriage or Cartage by Land mentioned
in s^d agreement: . . . [one word unclear] s^d Bateman apprehends that he
ought not to pay a penny of the Summe, and the more for that the s^d Taft
hath dealt most Injuriously by him in makeing s^d frame wch is the weakest
– slenderest and the most dozed timber that hath beene Seen to be putt
into any building of the like dimentions in the Land, as may appeare by
Sufficient Evidence: most of the timber Wañy & on many of the Suñers
The Bark left on to make it there Square and wch Indeed was the Occasion
of all this Trouble[.] Whereas Taft hath Spent many dayes here Since the
action was heard it is causelessly, for I tendred him more then was Jussly
due to him as Soone as ever the Action was determined by this Court So
that upon a Just and honest Acco^t there is not five pound due to the said
Taft. . . .¹

1. Suffolk County Court Records, Office of the Clerk of the Supreme Judicial
Court for Suffolk County, Boston, Mass., docket no. 1916.

BOSTON: COLE-SEDGWICK HOUSE

Deed from Samuel Cole of Boston, innholder, to Capt. Robert Sedgwick of
Charlestown, "last Day of February," 1638, for £200 lawful money.

. . . all that parts of one new mansion house in Boston aforesaid wherein
the said Samuel . . . lately dwelled . . . wch lyes to the south end of the

said house beyond the sommer or beame wch lyes overthwart the great
chamber, and up and downe by the said beame from the bottome of the
seller to the top of the house, and in breadth from east to west the full extent of the said house and shedds adoiyning (excepting roome on the south
parte of the said beame, next to it, for the making of a stacke of brick
chimnneys from the seller to the top of the said new house, for that part
of the same house assured to the said Thomas Marryot & others) . . . And
also the old house and leantoos. . . .

*Articles of agreement between Samuel Cole of Boston and Capt. Robert
Sedgwick of Charlestown, September 1, 1638.*

1. Imprimis the said Samuel Cole for himselfe and his wife and their
heires shall for two hundred pounds firmly convey & assure unto the said
Captaine Sedgwicke, his heires and assignes for ever, all that parte of the
new house wherein the said Samuel lately dwelled in Boston aforesaid, and
the old house adjoyning wth the shedds, court yard, garden and appurtenances, to be divided from that parte of the said new house and garden wth
the appurtenances assured to Thomas Marryot & others, and the old house
and leantoos, yard and garden thereto belonging, wth the appurtenances.
2. Itm̃, the said Captaine Sedgwicke is to find one hoggshead of lyme
and the said Samuel Cole shall therewith cause to be mended the backe of
the chimney of the leantoo and the rough cast of the outsyde of the new
house, the said Samuel finding all other materialls necessary thereunto.
3. Itm̃, the said Captain Sedgwicke shall have the buildinges and materialls of the stable, hogstyes and house of office on that part of the said new
house, yard & garden assured to Thomas M. & others now standing, to be
removed by the said Captain Sedgwicke when he will, or when he shall
be required so to doe by the said Thomas M. and others or their assignes.
4. Itm̃, that the said Captaine Sedgwicke, his heires and assignes, shall at
their costs & charges cause the premises to him and them to be granted, to
be divided from that parte of the said new house and garden and yard assured to Thomas Marryot and others as aforesaid, and remove & build
chimneys & doe all other things, as the said Samuel Cole is bound to doe
by a certaine writing under his hand & seale made unto the said Thomas
Marryot and others Dated the tenth of Aprill last past, whereof the said
Captaine Sedgwick may take a coppy.
5. Itm̃, the said Captaine Sedgwicke shall at his cost and charges cause
to be clapboarded round the house frame of the said Samuel Cole now in
rearing next M. Greenesmith's in Boston precincts, and cause to be layd
two floares in the said house wth boards, and shall pay for the thatching of

the said house, and lend the said Samuel Cole a lighter to fetch the thatch for the same.[1]

1. Edward Everett Hale, Jr., ed., *Note-Book kept by Thomas Lechford, Esq., Lawyer, in Boston, Massachusetts Bay, from June 27, 1638, to July 29, 1641* (Cambridge, Mass., 1885), pp. 51–57.

BOSTON: HOUSE FOR HENRY ELLIS

Deposition of Richard Jacques, aged 21, March 31, 1679.

. . . [who] saith that about fiue or six years sence my father built a house for Henry Elles at Boston neare m[r] Atkisons house and mad 2 Great windows in the frunt of the house and a Geablend in the frunt and Coured all the outsid of the hous with Clabords and shingl and laid all the floors and made two pare of stairs and made a Closet in the Chamber with partisions to the Roomes and dors to the same[;] and in the somer my father Raised the frame of the hous and be fore the wintr set in we finished the same so that the masones stand[?] not for owr work[;] and allso windos sutab. for eury Roome.

1. Essex Quarterly Court Files, Office of the Clerk of the Superior Court for Essex County, Salem, Mass., xxx, 116.

BOSTON: HOUSE FOR THE LATIN SCHOOLMASTER

Contract with carpenter, November 24, 1701.

Agreement made between the Select men and Cap[t] John Barnet viz[t]

That the Said Barnet Shall Erect a House on the Land where M[r] Ezekiell Chever Lately dwelt of forty foot long, Twenty foot wide and Twenty foot Stud wth four foot Rise in the Roof, to make a Cellar floor under one halfe of S[d] house and to build a Kitchin of Sixteen foot in Length & twelve foot in bredth with a Chamber therein, and to Lay the floors flush through out the main house and to make three paire of Stayers in y[e] main house & one paire in the Kitchin and to Inclose S[d] house & to do and compleat all carpenters worke and to finde all timber boards, Clapboards, nayles, glass and Glaziers worke & Iron worke. and to make one Celler door and to finde one Lock for the Outer door of Said House, And also to make the Case[mts] for S[d] house, and perform S[d] worke and to finish S[d] building by the first day of August next.

In consideration whereof the Select men do agree that the S[d] Cap[t] Barnet Shall have the Old Timb^r, boards, Iron work & glass of the Old house now Standing on S^d Land and to pay unto him the Sum of One hundred and thirty pounds money that is to say forty pounds down in hand & the rest as the worke goes on.

Contract with mason, November 24, 1701.

Agreement made between the Select men and Mr John Goodwin vizt

That the Said John Goodwin agrees to do and perform the masons worke of the house now to be built on the Land where m^r Ezekiell Chever Lately dwelt. S^d house to [be] of the dementions agreed for wth Capt John Barnerd. The S^d Goodwin to digg and Stone a Celler under the Largest end of S^d House, to under pin the whole house & Kitchen. S^d Cellar to be Six foot & four Inches deep under the Cell, the wall to be Laid with Lime and Sand Morter, to turn an Arch in S^d Celler and to build a good Stack of brick Chimneys, wth three Lower room Chimnyes[,] two Chamber Chimnyes and one garret Chimney, to fill Lath and plaster all the walls under the plate of Said house and Kitchen, to Ceile two floors through out the S^d House and plaster the Gable ends and under the Staires within Sight, and to plaster the Clossets and all the brickworke as high up as the Garrett, to lay the Hearth of the Chimnyes with two rows of Tile in the Lower rooms and Chambers, and to plaster the Coveing, and to point the garret and Purge [parge] the Chimnyes with good Lime morter; and at the Said Goodwins Charge to finde all Stones, brick, Lime, Sand, Lath, Haire, nayles and other materialls for the Said worke, and to Compleat & finish the Same by the first day of August next.

In consideration whereof the Select men Shall pay unto the S^d John Goodwin the sum of Ninety pounds money, with the free Liberty of his useing all the Stones and Brick of the Old house now there Standing for his own use, and to have forthwith an order for Twenty pounds in part of paym^ts

Meetings of the Selectmen.

[*Mar. 2, 1702.*] The Said House to have two windows in each Roome one in the front & the other at the end.

[*June 3, 1702.*] Ordered that Capt John Barnerd do provide a Raysing Dinner for the Raysing the Schoolmasters House at the Charge of the Town not exceeding the Sum of Three pounds.

[*Oct. 13, 1703.*] Ordered that Mr John Barnet take the Care of geting a Sufficient fence & gate made at the Latten Schoolmasters House & also for ye makeing a House of Easment there.

[*Oct. 30, 1703.*] Ordered that Mr Thomas Child [painter] do the following work ab[t] the Latten Schoolmasters House viz[t] finish the Gate & prime the fence, finish the Out side work of the house. And to prime the Inside worke of the Same, and to be paid what is reasonable for the Said work.

[*Nov. 30, 1703.*] Ordered that David Crouch & his mate have a noat for 12/8 for worke in diging a Vault &c. for the Schoolmasters Hous.

[*Sept. 13, 1708.*] Mesu[rs] Daniell Oliver & Daniel Powning are desired to gett gutters & other necessary repaires to be done at y[e] School masters House.[1]

1. *A Report of the Record Commissioners of the City of Boston, Containing the Records of Boston Selectmen, 1701 to 1715* (Boston, Mass., 1884), pp. 11–12, 17, 23, 28 and 79.

BOSTON: HOUSE FOR THOMAS ROBINSON

Building contract, August 25 (?), 1660.

This witneseth that I Jobe Lane of Malden Acknolleg my selfe to stand ingaged unto mr Thomas Robeson of sittuat for the Raysing of A frame for A dwelling house Apon y[e] Land of the sd Robinsons in Boston Joy[n]-ing unto the Land of m[r] Pottar . . . [one word unclear] the demensions of the frame is to be as followes viz forty two foot Longe[,] nintene foot weyd and Eighten Inches Jutte, for the hight is to be fiftene foot betwixt Joynts[,] and two stule windose and the Rest Clerstorey windose so many as in the Judgment of men[?] is nedfull, and on[e] and twenty foot of the sayd frame [sic]. I the sd Lane promise to find sommers and Joyse for A seller floure[;] all these timbers the which I mack use of Abought the Aboue sd frame shall be timber sold in seson and the frame shall be Euery waye sub-stanshall Acording to the Judgment of men and further I do promise to Rayse the sayd frame at or befor the 14th of Nouember Next in this yere 1660 and for and in Considarashon Aboue sd I the sayd J [sic] Joseph Rock do Ingag my selfe in the behalfe of my Brother and Thomas Robinson to paye unto the sd Job Lane the somme of fifty pounds starling the which is to be payd by the hands of my mother mrs Mrtha Coggan the which is in full of Legesayes duw from the sd m[rs] Coggan unto my sistar mary Robe-son and hur Children as maye Apere p the will of my father m[r] John Coggan desed: now ther being An Agrement mad betwixt me the Aboue sd Lane and m[rs] Coggan for A corne mill at Malden, I do promise to buld the Aboue sd frame and [it] is to be in part of paye unto m[rs] Coggan for the sd purches[,] all which is by the Consent of my mother m[rs] Marthah Coggan. . . .[1]

1. Lane Family papers, privately owned.

BOSTON: HOUSE FOR JOHN WILLIAMS

Building contract, January 23, 1678/1679.

This Agreement made Between James Townsend of Boston in New England housewright of the one part And John Williams of s^d Boston Boateman on the other part Witnesseth that the s^d James Townsend doth hereby covenant promiss and agree (in consideration of the payments and other the Covenants hereafter in these presents expressed) to fframe erect Set up and finish for him the s^d Williams upon his Land in Boston in the place where his now dwelling house standeth (which is to bee taken down by the s^d Townsend) A Tenement or dwelling house according to the dimentions following. Viz^t to contain in Length thirty four foote more or less as the Land will beare, and in breadth twenty foote, and ffifteen foote Stud with two jetts in the front next the Street, and a Leanto of ten foote wide joyning to the backside to reach throughout the whole length of s^d house, to Stone a Cellar underneath the s^d main house throughout the whole length and breadth thereof, to build a Stack of good brick Chimny's to the s^d house to contain six fires, one in the Cellar, three upon the first ffloore and two in the Chambers, to inclose and cover the sides and Roofe with Clapboards and shingles, to make and place four great casement frames in the front of s^d building, two cleer storey windows in the gables and two in the Cellar wall and to make outside dores and Staires into the Cellar, to fill lath & plaister the walls of s^d house throughout, to lay a ffloor of boards upon Sleepers in the Cellar, to make up all partitions, to make and hang all dores Staires, and to lay all the ffloors of s^d house with good merchantable well Seasoned pine boards, to make & put up pyramides and flewboards at the gables, and generally to do all Carpentry and masons worke whatsoever necessary to the compleating and finishing of the s^d Tenement or building to make it tenantable, although not herein perticularly expres't (Ceiling of the Roomes excepted)[;] all the timber used in and about the frame of s^d house to bee of good sound well seasoned Sizable white and black oake, all which workes and materials for the same (Clapboards Shingles hinges and locks excepted) are to bee found made and done strong substantiall & workemanlike at the proper cost and charge of the s^d James Townsend, the fframe to bee raysed at or before the first day of May and the whole worke to bee fully done and finished on or before the last day of July next insuing the day of the date of these presents. In Consideration of which workes to bee done and finished in all respects as is above expres't and materials for the same, the abovenamed John Williams doth hereby covenant promiss and agree to allow unto the s^d James Townsend his present dwelling house, all the timber boards & bricks belonging thereunto (hee takeing down the same) and to pay or cause to bee paid unto him his heires Exec^rs Adm^rs or Assignes the full Sume of One hundred and thirty pounds currant mony of New England in manner following Viz^t thirty pounds at the Ensealing of these presents, ffifty pounds at the rayseing of the frame, and ffifty pounds more when the whole worke is done and finished as aboves^d Also to digg the Cellar and to finde and provide all Shingles clapboards hinges and locks for the s^d building at his own cost & charge ffor the true performance of which abovewritten Covenants Agreements and payments the party's to these presents each one for his respective part doth binde himselfe his heires Exec^rs and Adm^rs unto the other his heires Exec^rs Adm^rs & Assignes in the penall Sume of two hundred pounds lawfull money of New England to be well and truly paid by the defective part[y]. . . .

Memorand^m It's agreed that the foreside and end of the house is to bee boarded underneath the Clapboards up to the first jette

Deposition of William Dawes, mason, aged about 62, January 26, 1680.

. . . being desired by James Townsend to go with Deacon Allen to pass their Judgement upon a house built by the s^d Townsend for John Williams . . . I do judge it to bee done workemanlike according to covenant and that hee has done rather more then less hee was obliged by covenant, as the plaistering the walls of the Cellar and the pointing the garret[,] and that it is not usuall to Seel the jetties when the Roomes are not Seeled.

Deposition of Thomas Ghent, aged about 37, January 26, 1680.

That some time last Spring John Williams the Boatman imployed me to digg a Cellar for him, where his dwelling house now standeth. wch house was built by James Townsend and this deponent testifieth that the s^d Cellar was not digged and finished untill the last Election day in the morning being the 28 of may. 1679. my Selfe and one more man being imployed about it.

Deposition of Cornelius White, aged 30, sworn in court January 27, 1680.

. . . as to that peice of worke that hee the s^d White tooke of James Townsend, wch was the Cellar of John Williams and by my agreement with him was to bee ready to go to worke upon some time in march. 79. the which Cellar was not ready by reason of the default of the s^d Williams untill the middle of may last & farther Saith not.

Deposition of Peter Weare, aged about 29, sworn in court January 27, 1680.

. . . [who] testifieth and Saith that hee being Emploied by James Townsend about the framing & finishing of the house of John Williams from the first to the last and that it was done Substantiall and workemanlike by the middle of October and further that the s^d Williams did say severall times in my hearing that hee could not finde any fault in the worke, ffarther after the s^d Townsend had framed the house in wideness and Length according to his Covenant, hee was forced to cut off Six or Seven inches of the Length of it which was no small hinderance to the s^d Townsend and farther Saith not.

Deposition of Gamaliel Rogers, aged about 22, sworn in court, January 27, 1680.

. . . sometime in July last past I was at worke at Goodman Williams house, and hee would not let me go forward with my worke, because hee would have it boarded under the Clapboards and the same day James Townsend came down and they had some discourse about it, and the s^d Williams was as I thought very well Satisfied about the boarding, and I went forwards with my worke and afterwards I heard the s^d Williams Say that hee the s^d Townsend should allow him boards for the fence.

Deposition of Cornelius White, aged about 30, sworn in court January 28, 1680.

. . . [who] testifieth and Saith that that end of John Williams his house joining to m^rs Pugliss^s could not bee filled because there could not bee boards put up to fill against by reason it stood so neer it. And that the middle wall in s^d Williams house between the main house and the Leantoo is boarded with plaine boards on one side, and filled lathed and plaistered on the other side which is not usuall and further Saith not: This Deponent adds that it is not usuall to fill gable ends where a house jetts[.] John Pearse aged about 70 yeares testifieth to all abovewritten

White adds that W^ms did motion to have that end of the house filled, but I shewed unto him the inconvenience and improbability of doing it; wherewith W^ms seemed to bee well Satisfied.

Deposition of Obadiah Reed, Francis Dodson and Thomas Atkins, "being desired by John Williams of Boston to veiw and examine what his new dwelling house doth want to bee finished," sworn in court January 27, 1680.

Inprimis. The mantle tree in the Cellar not faced.
2ly. The mantle tree in the Leanto Chimly not faced.
3ly. One Partition in the Cellar and a dore left undone
4ly. Two Partitions in the Garret not done, and never a dore to them.
5.   Three pair of Stairs and but one dore to them all.

6. Seventeen dores in the house, and not one latch, katch. or bolt to any one of them

7ly. ffive gable ends to the house and not one of them fil'd.

8ly. Two Jetties not close[d] in the foreside: the one end and the foreside should have been boarded underneath the clapboards wch is not done.

9ly. One Pyramid and one gutter on the backside of the house not done

10. One guttar on the foreside of s^d house not done, so that the house is much damnified for want of it.

11. One end of the main house and Leanto from the bottom to the top which hath no filling at all in it:And the Cheekes

12 the Cellar dore, which should have been done up with brick and Lime, is not done, which should have been done.

13. One Partition upon the wing of the Leanto Chimney not done

14. Some of the Windows in the house open between the Window frames and the posts.

15. The Partition in the Leanto is not done as it should bee by a workeman.

16. The Cellar Stairs that go out to the Street are neither fastned with Spikes nor with trunnells.[1]

1. Suffolk County Court Records, Office of the Clerk of the Supreme Judicial Court for Suffolk County, Boston, Mass., docket no. 1833.

BOXFORD: HOUSE FOR DAVID PEABODY

Building contract, April 13, 1726.

Know all men by these presents that I: Benjamin porter of Boxford in the County of Easex in New england: joyner haue Bargained and promised for to build and finish a dwelling house for Dauid peabody of the aboue sd town County and Contary yeoman: of the dementions here after Expresed: viz Two frams: the one to be twenty foott in weidth and seuenteen foot Long: and to be the same height as is his old house is which is upon his farme whear Thomas Carr is sd peabodys Tennant and is to be Joyned to the End of sd old house: and the sd house is to be Cou[er]ed on the fore side: and the Rufe to [be] borded and shingled with white pine shingels: short shingels: and the fram to [be] Clabborded all Round: and the fore side of sd house all with white pine or Ceader shingels and Clabords[.] And to build sd peabody a Back Rume of Eighteen foott square: seuen foott stud in height: and to bord the Rofe and to short shingell the Rofe and Clabbord all the Rest of the frames and [do] all the out side woork of both[.] the aboue sd frams is to [be] finished by the first day of december next ensuing the Date of these presents: and the aboue sd Benjamin porter Joyner is To make and put up six windows to the hiest frame: aboue and below: three to a Rome[,] And Two windows to the back Rome[;] and all the windows to be of the bigness as they are generaly made now to housing newly built here abouts in the neighbourhood[;] and to glaze all the windows and to Lay three flowers in the Rome and one of them to be plained: Two pe[rti]tions by the fire way one aboue and one below: and to be done handsome plained woorke: and the sd windows To be Lined[;] and Two flowers too the Back Rome: and one pe[rti]tion by the fire way in the back Rome: and the sd porter is To find bords and nayls[,] Clabords and shingels and glase and all the meterals for the finishing of all the aboue sd woorke: only the said Dauid peabody is to Leat the said Benjamin porter haue the Libberty for to gitt what timber he shall haue ocation for to make use of for the building of sd woorke and finishing of it of[f] from the sd farm whear sd Carr sd Tenant Liues upon which sd housings are to be built . . . And the aboue sd peabody is [to] giue to ye sd porter or his heiers a good and Lawfull deed of Conuaince of Twenty acres of Land out of his aboue sd farm and if the sd peabody shall Truly Execute sd deed to sd porter That then the said porter doth hereby bind and oblidge himself his heiers Executors and Administrators in the sume of one hundred pounds in pasiable money of newengland unto the said peabody his heiers Executors Administrators and assiens for to haue all the aboue Buildings finished as aboue Expressed by the time aboue Expresed. . . .[1]

1. Unrecorded deeds, etc., 1721–1840, Peabody-Osgood Family papers, The Essex Institute.

BOXFORD: HOUSE FOR THE POOR

Town meeting, February 5, 1706.

. . . voted by the Towen to bueld a houes for the pooer of the Towen . . . thorty foout in lenth and fourteen foout in bradth and six foout stud with a conveniant sealler vnder one Eand of it: also the Towen have Chosen three men to a gree with sum man or men of our Towen to bueld and finish this a bove saied houes and sealler according to the sound discresion of thes three men . . . vpon the Towens Cost and Charg[1]

1. Sidney Perley, ed., "Boxford Town Records, 1685–1706," *The Historical Collections of the Topsfield Historical Society*, v (1899), 101.

BRADFORD: HOUSE FOR PHILIP NELSON

Building contract, no date (probably early in 1663).

Be it knowne unto all men by the presents that John willcott of Newbury in the county of Essex in new England carpenter, for and in considderation of a pcell of land by estimation three hundred acres more or less lyeing & sittuate in Rowley aforsayd doth acknowledge himselfe to owe & to be indebted to Phillip Nellson of Rowley in the county aforesayd, his heires, executors, administrators, or assignes, the full & just suṁ of two hundred pound, to be payd att time and in kind as followeth, one hundred pound he is to pay in the building a house & barne upon the land of the sd Phillip Nellson at Merrimack [Bradford], which house he is to build, and to make it thirty foure foote long and nyne foote stud, and sixteene foote wyde, and he is for to cover the Roofe of the sayd house with good & well seasoned pine boards, and to be duble boarded, & to be well and substantially nayled, and the syds & the ends of the sayd house he is for to clabord with good & substantiall clabord, and to be well claborded and nailed, also he is to make six windows to the sayd house, the four lower windows are to be two foote long, and two of them are to have three lights a peece, & the other two are to have two lights a peece, & the other two windows at the ends of the house he is to make with three lights a peece, and to find glase to all the forsayd windows, and for to naile up the sayd glase, also he is to make three dores to the sayd house, one out dore, & two inward dores, all which three dores are to be made of good & will seasoned pine board and he is to finde hookes & hinges to the sd dores, and to hang the same, and he is for to make and to lay four floores to the sayd house, two lower floores and two chamber floores, which are to be well & close layd, and to be covered with good & well seasoned pine boards, & to be well and sustantially nayled and he is for to make a good dubble chimnye to the sayd house, and to daub the same, makeing a good back to the sayd chimnyes, and he is to daub the ends of the sayd house unto the top of the house, and syds unto the wall plates, with a suficient thicknes of clay, and for to make a good oven to the sd house, and to make one paire of good staires to go into the chambers of the sayd house, which house is to be finished as thus expressed at or before the last of may in the yeare one thousand six hundred sixty & three. . , . the other hundred pound is to be payd in corne, or in neate cattle . . . not to exceed above seaven years of age, except it be oxen which are not to exeed aboue nyne years of age. . . .[1]

1. Essex Quarterly Court Files, Office of the Clerk of the Superior Court for Essex County, Salem, Mass., XXIV, 115.

CHARLESTOWN: HOUSE BELONGING TO THE TOWN

Lease (with contract) to John Wesson, yeoman, of Charlestown, January 26, 1705.

. . . one Certain Tract or parcel of Land, scituate, lying and being within the Limitts and bounds of Charlstown aforesaid, and belonging to said Towne, Conteining ninety-one acres and one-half: be the same more or less . . . And [Wesson] also shall and will Erect, Build and finish upon said Land A Dwelling house which shall be Twenty foot Long, and Eighteen foot wide, nine foot stud Between Joynts and A Leanto at the End Twelve foot Long the width of the house, six foot stud, and shall Digg and sufficiently ston a Conveinent seller under said house, and shall build and carry up A Double Stack of Brick Chimneys to A Conveinent height above the house, and shall lay Two good floors in said house, and shall fill the walles Between the studds and ceile them with plained boards or Lime morter, and shall make Conveinent stairs, and shall board or clabboard the outside of said house, and board and Shingle the Roofe to make it every Way thite, and make Conveinent Lights in said house and Glaze them. . . . And the said Land, together with all the buildings theron that shall be erected theron as afforsaid, So well and Sufficiently repaired and Amended, With the orchard well fenced intire, and all the Land he shall Improve sufficiently fenced as aforsaid, at the end of said Term of Twenty-one years shall and will peaceably and quietly yield up and Surrender the same unto the . . . s^d Towne of Charlstowne. &c., &c.[1]

[Identical leases with respect to buildings and the improvement of lands were drawn by the Town's committee with Stephen Williams, yeoman, of Woburn on February 23, 1705, and Thomas Gould, husbandman, and Daniel Gould, cordwainer, of Charlestown on August 14, 1705, for other tracts of land in Charlestown belonging to the town.[2]]

1. *A Report of the Record Commissioners Containing Charlestown Land Records, 1638–1802,* 2nd ed. (Boston, Mass., 1883), pp. 171–172.
2. Ibid., pp. 174–175.

CHARLESTOWN (LOVELL'S ISLAND): HOUSE BELONGING TO THE TOWN

Lease (with contract) to George Worthylake, planter, of Boston, August 3, 1696.

. . . all That the Island commonly called and Known By the name of Lovels Island . . . for the term of Twenty six years from thence Nex ensuing, yeilding and pay therfor, &c., the yearly Rent or sum of Ten pounds Current money of New England. . . .

And the said George Worthylake for himself, &c., doth hereby covenant, &c., that he, the said George Worthylake, his heirs, execut^rs and admistrat^rs, or Asigns, or some of them, shall and will erect, build and finish A Dwelling house upon the said Island which shall be Twenty foot Long, Sixteen foot wide, and eleven foot stud; and shall digg and well and sufficently stone A good convenient Celler under the said house, and shall Build and cary up a good Strong Stack of chimneys, to Be built with Stone from the foundation to the mantletree, and from the mantletree upward with good bricks, to A convenient height above the roofe of the house, and Shall Lay two good floores in the said house, and shall fill the Walls between the studds and ceile them with good plained boords; and shall make two paire of stairs, one pair down into the Celler, and the other pair up into the Chamber; and shall board the Walls of the said house, and board and well Shingle the roofe so as to make it every way thite; and Shall make convenient Lights in the said House and well Glaze the same; and shall at his and theire owne proper Cost and Charge from time to time, and at all Times During the aforsaid Term, when and often as need shall Require, Well and Sufficiently repair, support, maintaine, and Amend the said Dwelling house and the barne Now Standing one the said Iland, With all needfull and necessary repairations whatsoever, etc.[1]

1. *A Report of the Record Commissioners Containing Charlestown Land Records, 1638–1802*, 2nd ed. (Boston, Mass., 1883), pp. 172–173.

DANVERS: PARSONAGE

Town meeting, 1673, 1681.

"In this second year of the organization of the parish [Salem Village], 1673, it was voted to build 'an house for the minister:' the dimensions to be '28 foot in length, 13 foot between joynts and 20 foot in breadth, and a leentoo of 11 foot at the end of the house.' But this does not appear to have been carried into effect; for seven years later, in February, 1680 (1681 N.S.), we find the vote renewed: 'the Dementions of the House are as followeth: 42 foot long, twenty foot Broad: thirteen foot stude, fouer chimleis, no gable ends.' "[1]

1. Charles B. Rice, *Proceedings at the Celebration of the Two Hundredth Anniversary of the First Parish at Salem Village, now Danvers, October 8, 1872* . . . (Boston, Mass., 1874), p. 21.

DEDHAM: "HOUSE IN THE CHURCH LOTT"

Town meeting, February 18, 1669.

... considering that ther is some remote Lands belonging to the Towne not like to be vsefull to any man dwelling at home in the Towne ... [it] might by contract with any man of our Towne pcure and paye for the felling crosse cutting heweing saweing frameing and with conueanient help the rayseing of an house in the place afore said betwixt 40 and 50 foote longe[,] 18 or 20 foote wide[,] 13 foote betweene joynts[,] double floard[,] with windowes and all the building sufficient for strength and conueaniencie as the case may be more at full be described.[1]

1. Don Gleason Hill, ed., *The Early Records of the Town of Dedham, Massachusetts, 1659–1673* ... (Dedham, Mass., 1894), pp. 165–166.

HAVERHILL: HOUSE FOR ROBERT SWAN

Building contract, February 28, 1681.

John Whittier doth herby couenant with robert Swon [both of Haverhill] to buld or erect and finsh a dwaling hous for hm for work demensions and tim as foleth[:] yᵉ frame is to be eight and forte foote long[,] twente foot wid[,] thurten foot and a half Betwen ioynts[;] the ends and sids to be claborded exapting that part which will be betwen the ould hous[;] and that the rof to be coured with bords and short shingles[;] to make nine windo frames and too par of cagement frames[;] to lay six floors[;] to mak fouer pertiones ioyening to the chimles or ner to them[;] to mak one outside dor and fiue other dors and to mak thre par of stairs[;] and the sᵈ John to cut the timbers upone the sᵈ raberts rit [right] ether of land or comen: the sᵈ robert Swon doth herby couenant upon notes given to him of the timber being cut to and with yᵉ sᵈ whittier to draw or cause to be brout in plas wher the sᵈ frame is to be raised all the timber so that the sᵈ John be not hindred nor disapoynted or want the same to work upon[;] the sᵈ robert Swon doth herby couenant with the sᵈ John whittier to prouide and bring in to plac at his own proper cost and charg all clabords bords shingls Joys or slittwork nails and ioyrn work whatsoeuer[;] the sᵈ robert allso when the frame is fit for to be raised is to find all nasesere hands and halp for the Joyneing with yᵉ sᵈ Jon to rais it[;] the fram is to be raised at or befor the 15ᵗʰ day of ogest ensuing the dat herof and one rom to be inclosed and couered and one flore to be laied as sone as yᵉ sᵈ John can and all the rast of yᵉ work to be done at or befor the last day in the yer on thousand six hundred eighte and thre[;] It is to be understod by ye word finish in ye first line is onely ment to doe ye carpendors work aboue menisoned which is to be done wall and workmanlik:

The s^d Robart Swon doth herby couenant with ye s^d John whittier in consideration of the s^d work by hm to be done to pay to him or his heirs or assines the . . . [torn] sum of fiue and thirte pound in maner followeng[:] that is fouer and twenty dayes work and fouer bushels of indan corn upone demand[;] twelve pound to be paied at or before ye ninth of octtober next ensuing ye dat her of: the one half to be paied in marchantabl corn than at pris curant otes exapted[,] the other half to be paied in good sound nate catel to be fat and fit for ye slaiter bules exapted[;] and thirten pound mor to be paied at or befoer the last day of aprel ensuing the dat herof in ye yer 16 hundred eighte and thre: twalue pound [of this amount] to be payed in marchantabel corne than & at pris curant ots exapted and and [sic] twenti shilens in curant monee of new england

and the said rabart Swone doth herby couenant with ye s^d John that he or any under or for him shall haue thre diet dureing the time that he or thay shall be at work at his hous and the s^d Jon to alowe ye s^d robart fowr shilens a wek for his diet[?] which is to be alowed out of ye last paiment that is not yet mentioned and the remainder to be paid the s^d John in nat catell under nine yers on at or befoer ye last day of october in ye yer 16 hundred eighte and thre. . . .[1]

1. Essex Quarterly Court Files, Office of the Clerk of the Superior Court for Essex County, Salem, Mass., XLI, 10.

Ipswich: Addition to the House of Richard Jacob

Building contract, September 27, 1659.

Thes presents wittneseth that I william Auerill of Ipswich Carpenter haue undertaken a peece of building of Richard Jacob of Ipswich in manner as followeth[:] Viz one Bay of building of 18 foot square and 13 foot in the stud : as allso to provide Clabbord and shingle for the forsaid building and to Lay them[.] Allso he is to Lay three flors with Joys and bord and to make 4 windows[,] too stole windows of 5 Lights a peece and to Claristory windows of 4 Lights a peece[;] also a garret window[,] to Casments betwene studs[;] prtitions and dors to Close the Roms Compleat[;] as allso to Remoue a Little Rome and Close it to his house and make it tite betwene[.] allso to make a table and frame of 12 or 14 foot Long and a joyned form of 4 foot Long and a binch Behind the table[.] for and in Consideration of all the foresaid premises I the forsaid William do Ac-

knowledg to haue Receued the sum of twelue pound as full satisfaction
And for the du performance heerof I the foresaid William do bind my
selfe Executors administrators and assins in the forfite of twenty four
pound to finish Compleatly by the Last of august next Ensuing the date
heerof[;] and the said Richard for his part is to draw all the timber and
bord for Couering and to find Couenyant help to Raise and frens[?] and
bords and nails[,] only shuch timbr as is defective through the said Williams defalt he is to prouid at his own proper Cost to mak the worke
substantial all according to the tru intent of the bargan aboue writen

Deposition of Thomas Whittered, March 26, 1661.

This deponent saith I being at worke at sargant Richard Jacobs house the
latter end of last summer hee hired mee to hew a grounsill and mortis it to
putt into the side of his ould house that stands whare the new house is to
be sat (as I under stood by Richard Jacob)
I testify allso that the grounsill of the ould house is Rotten and the new
sill is nott put in to this day though it is to be understood I wrought by the
day and was not ingaged to put it in: the house as it then stood and still
Remains is incapable of being Remoued as I conceiue: I furder Testify that
the frame of the new house did not want much of being fitt to Raise when
I was there att worke about the grounsill: also there was a considerable
quantity of shingle and clapboard for couering then wrought out and still
piled up in sargant Jacobs yard done by william auerell as I am a wittness
of[;] allso the Celler that the ould house is to stand ouer is without sleepers
open to this day

*Deposition of Samuel and Thomas Jacob, aged about 20 and 22, sworn in
court, March 26, 1661.*

This deponent [sic] testifyeth that in the Case depending betwene ther
father and william auerill that there was a sell prouided Redy for the old
house and the Resen why it was not put in was becase the walls should not
be broke downe before the other house was Redy to be set up

Deposition of Thomas Clarke of Noddles Island, March 26, 1661.

[who] sayeth that I cleaft out for william Auerell about twelue hundred
of clapb[oard] and shingle in Richard Jacobs yard for couering about the
time that the Jurymen was chosen for last september court to be held at
ipswich: sum of the clapboard stufe was brought home to sarg^t Jacobs
house while I was there at worke:[1]

1. Essex Quarterly Court Files, Office of the Clerk of the Superior Court for Essex
County, Salem, Mass., VI, 70–71.

Ipswich: House for Samuel Symonds

Letter from Samuel Symonds to John Winthrop, Jr., of Ipswich, after February 8, 1638.

. . . Concerneinge the frame of the howse I thanke you kindely for your love and care to further my busines. I could be well content to leave much of the contrivance to your owne liberty vpon what we have talked together about it already. I am indiferent whether it be 30 foote or 35 foote longe[,] 16 or 18 foote broade. I would have wood chimnyes at each end, the frames of the chimnyes to be stronger then ordinary to beare good heavy load of clay for security against fire. you may let the chimnyes be all the breadth of the howse, if you thinke good[;] the 2 lower dores to be in the middle of the howse one opposite to the other. be sure that all the dorewaies in every place be soe high that any man may goe vpright vnder. the staiers I thinke had best be placed close by the dore. it makes noe great matter though there be noe particion vpon the first flore[;] if there be, make one biger then the other. for windowes let them not be over large in any roome, and as few as conveniently may be. let all have current shutting draw-windowes, haveing respect both to present and future vse. I thinke to make it a girt howse will make it more chargeable then neede. however, the side bearers for the second story being to be loaden with corne etc. must not be pinned on but rather eyther lett in to the studds or borne vp with false studds and soe tenented in at the ends; I leave it to you and the Carpenters. In this story over the first I would have a particion, whether in the middest or over the particion vnder I leave it; In the garrett noe particion, but let there be one or two lucome windowes, if two, both on one side. I desire to have the sparrs reach downe pritty deep at the eves to preserve the walls the better from the wether. I would have it Sellered all over, and soe the frame of the howse accordengly from the bottom. I would have the howse strong in timber though plaine and well brased. I would have it covered with very good oake-hart inch board *for the present*, to be tacked on onely for the present as you tould me; let the frame begin from the bottom of the Seller, and soe in the ordinary way vpright for I can hereafter (to save the timber within grounde) run vp a thin brickworke without. I thinke it best to have the walls without to be all clapboarded besides the clay walls. It were not amisse to leave a dore-way or two within the Seller that soe hereafter one may make comings in from without, and let them be both vpon that side which the lucome window or windowes be.

I desire to have the howse in your bargaineing to be as compleatly mentioned in particulars as may be, at least soe far as you bargaine for, and as speedily done alsoe as you can. I thinke it not best to have too much timber

felled neare the howse place westward, etc. Here are as many remem-
brances as come to minde. I desire you to be in my stead herein, and what
ever you doe shall please me. . . .[1]

1. *Winthrop Papers* (Boston, Mass.: The Massachusetts Historical Society, 1929–
1947), IV, 11–12. See also Thomas F. Waters, "A History of the Old Argilla Road in
Ipswich, Massachusetts," *Publications of the Ipswich Historical Society*, IX (1900), 23–29.

MARLBOROUGH: PARSONAGE

Building contract, April 5, 1661.

This Indenture made the fifth day of Aprill one Thousand six hundred
sixty & one, by & between obadias Ward, Christopher Banyster, & Richard Barnes of the Towne of Marlborough on ye one party; And the In-
habitants & all the Proprieto^{rs} of the same Towne on ye other party
Witnesseth That ye s^d obadias Ward Christoph: Banyster & Richd Barnes
hath covenanted, promised, & Bargained to build a fframe for A Ministers
house, every way like to ye fframe y^t Jno Ruddocke hath built for himselfe
in the affores^d Towne of Marlborough: the house or fframe is to bee A
Girt house Thirty six ffoote Long, eighteene foote wide, & twelve ffoote
(bettweene Joyntes) & A halfe; the studs standing & such A distance that A
foure foote & A halfe Claboard may reach three studs: & two ffloores of
juice, & foure windows on the foreside, & two windowes at the west end
& two Gables on the foreside of ten foote wide; & eight ffoote Sparr, with
two small windows on the fforeside of the Gables[;] & they are to ffell all
the timber & bring it in place, & do all y^t belongs to the fframe, only the
Towne is to helpe raise the affores^d fframe, & all this worke is to bee done,
& ye fframe raised within A ffortnight after Mich^{ll} tyde: And this being
done the Towne of Marlborough doth promise & engage to pay unto
them the s^d obadias Ward, Christopher Banyster & Richd Barnes, the sume
of ffifteene Pounds in Corne within fourteene daies after the house is
raised the one half of it, & the oth^r halfe some time in March[;] the whole
pay is to bee one third in wheat, & one third in Rie, & the oth^r third in
Indian Corne[;] the halfe in wheat & Rie is to bee paid fourteene daies aft^r
the house is up in wheat & Rie, & the oth^r halfe in Rie & Indian some time
in march: wheat at foure shillings & six pence A bushell, Rie at foure
shillings A bushell, & Indian at three shillings A bushell. . . .[1]

1. Franklin P. Rice, ed., *First Records of Marlborough, Massachusetts* (Worcester,
Mass.: Published by Franklin P. Rice, 1909), pp. 12–13.

READING: HOUSE FOR SAMUEL FITCH

Will of Zachariah Fitch of Reading, May 3, 1662.

. . . my mind & will is that my Sonne Joseph & my sonn Benjamin shall (with the helpe of my sonne Samuell of his owne hand) build my sonne Samull a house uppon his Lott by Beare hill Twenty fower foote Longe & Eighteene foot wide and Twelue foot heigh in the stod & Couer itt & Clabbord or board itt: & fence in the Lott att Beare hill with a good suffitient fenc of fiue Rayles . . . By that time that my Sonne Samuell Comes to the Age of Twenty Two yeares. . . .[1]

1. Middlesex County Probate Records, first ser., docket no. 7724.

SALEM: HOUSE FOR JONATHAN CORWIN (1)

Contract with mason, February 19, 1675.

Articles and Couenants made agreed upon and Confirmed betweene Mr Jonathan Corwin of Salem mercht & Daniel Andrewes of [blank] of the other part, Concerning a Parcell of worke as followeth. viz:

Inprimis, the said parcell of worke is to be bestowed in filling, plaistering & finishing a Certaine Dwellinghouse bought by the said owner of Capt. Nathll Dauenport of Boston, & is scituate in Salem aforesaid towards the west End of the towne, betweene the houses of Rich Sibly on the west and Deliuerance Parkman on the East, & is to be performed according to the following Directions. viz:

1. The said Daniel Andrewes is to dig & build a Cellar as large as the Easterly roome of said house will afford (& in the said roome according to the breadth & length of it) not exceeding six foot in heigth, & to underpin the Porch & the remaining part of the house, not exceeding three foote in height, also to underpin the kitchen on the North side of the house, not Exceeding one ffoote, the said kitchen being twenty foote long & Eighteene foote wide, & to make steps with stones into ye Cellar in two places belonging to ye Cellar, together with stone steps up into ye porch.

2. ffor the Chimneys he is to take downe the Chimneys which are now standing, & to take & make up of the brickes that are now in the Chimneyes, & the stones that are in the Leanetoo Cellar that now is. & to rebuild the said Chimneys with fiue fireplaces, viz: 2 below & 2 in the Chambers & one in the Garrett. Also to build one Chimny in the kitchen (with ouens and a ffurnace) not Exceeding 5 foote aboue the top of the house.

3. He is to sett the Jamms of the 2 Chamber Chimneys, & of the Easter-

most roome below with Dutch tyles the said Owner finding the tyle, also to lay all the hearths belonging to yᵉ said house, & to point the Cellar & underpinning of yᵉ house, & so much of the 3 hearths as are to be laid with Dutch tile, the said Owner is to find them.

4. As for Lathing & plaistering, he is to lath & Siele the 4 roomes of the house, betwixt yᵉ Joyce ouer head, & to plaister the sides of the house with a Coate of lime & haire upon the clay, also to fill ye Gable Ends of the house with bricke, & to plaister them with Clay,

5. to Lath & plaister the partitions of the house with Clay & lime, & to fill lath & plaister with bricke & Clay the porch & porch Chamber, & to plaister them with lime & haire besides, & to siele & lath them ouerhead with lime, also to fill Lath & plaister the kitchen up to yᵉ wallplate, on euery side.

6. The said Daniel Andrewes is to find lime, bricke, Clay, stone & haire, together with labourers & workemen to helpe him, & generally all materialls for the Effecting & Carrying on of the aforesaid worke, Except laths & nailes.

7. The whole worke before mentioned is to be done finished & pformed att or before the last day of August next following, provided the said Daniel or any that worke with him be not lett or hindred for want of the Carpenters worke.

8. Lastly in Consideration of all the aforesaid worke so finished & accomplished as is abouesaid, the aforesaid owner is to pay or Cause to be paid unto yᵉ said workeman the summe of fifty pounds in money Currant in New England, to be paid at or before the finishing of the said worke. . . .[1]

Mason's receipt, March 12, 1675.

Resᵈ this 12ᵗʰ March 1674/75 of Jonathan Corwin of Salem yᵉ ffull & Just Suñe of Eight poundes being in Concideration of our last bargaine. Viz. yᵉ Cellar to be under yᵉ whole house & yᵉ Stack of Chymnyes to Come fro yᵉ Bottome of yᵉ Cellar. . . .

Daniel Andrus [crossed out][2]

1. Corwin Family mss, American Antiquarian Society.
2. Jonathan Corwin, Account Book, ms, vol. for 1656–1679, American Antiquarian Society.

Salem: House for Jonathan Corwin (2)

Memorandum, September 12, 1679.

the house yᵗ Thomas fflint is to build for mee is accordᵍ to these following Demensions

Length. 24 foot from inside to inside

Breadth. 18 foot Ditto

Height of stud. 10 foot betwene wall plate & groundsell.

wth 3 Length of Joyce[;] to Jett att ye end Next ye Street 2 ffoot wth hansom pindulu's [or pindula's;] one Gable end on ye west Side & towards ye North End together wth Sleepers for the Lower ffloore

Y^e frame to be Compleatly Raysed wth ye Joyce ffitted for itt by ye Last day of Nouember Next for wch work Jonathan Corwin is to allow to Thomas fflint twelve poundes in good English Goods price Currant. . . .[1]

1. Jonathan Corwin, Account Book, MS, vol. for 1656–1679, American Antiquarian Society.

SALEM: ADDITION TO THE HOUSE OF GEORGE EMERY

Building contract, 14: 6mo: 1658.

There is a grement betwene Mr Gorge emery of salem and John Norman of manchester housecarpenter and the said norman is to build a porch seuen ffoot 4 enches stud[,] 8 ffoot of frame braced and tenneted in to the stud[,] jetted ouer 14 enches and [?] three wayes and to couer it and shingle the gutters[;] to make one wendow & one doore and stayers in to bothe chambers and to make one gable end a Leuen ffoote broad and to couer it and shingle the gutteres and a cleare storrey wendow for ye gableend and a stoole wendow acording to the Lower wendow and three ffloores of boards in the new roome and three ffloores of boards in the porch and to make 3 doores and to ffinnes all this worke spesseffid and to due the porch and windowes within two monthes from the date hereoff . . . and ffind boardes to ffines thes worke and clabbordes . . . and the said norman is to haue in consedderation for this worke speseffid twelfe poundes and he is to haue a gray mare at 12 pound prise going into two yeares ould or else the saddle mare at 16 poundes. . . .

Deposition of John Gedney and Phillip Cromwell, 22: 1mo: 1661.

. . . [who] sayth that some time the last sumer John Norman & m^r Emery of Salem made an agreement that John Norman was to sett up a gable end upon the old p̅te of m^r Emerys house & to shingle the east sid of the house, & to sett up weather boards, m^r Emery providing y^m[,] for wch with worke don before John Norman was to haue a yong ambling mare & a colt if shee had any, m^r Emery to warrant her with colt when he put her out

Carpenter's bill of costs (undated).

	£	sh	d
for bullding of a porcht	6	10	0
for 2000 of bowrds and working of them	8	0	0
for 200 & 50 clapbowrd and working of them	1	10	0
for 6000 of shingell & laying of them	6	12	0
for seting up of a Gabell end	1	10	0
for making of 3 windowes	1	0	0
for makeing of 3 dowers	0	5	0
for makeing of a pare of stayers & cassin of them	0	10	0
	25	17	0[1]

1. Essex Quarterly Court Files, Office of the Clerk of the Superior Court for Essex County, Salem, Mass., VI, 85–87.

SALEM: HOUSE FOR THOMAS MAULLE

Memorandum, account book of Joshua Buffum, carpenter, 20: 10 mo: 1678.

A house ingaged for to bee bilt for thomas maulle ye 20 day of the 10 month 1678 and all to be fineshed by ye last of ye 8 month 1679[:] thes house is to bee in lenth 35 fute and 20 fute in brith[,] the stoud 14 fute in haith

The aboue said house wass all compleated by the 30 day of ye 8 month 1679 acording to Thomas Maoules dariction

the cost of ye house in nailes	06–03–10
for byeng and cartind of tymber	06–16–00
for sawing	05–05–00
for clabordes	03–15–00
for bordes	10–00–00
for shengell	05–15–00
for carting of clay	01–05–00
for Engenes [Indians'] helpe aboute making morter	02–00–00
in lyme and hare	03–14–00
for windos making and stayeres making	01–05–00
for Iorne worke beside casmentes and	
selere dore	01–10–00
	[£]47–08–10[1]

1. Henry W. Belknap, *Trades and Tradesmen of Essex County, Massachusetts* . . . (Salem, Mass.: The Essex Institute, 1929), p. 56.

SUDBURY: HOUSE ON JOHN GLOVER'S FARM

Lease from John Glover of Harvard College, Cambridge, student, and Henry Dunster, "president of the said College Father in Law, Guardian Elect, and Tutor to the Said John," to Edmund Rice of Sudbury, husbandman, September 29, 1647.

. . . John Glovers whole farme, lying abutting northward on the said Henry Dunsters Lands, Severed by Sudbury Line, and so on to Cochittuate brooke . . . from the 29th of September 1647 to the 29th of September 1657. . . .

Item. That the said Edmund shall within the first 5 or 6 years, build one dwelling house on the premises 30 foote long, 10 foote high stud, one foot sill from the ground, 16 foote wide, 2 fire roomes, both below, or the one above, and the other below. All dores well hanged, and staires with convenient fastnes of locks or bolts, windows glased, and well planked under foote and boarded sufficiently to lay corne in, in the story abovehead, and the same keep in good and sufficient repaire unto the end of the said terme of ten years compleated.[1]

1. Robert W. Lovett, ed., *Documents from the Harvard University Archives, 1638–1750* (Boston, Mass.: Published by The Colonial Society of Massachusetts, 1975), p. 22.

TOPSFIELD: HOUSE FOR WILLIAM PERKINS

Building contract, March 16, 1691.

Thease preasents witnesseth y^t I Joseph Hale of Newbury in ye County of Essex in New England doe bind my self my Heyers Executors or Administrators to Heugh frame and seat up and doe all ye Carpenters woorke of a House of 25 foot Long and 20 foot wide and 14 foot stud, for william Pearkins of Topsfield in ye above sd County at or be fore ye first of march next Insueing ye date heare of[.] ye woork is to be compleatly finished, & ye aboue sd william Pearkins doe like so In gage my self my heyers or Executors to provid for ye above sd Joseph hale meat drink and Lodging all ye time y^t ye above sd woork is doing, and Likewise to bring all ye Tymber into Place y^t is needfull for ye building and to provide sutch as shall be sutable for ye same, and Likewise to provide Boards shingles and nailes sutable for ye woorke, In Consideration of Twenty seaven Poundes wch ye above sd william pearkins have Given bill for ye payment of. . . . The poasts are to be split and studs and Joyst sawd[1]

1. "Towne Family Papers," *The Historical Collections of the Topsfield Historical Society*, XVIII (1913), 4–5.

Index

Abbot, Benjamin, 125
Abbot House, Andover, 125
Alden, John, 55
Allerton, Isaac, 45, 50
Allerton House, Kingston, 45; construction, 51; dating, 51–52; second house, 52
American Architect and Building News, 107
American Traveller, Boston, 174
Andover, Mass., Abbot House, 125
Andrews, Daniel, 171, 217–218
Andrews, Joseph, 187
Andrews, Thomas, Sr., 144
Andrews, Thomas, Jr., 144
Andrews House, Hingham, 144–145
Appleton, Samuel, 183
Appleton, Samuel, Jr., 160, 183
Appleton, William Sumner, 126, 143, 144, 149, 152, 161, 163, 166n, 167n, 186n, 189, 190n
Appleton-Taylor-Mansfield House, Saugus, 160, 183–184
Archaeology: applied to architecture, 43; focus, 44; visibility, 44; applied to whaler's tavern, 45–49; to Allerton house, 49–53; to Winslow house, 58
Arlington Street Church, 89n
Atkins, Albert H., 191
Atkins, Thomas, 206
Atlantic Monthly, 88
Austin, Thomas, 131
Averill, William, 213–214

Babson, John J., 142
Back Bay, 89n
Bailyn, Bernard, 19
Baker, Roy W., 126, 157, 165, 186, 190
Balch, John, 126
Balch Family Association, 126
Balch House, Beverly, 126–127
Bancroft, Ellen, 128n

Bancroft, Robert Hale, 128n
Banister, Thomas, letters about house of, 194–196
Banyster, Christopher, 216
Barnard, Matthew, 128
Barnard, Matthew, House, Boston, 128
Barnard, Rev. Thomas, 167
Barnard, Parson Thomas, House, North Andover, 113, 114, 167–168, 188
Barnes, Richard, 216
Barnet, Capt. John, 201, 202
Barnstable County, 118
Barry, Sir Charles, 101n
Bartoll, Samuel, 172
Bass, John, 168
Bass House, Quincy, 168
Bateman, John, building contract for house of, 196–199
Batter, Edmond, 177
Baxter House, Quincy, 168
Beacon Street, Boston, 87, 89, 92, 94, 111
Bean, Gilbert L., 131
Belcher, Jonathan, 78
Belknap, Henry W., 220n
Bellarmine jugs, 45
Bentley, Rev. William, 172, 182, 187
Beverly, Mass., 118; Balch House, 126, 127; Rev. John Chipman House, 126; Hale House, 128; building contract for parsonage in, 193–194
Beverly Historical Association, 126, 128
Bishop's Alley, 75, 77
Blague, Nathaniel, 11
Blake, Abigail (Preston), 66
Blake, Agnes, 67
Blake, Clarence, 72
Blake, Ebenezer, 65, 66, 67
Blake, Elizabeth, 67
Blake, Elizabeth Clap (Mrs. James), 62, 67
Blake, Hannah, 67
Blake, James, 62, 67, 68–69

Blake, James, House, Dorchester, 61–74; published tradition, 61–62; ownership, 62–69; structural history, 69–74
Blake, John (1657–1718), 67, 69
Blake, John (d. 1772), 66
Blake, Josiah, 67, 69
Blake, Rachel, 65, 66
Blake, Samuel, 61–62, 62n, 69, 69n, 137n
Blake, William, 67
Blanchard, Grace, 188
Blanchard-Wellington House, Medford, 163–164
Blaney, Joseph, 186
Blaney, Joseph, House, Swampscott, 186
Blettsoe, Thomas, 194–196
Boardman, Abijah, 184
Boardman, Stephen, 151
Boardman, William, 184
Boardman, William, Jr., 184
Boardman House, Saugus, 184–186
Booth, Robert, 161, 178
Boston, 4; views, 83; loss of First Period buildings, 121; Matthew Barnard House, 128; Bridgham House, 129; Clough-Vernon House, 129; Paul Revere House, 130; Stanbury House, 131; papers relating to house of William Rix, 194; to house of T. Banister, 194–196; to house of John Bateman, 196–199; to Cole-Sedgwick House, 199–201; deposition on house for Henry Ellis, 201; contract for schoolmaster's house, 201–203; for house of John Williams, 204–207; see also Revere, Paul, House
Boston City Hall, 89n
Boston Herald, 74n
Bostonian Society, 88n, 129
Bowen, Abel, 85, 86
Bowles, Joseph, 146–147
Bowles-Smith House, Ipswich, 146–147
Boxford, Mass.: contract for house in, 207–208; contract for House for the Poor, 208
Brackenbury, Richard, 176
Bradford, William, 52
Bradford, Mass., contract for house of P. Nelson, 209
Bradstreet, Anne, House, N. Andover, 113
Bradstreet, Gov. Simon, 172
Braintree, Mass., 131

Bredon, Thomas, 9, 13
Bridgham, Henry, 129
Bridgham House, Boston, 129
Briggs, Asa, 101n
Brigham, Charles, 95–97, 95n, 98n
Bristol County, 118
Brooks, Alfred Mansfield, 142–143
Brooks, Rev. Phillips, 85
Brown, Frank Chouteau, 152, 171, 176, 191n
Brown, John, Sr., 143
Brown, Moses, 167
Brown, Nathaniel, 143
Brown, William, Jr., 170
Brown House, Hamilton, 143–144
Browne, Capt. Abraham, 188–189
Browne, James, 197
Browne, Samuel, 189
Browne, Col. William, House (Sun Tavern), Salem, 170
Browne House, Watertown, 188–189
Bryant, Abraham, Jr., 169
Bryant, J. F. Gridley, 89n
Bryant and Gilman, 88
Budrose, Philip A., 180
Buffum, Joshua, 220
Bulfinch, Charles, 82; State House, 94, 111
Bunting, Bainbridge, 99n
Burnham, Ralph W., 117, 149–150, 156; Ross Tavern owned by, 157; Wilson-Appleton House restored by, 160; Benaiah Titcomb House re-erected by, 167
Burnham, Thomas, 148–149
Burnham House, Essex, 138–139
Bushee, Florence Evans, 165

Caldwell, Dillingham, 147
Caldwell, John, 147
Caldwell House, Ipswich, 147–148
Call, Mary, 146
Call, Philip, 146
Cambridge, Mass., 102; Hooper House, 102–104; Carey House, 104–105; Cooper-Frost-Austin House, 131–132
Cambridge Historical Commission, 102n
Candee, Richard, 48
Cape Ann, 176
Cape Ann Scientific, Literary and Historical Association, 142–143

Capen, Rev. Joseph, 187

Capen, Parson, House, Topsfield, 144, 187

Capen House, Dorchester, 137–138, 139

Carey, Arthur Astor, House, 102, 104–105, 108, 109

Cary, Col., 31

Cellars, absence, 52

Ceramics, in dating of houses, 52

Chamberlain, Allen, 169–170, 170n

Chamberlain, Mellen, 191n

Chandler, Joseph Everett, 4n, 6n, 130, 132, 134, 145, 169, 176, 182

Charlestown, Mass., leases and contracts for houses in, 210–211

Charter House, see Clough-Vernon House

Cheek, Richard, 136

Chelmsford, Mass., 132

Chever, Ezekiel, 201, 202

Chicago, 108, 109, 111

Chickley, Anthony, 8–10, 13

Child, Thomas (distiller), 76

Child, Thomas (painter), 202–203

Chiltonville, Mass., 57

Chipman, Rev. John, 126

Chipman, Rev. John, House, Beverly, 126–127

Christ Church, Salem St., North End, 75, 76; steeple, 77, 83

Claflin, Robert, 189

Clap, Ebenezer, 62

Clap, Elisha, 65, 66

Clark, Benjamin, 162

Clarke, Thomas, 214

Clough, William, 129

Clough(?)-How House, Boston, 129

Clough-Vernon House, Boston, 129

Coffin, Joshua, 164, 165

Coffin, Tristram, Jr., 164

Coffin House, Newbury, 164

Coggan, Martha, 203

Cole, Samuel, 199–201

Cole-Sedgwick House, Boston, 199–201

Coleman, William, 17n

Coles, William A., 99n

Colling, James K., 101

Collins, Robert, 148

Collins, Susanna, 10

Collins-Lord House, Ipswich, 148, 157

Cologne stonewares, 52

Colonial Revival, 104, 105; influence of Hancock House on, 105–106, 111; Peabody on, 107

Colonial Society of Massachusetts, 76n

Columbian Exposition (1893), Chicago, 108, 109, 111

Conant, Exercise, 126

Concord Antiquarian Society, 156

Conolly, Horace, 182

Cooper, John, 131

Cooper, Samuel, 131

Cooper, Walter, 131

Cooper-Frost-Austin House, Cambridge, 131–132, 133

Copley Square, Boston, 75; Museum of Fine Arts in, 102

Corwin, George, 171

Corwin, Jonathan, 171; mason's contract for houses of, 217–218; memoranda by, 218–219

Corwin, Mrs. Sarah, 171

Corwin House (Witch House), Salem, 171

Costello, Marion A., 139

Cotton, John, 9

Crocetti, Ernest A., 152

Cromwell, Phillip, 219

Crouch, David, 203

Cummings, Abbott Lowell, 113–121, 131n, 168n, 186n; on Royall House, 26; documents compiled by, 193–221

Currier, John J., 166n, 167

Curtis, Greeley, 96–99

Curtis, Greeley, House, Manchester-by-the-Sea, 87, 88n

Cushing, Daniel, Sr., 145

Cushing, Peter, 145

Cushing House, Hingham, 145

Dabrowski, Richard C., 132

Daily Evening Traveller, Boston, 131n

Dalrymple, Miss E. W., 173

Dane, John, 151

Danvers, Mass., 132; Darling-Prince House, 132; John Holten House, 132, 134; Rebecca Nurse House, 134; Porter-Bradstreet House, 134; Rea-Putnam-Fowler House, 135; Parsonage, 211

Darling-Prince House, Danvers, 132

Dating of historic buildings: difficulty, 113–115; methods, 115; categories of

First Period, 116–117; photographic evidence, 119; Old Style, 125
Davenport, Rev. Addington, 79
Davenport, Capt. Nathaniel, 171, 217
Davenport, Capt. Richard, 171
Davis, A. J., 93n
Davis, John, 194
Dawes, William (b. c. 1618), 205
Dawes, William (1745–1799), 31
Dedham, Mass.: Fairbanks House, 113, 135–137; "House in the Church Lott," 212
Deetz, James, 43–59
Demers, Frank A., 115n, 125
Dendochronology, 114, 115
Detwiller, Frederic C., 3n
Dewing, Arthur Stone, 125
Dexter, H. Clark, Jr., 139
Dexter, Harold C., 140
Dexter, Thomas, 183
Direct Tax, 128, 130
Doane, Alvan L., 140
Dodge, Robert G., 155
Dodson, Francis, 206
Dole, Richard, 167
Dole-Little House, Newbury, 164–165
Dorchester, Mass.: Blake House, 61–74, 137; Capen House, 137–138; Pierce House, 138
Dorchester Beacon, 72n
Dorchester Historical Society, 61, 62–63, 72, 137
Dow, Arthur W., 152
Dow, Eugene, 169
Dow, George Francis, 140n, 153n, 184n, 187, 187n, 189
Downing, Emanuel, 172
Downing, George, 172
Downing, Lucy, 172
Downing-Bradstreet House, Salem, 172
Drake, Samuel Adams, 128n
Drawings: by Sturgis, 88, 101–102; measured, 99–101
Dudley, Gov. Thomas, 154
Dunster, Henry, 221
Du Pont, Henry Francis, 150; see also Winterthur Museum
Duxbury, Mass., 55

Egan, C. Edward, Jr., 146n
Ekholm, Erik, 45

Eliot, Charles W., 103
Ellery, William, 142
Ellis, Henry, deposition on house for, 201
Emerson-Wardwell lot, Ipswich, 151
Emery, George, papers relating to addition to house of, 219–220
Emmerton, Caroline O., 176, 182
Endicott, Gov. John, 176
Endicott, C. M., 176
England: architectural parts imported from, 88, 101; use of measured drawings in, 101; structural comparisons with houses in, 115
English, Philip, 172
English, Philip, House, Salem, 172–174
Essex, Mass.: Burnham House, 138–139; George Giddings House, 140; Story House, 140–141; Benaiah Titcomb House moved to, 167
Essex County, 115; First Period houses, 117–118
Essex Institute, Salem, 88n, 170, 177, 183

Fairbanks, Jonathan, 113, 135
Fairbanks House, Dedham, 113, 135–137
Farrington, George Pickman, 171
Fayerweather Street, Cambridge, 102
Fearn, Elizabeth, 65, 66
Federal Writers' guide to Massachusetts, 114
Finney, Arthur L., 23–33
Fire of 1676, Boston, 9, 12, 13, 14, 128, 130
First Ironworks Association, Saugus, 184
First Period (1620–1725): wooden buildings, 4; development in, 56; statistics, 113, 116–117, 120; difficulty of dating buildings, 114; categories, 116–117; new discoveries, 118–119; demolition of buildings, 119–121
Fiske, Thomas, Jr., 189
Fiske, Captain Thomas, House, Wenham, 189–190
Fitch, Benjamin, 217
Fitch, Joseph, 217
Fitch, Samuel, 217
Fitch, Zachariah, 217
Fitts, Isaac, 157
Flint, Thomas, 218–219
Floyd, Margaret Henderson, 87–111, 101n

Focus: in archaeological evidence, 44; in whaler's tavern excavation, 45; in Allerton House, 50

Forbes, Esther, 4n

Forbes, Harriette M., 119, 160

Forman, Ian F., 153

Fowler, Joseph, 190

Frechen stoneware, 45

French, Mrs. George A., 62n

French, John, Sr., 187

French, John, Jr., 187

French-Andrews House, Topsfield, 187–188

Fulton, Sarah Bradlee, Chapter, D.A.R., 31, 33

Gage, Gen. Thomas, 31

Gale, Ambrose, House, Marblehead, 161

Gardner, Ann (Mrs. Joseph), 172

Gardner, Joseph, 172

Gear, Kate, 31

Gedney, Eleazer, 174

Gedney, John, 219

Gedney, Martha, 174

Gedney House, Salem, 174, 175

Georgian style, 26

Gerrish, Joseph, 189

Ghent, Thomas, 205

Giddings, George, 140, 148

Giddings, George, House, Essex, 140

Giddings-Burnham House, Ipswich, 148–149

Gilman, Arthur, 88, 94, 96n

Glassie, Henry, 53

Globe Tavern, Salem, 172

Gloucester, Mass., 142–143, 169–170

Glover, John, lease of house, 221

Goddard, Giles, 197, 198

Goelet, Francis, 82

Goldsmith, John, 77

Goldsmith, Zaccheus, 190

Goldsmith-Pickering House, Wenham, 190

Goodwin, John, 202

Goodwin, Nathaniel, 129

Gould, Daniel, 210

Gould, Thomas, 210

Great Island, Wellfleet, whaler's tavern, 44–45

Greene, G. Holden, 145

Greene, Thomas, 76, 78–79

Hale, Edward Everett, Jr., 194n

Hale, Rev. John, 128

Hale, Joseph, 221

Hale, Col. Robert, 128

Hale House, Beverly, 128

Hall, James, 55

Hall, changing features, 102

Hamden County, 118

Hamilton, Mass.: Brown House, 143–144; Whipple-Matthews House, 144

Hampshire County, 118

Hancock, John, 93

Hancock, Thomas, 88

Hancock House, 87–111; description, 88–92; exterior, 90–91; interior, 91–92; proposed demolition, 94; staircase, 94–99; measured drawings, 101–102; style reflected in later houses, 102–105, 108, 109–110; architectural importance, 105, 109–111

Handel, George Frederick, 80

Hapgood, Hezekiah, 186

Hapgood House, Stow, 186

Harris, Job, 155n

Harrison, Peter, 75

Hart, George, 150

Hart, George, House, Ipswich, 150–151

Hart, Thomas, 149

Hart House, Ipswich, 117, 149–150

Harvard Bulletin, 93n

Harvard College, 93, 102n, 221

Haskell, William, 190

Haskell House, W. Gloucester, 190–191

Haverhill, Mass., contract for house of R. Swan, 212–213

Hawes, Benjamin, 63, 65

Hawes, John, 63, 65, 66

Hawes Fund, Trustees of, 63

Hawley Street, Boston, 75

Hawthorne, Nathaniel, 90n

Hayward, John, 197

Headlam, Cecil, 195n

Hicks, Timothy, 177

Hill, Don Gleason, 90, 137, 212n

Hingham, Mass.: Peabody on architecture of, 107; Parish House in, 108–109, 110; Andrews House, 144–145; Cushing House, 145; Cushing-Robinson House, 146; Woodcock-Langley House, 146

Hingham Historical Society, 145
Historic American Buildings Survey, 88n
Historic Houses in Andover, Mass., 125
Historic Salem, Inc., 171, 180
Hobart, Caleb, 198
Hobart, Rev. Peter, 146
Hodges, Capt. Joseph, 177
Hodgson, Charles, 72
Holden, Wheaton A., 106n
Hollis Street Meeting House, 83
Holten, John, House, Danvers, 132, 134
Homes of Our Forefathers (Whitefield), 100
Hooper, Benjamin, 174
Hooper, Edward W.: house of, Cambridge, 102–104; interior of house, 105, 106
Hooper, John H., 30, 164
Hooper, Rev. Mr., 82
Hooper-Hathaway House, Salem, 174, 176
Hornblower, Henry, 56
House of Seven Gables (Turner House), Salem, 176, 180–183
House of Seven Gables Settlement Association, 183
Hovey, Daniel, 151
Hovey, Thomas, 151
Hovey-Boardman House, Ipswich, 151
How, James, 129
Howard, John, 152
Howard, Robert, 6, 8, 13, 15, 130; identification, 15–16; tax on house of, 16–17; house built for, 17–18; description of house, 18–20; commercial career, 19–20; *see also* Revere, Paul, House

Howard, Samuel, 152
Howard, William, 151–152
Howard, William, House, Ipswich, 151–152
Hubbard, Richard, 143
Hubbard, William, 143
Hunt, Lewis, 176
Hunt, Lewis, House, Salem, 176
Hunt, Richard Morris, 99n
Hutchinson, Eliakim, 194

Indicott, John, 77, 78
Ingoldsby, Ebenezer, 197
Ipswich, Mass., 117; First Period houses, 118; Bowles-Smith House, 146–147;

Caldwell House, 147–148; Collins-Lord House, 148; Giddings-Burnham House, 148–149; Hart House, 149–150; George Hart House, 150–151; Hovey-Boardman House, 151; William Howard House, 151–152; Knowlton House, 152; Austin Lord House, 153; Nathaniel Lord House, 153–154; Lummus-Low House, 154; Manning House, 154–155; Paine-Dodge House, 155; Capt. Matthew Perkins House, 155–156; Perkins-Sutton House, 156; Ross Tavern, 156–157; Whipple House, 157–159; Wilson-Appleton House, 159–160; contract for addition to R. Jacob house, 213–214; letter on house for S. Symonds, 215–216
Ipswich Historical Society, 157, 158n
Irish Meeting House, Boston, 83
Ironworks, Saugus, 183
Isham, Norman, 126, 127, 144
Ives, Thomas, 176

Jacob, Richard, papers relating to house of, 213–214
Jacob, Samuel, 214
Jacob, Thomas, 214
Jacques, Richard, 201
Jamestown, 56
Jeffs, John, 4
John Hancock Insurance Co., Boston, 88n
Johnson, James, 194
Jones, Alvin Lincoln, 137n
Jordan, Abraham, 80
Julien, Jean Baptiste Gilbert Payplat dis, 129

Kenton, Robert, 79
Kettell, Russell H., 156n
Kiefer, Matthew J., 61
Kimball, Fiske, 4n, 113, 115
Kimball, Philip, 149
King's Chapel, Boston, 30, 75, 76; school of, 77
Kingston, Mass., Allerton House, 45, 49–53
Knowlton, Nathaniel, 152
Knowlton, Deacon Thomas, Sr., 152
Knowlton House, Ipswich, 152

Ladd, Ralph, 150n

Lake, Daniel, 188
Lake, Eleazer, 188
Lane, Job, 203
Langley, John, 146
Lapham, Alice G., 126
Laskin, Timothy, 176
Latin schoolmaster, house for, 201–203
Lattimer, Christopher, 161
Lebovich, William, 3n, 6
Lee, Gen. Charles, 31
Lidgett, Mrs. Peter, 23
Lincoln, Mass., Whittemore-Smith House, 160
Little, Arthur, 100
Lord, Austin, House, Ipswich, 153
Lord, Mrs. Charlotte, 149
Lord, James, 153
Lord, Nathaniel, 146, 154
Lord, Nathaniel, House, Ipswich, 153–154
Lord, Robert, Sr., 148, 154
Lothrop, Thomas, 193
Lovell's Island, Charlestown, 210–211
Lovett, Robert W., 221n
Luce, Peter, 76
Lummus, Jonathan, Sr., 154
Lummus-Low House, Ipswich, 154

Macdonald-Miller, Rev. Donald, 187
Manchester-by-the-Sea, 88n, 99, 102
Manning, William, 170
Manning House, Ipswich, 154–155
Mansfield, Paul, 176
Marblehead, Mass.: Ambrose Gale House, 161; Norden House, 161–162; Parker-Orne House, 162
March, Hugh, 165
Marlborough, Mass., contract for parsonage in, 216
Marryot, Thomas, 200
Marshall, John, 168
Marshfield, Mass., 58
Massachusetts, Commonwealth of: research on old houses, 118; First Period buildings, 121
Massachusetts Historical Society, 88n, 108
Massachusetts Magazine, 90
Massachusetts Shipping Register (1697–1714), 19

Massachusetts State Building, Chicago, 108, 109–110, 111
Mather, Cotton, 14
Mather, Rev. Increase, 8–9, 10, 20; house built for, 9, 13, 130
Matthews, Nathan, 144
Maulle, Thomas, memorandum on house for, 220
Mayo, John, 14
Mayo, Elna Jean, 14n
McGinley, Paul J., 147
Medfield, Mass., Peak House, 162–163
Medfield Historical Society, 163
Medford, Mass.: granite ashlar from, 90; Blanchard-Wellington House, 163–164
Merchant, William, 153
Merrill, Richard, 133, 185
Metropolitan District Commission, Boston, 169
Metropolitan Museum of Art, New York, 117, 150
Middlesex County, First Period houses, 118, 119
Milton, Mass., Capen House moved to, 138
Montgomery, Charles F., 196n
More, William, 81
Morris, William, 101
Morrison, Hugh, 4n
Morse, Anthony, 167
Mountford, Arnold, 45
Mullett, Arthur B., 96n
Murray, Martha Lucy, 150
Museum of Fine Arts, Boston: Copley Square, 102n; Huntington Avenue, 155

Nantucket, island of, 118
Narbonne House, Salem, 176–177
National Museum, Independence Hall, Philadelphia, 88n
National Museum of History and Technology, Washington, 141, 151, 165
National Park Service, 160, 177, 184
National Society of Colonial Dames of America, 169
Nelson, Philip, contract for house of, 209
New England Chapter, Society of Architectural Historians, 6n
New England Interiors (Little), 100
New South Meeting House, Boston, 83

Newbury, Mass.: Coffin House, 164; Dole-Little House, 164–165; Noyes House, 165; Swett-Ilsley House, 165–166

Newburyport, Mass., Benaiah Titcomb House, 167

Newport, R.I., 76

Norden, Nathaniel, 161

Norden House, Marblehead, 161–162

Norfolk County, 118

Norman, John, 193, 219

North Andover, Mass., Parson Barnard House, 167–168

North Andover Historical Society, 167

North Devonshire Sgrafitto ware, 45

North End, Boston, value of property, 15n

North Square, Boston, 4, 6, 8; leveled by fire, 14

Norwood, Francis, Sr., 170

Norwood, Joshua, 170

Noyes, Isaac, 166

Noyes House, Newbury, 165

Nurse, Rebecca, 134

Nurse, Rebecca, House, Danvers, 134

Nurse, Samuel, 134

Nutting, Wallace, 184

"Old Chelmsford" Garrison House Association, 132

Old Feather Store, see Stanbury House

Old Garrison, Chelmsford, 132

Old Ship Church, Hingham, Parish House, 108–110

Old South Meeting House, Boston, 83

Old State House, Boston, 109

Old-Time New England, 88n, 121, 167n

Oliver, Daniel, 203

Orcutt, William Dana, 62

Osborn, Henry, 153

Osborn, John, 153

Otis, John, Sr., 146

Otis, John, Jr., 146

Owens, William W., Jr., 142

Paine, Elizabeth, 155

Paine, Robert, Sr., 155

Paine, Robert, Jr., 155

Paine-Dodge House, Ipswich, 155

Palladio Londinensis (Wm. Salmon), 30

Parker, David, 162

Parker, Winthrop D., 169

Parker-Orne House, Marblehead, 162

Parker Tavern, Reading, 169

Parkman, Deliverance, 177, 217

Parkman House, Salem, 177–178

Patch, James, 193

Peabody, David, contract for house of, 207–208

Peabody, Elizabeth (Prince), 132n

Peabody, James B., 75–86

Peabody, Robert Swain, 106; Parish House by, 108–109; Mass. State Building by, 109–111

Peak House, Medfield, 162–163

Pearse, John, 206

Pelham, Peter, Jr., 80

Penniman, J. R., 173

Perkins, Abraham, 148

Perkins, Judith, 143

Perkins, Capt. Matthew, 155, 156

Perkins, Matthew, Jr., 156

Perkins, Capt. Matthew, House, Ipswich, 155–156

Perkins, William, contract for house of, 221

Perkins-Sutton House, Ipswich, 156

Perley, Sidney, 126, 132, 134, 134n, 135, 162n, 170, 171n, 173, 176, 178, 180, 208n

Philadelphia, Centennial Exhibition in (1876), 100, 106, 120

Pickering, Alice, 179

Pickering, John, Sr., 178–179

Pickering, John, Jr., 179

Pickering, John (10th), 179

Pickering, Jonathan, 178

Pickering, Col. Timothy, 179, 190

Pickering House, Salem, 178–179, 192

Pickman, Samuel, 179

Pickman, Samuel, House, Salem, 179–180

Pierce, Catharine W., 189n

Pierce, John, 138

Pierce, Robert, 138

Pierce, Col. Samuel, 138

Pierce, Thomas, 138

Pierce, William, 191

Pierce House, Dorchester, 137, 138

Pigeon Cove, 170

Pilgrim Society, Plymouth, 55

Pinebank, Jamaica Plain, 88n, 95n

Pitt, William, 161

Pitts, Edmond, 145

Placzek, Adolf, 99*n*

Plimoth Plantation: archaeologists, 45, 49, 58; Bradford on, 52

Plymouth, Mass., 107, 115, 119

Plymouth Colony: archaeology applied to, 43–44, 49; sites studied, 44–45; Allerton House, 49–52; post-hole construction, 52–53; elongated buildings, 55

Plymouth County, 118

Pomroy, Daniel, 131

Porter, Benjamin, 207–208

Porter, Joseph, 134

Porter-Bradstreet House, Danvers, 134

Post-hole construction: Allerton House, 51; in Plymouth, 52–53

Post Office Building, Boston, 95

Pownall, Gov. Thomas, 83

Powning, Daniel, 203

Price, Rev. Roger, 77

Price, William, 76, 77, 78, 79–80, 83, 85–86

"Price-Burgis View of Boston," 83, 84, 85

Proctor, John, 157

Proctor, Thomas Emerson, 187

Province House, Boston, 121

Queen Anne Revival, 102

Quincy, Mass.: Bass House, 168; Baxter House, 168; Quincy Homestead, 168–169

Quincy, Edmund, 168

Quincy Historical Society, 168

Quincy Homestead, Quincy, 168–169

Quinsler, Antonia, 63

Quinsler, George J., 63

Randolph, Edward, 20

Rea, Daniel, 135

Rea, Joshua, 135

Rea, Zerubabel, 135

Read, Harold Comer, 4*n*

Reading, Mass., 217; Parker Tavern, 169

Reading Antiquarian Society, 169

Redding, Mr., 78

Reed, Obadiah, 206

Reservoir Street, Cambridge, 102

Revere, Paul, 130; views of Boston by, 83

Revere, Paul, House, Boston, 121, 128, 130; significance, 3–4; date of erection, 4

and 4*n*; date of ell, 4–6; single-build theory, 6 and 6*n*, 17*n*; title chain, 6–13; rebuilding, 13–18; tax on, 17; Howard as owner of, 18–20

Revere, Paul, Memorial Association, 3*n*, 6, 130

Rice, Charles B., 211*n*

Rice, Edmund, 221

Rice, Franklin P., 216*n*

Richardson, H. H., 75

Richardson Park, Dorchester, 63, 72

Rising, Donald B., 186

Rix, William, contract for house of, 194

Robb, Gordon, 179

Robbins, Chandler, 14*n*

Robbins, Roland, 55

Robinson, John, 175

Robinson, Thomas, contract for house of, 203

Rock, Joseph, 203

Rockport, Mass., Witch House, 169–170

Rogers, Gamaliel, 206

Roper, Stephen J., 3–21

Ropes family, Salem, 172

Ross, Jeremiah, 157

Ross, Philip W., 151, 154

Ross Tavern, Ipswich, 148, 156–157

Royall, Isaac, Sr., 23, 30; inventory of estate, 34–41

Royall, Isaac, Jr., 23, 26

Royall, Penelope, 23; *see also* Vassall, Mrs. Henry

Royall House, Medford, 23–33; Georgian details, 26; construction of west facade, 26–30; inventory, 30; later history, 31; garden, 33; inventory (1739), 34–41

Royall Professorship of Law (Harvard), 31

Salem, Mass.: First Period houses, 118; archaeological discoveries, 119; Col. William Browne House, 170; Corwin House, 171; Downing-Bradstreet House, 172; Philip English House, 172–174; Gedney House, 174, 175; Hooper-Hathaway House, 174, 176; Lewis Hunt House, 176; Narbonne House, 176–177; Parkman House, 177–178; Pickering House, 178–179, 192; Samuel Pickman House, 179–180; Todd House, 180; Turner House, 180–183; Ward House,

Salem, Mass., *continued*
    183; papers relating to house for J. Cor-
    win, 217–219; papers on addition to
    house of G. Emery, 219–220; memo-
    randum on house of T. Maulle, 220
Salem Village, *see* Danvers
Salmon, Catharine Louisa, 160
Salmon, William, 30
Saltonstall-Merrifield House, Ipswich, 150
Saltza, Philip W. von, 161
Sauer, Dr. David W., 140
Saugus, Mass.: Appleton-Taylor-Mans-
    field House, 183–184; Boardman House,
    184–186
Schofield, George A., 153n
"Scotch House," *see* Boardman House
Scully, Vincent, 107n
Seabury, Rev. Samuel, 79
Sears Pictorial History of the United States, 89
Second Church, Boston: ownership of Re-
    vere House, 8–10; rebuilding of meeting
    house, 12; rebuilding of Revere House,
    13–18; motives for rebuilding, 13–16
Sedgwick, Capt. Robert, 199–201
Sewall, Samuel, 168
Sewall, Capt. Samuel, 194
Sharpe, Edmund, 101n
Shatswell, Theophilus, 153
Shaw, Charles, 82–83, 83n
Shawmut Peninsula, 4
Sheathing, at whaler's tavern, 48
Shirley, Gov. William, 80
Shurtleff, Nathaniel B., 129n
Sibly, Richard, 217
Simmons, William, 153
Simonds, Thomas C., 62n
Simpson, John K., 131
Smith, Abbie S., 147
Smith, Ammi R., 147
Smith, Daniel, 155
Smith, Franklin Webster, 87
Smith, John, 138
Smith, Thomas, 153
Smith, Capt. William, 160
Snow, Caleb H., 129n
Society for the Preservation of New Eng-
    land Antiquities, 3n, 72, 129, 132, 137,
    139, 149, 164, 180; material relating to
    Hancock House, 87, 88; Cooper-Frost-
    Austin House, 131; Rebecca Nurse
    House, 134; Pierce House, 138; William

Howard House, 152; Capt. Matthew
    Perkins House, 156; Coffin House, 164;
    Dole-Little House, 165; Swett-Ilsley
    House, 165–166; Gedney House, 174;
    Boardman House, 185; Brown House,
    189
Society for the Protection of Ancient Build-
    ings, 101
Somerby, Henry, 164
Spoons, used in dating, 45, 52
Spring, James W., 164n
Staffordshire stoneware, 45
Stanbury, Susanna, 131
Stanbury, Thomas, 131
Standish, Miles, Duxbury homesite of, 55
Stanley, Matthew, 188
Stanley-Lake House, Topsfield, 188
Stark, James H., 62
Stark, Gen. John, 31
State House, Boston, 94
State War and Navy Building, Washing-
    ton, 96n
Stewart, William, 154–155
Stoneware, types used in dating, 45
Story, Seth, 140
Story, William, 140
Story, Zachariah, 140
Stow, Nathaniel, 169
Stow, Mass., Hapgood House, 186
Sturgis, John Hubbard, 87; drawings of
    Hancock House, 88, 101–102; staircase
    purchased by, 94–98; Cambridge
    houses by, 102–105; influence of draw-
    ings, 105
Sturgis, R. Clipston, 88n
Sturgis, Russell, 98n, 101n
Sudbury, lease of farm in, 221
Suffolk County, 118
Sullivan, Gen. John, 31
Summer Street, Boston, 75, 83
Sun Tavern, Salem, 170
Sutton, Gen. William, 156
Swampscott, Mass., Joseph Blaney House,
    186
Swan, Robert, contract for house of, 212–
    213
Swett, Stephen, 165
Swett-Ilsley House, Newbury, 165–166
Symonds, Samuel, letter relating to house
    of, 215–216

Taft, Robert, 196–199
Taxes, as estimate of value of Revere House, 17
Taylor, John, 184
Ten Hills Farm, Medford, 23
Thayer, Gen. Sylvanus, Birthplace, Braintree, 131
Thomas, M. Halsey, 128n, 130n, 169n
Tidd, Mrs. Jacob, 31
Titcomb, Benaiah, 167
Titcomb, Benaiah, Jr., 167
Titcomb, Benaiah, House, Newburyport, 167
Todd House, Salem, 180
Topsfield, Mass., 144; Parson Capen House, 187; French-Andrews House, 187–188; Stanley-Lake House, 188; contract for house of W. Perkins, 221
Topsfield Historical Society, 187
Towne, John H., 188n
Townsend, James, 204–205
Tree-ring analysis, 115
Trinity Church, Boston, 75–86; building of first, 76–81; first services at, 78, 79; organ, 80; costs, 80n, 81; bell, 81; changes in exterior, 81–82; described by contemporaries, 82–86
Trinity Church, Newport, R.I., 76
Turrell, Capt. Daniel, Sr., 6, 8; identification of, 10–11; member of Second Church, 11–13
Turner, James, 83
Turner, John, 180
Turner, John, Jr., 182
Turner House (House of the Seven Gables), Salem, 180–183

Union Marine Insurance Co., 170
Upham, William P., 171n
Upton, Elizabeth A., 182
Urban architecture, Revere House as, 4
Usher, Lt.-Gov. John, 23

Van Brunt, Henry, 99
Vassall, Leonard, 76
Vassall, Penelope Royall (Mrs. Henry), 23
Veren, Dorcas, 177
Veren, Hilliard, Sr., 177
Veren, Sarah, 177

Visibility: in archaeological evidence, 44; in whaler's tavern excavation, 45

Walker, Isaac, 17n
Walker, Sgt. Thomas, 6, 8; identification of, 10–11
Walker, Thomas, Jr., 11–13
Ward, Barbara M., 183n
Ward, Gerald W. R., 183n
Ward, John, 183
Ward, Obadias, 216
Ward House, Salem, 183
Ware and Van Brunt, 99
Washington, Gen. George, 31
Washington bedroom, Hancock House, 92, 105
Waters, Thomas Franklin, 147n, 148, 150, 151, 152n, 154, 156, 158n, 216n; restoration of Whipple House by, 157
Watertown, Mass., Browne House, 188–189
Watkins, Walter Kendall, 88n, 92n
Weare, Peter, 205–206
Webster, Kenneth, 138
Wendel, Daniel S., 148, 156n, 157
Wenham, Mass.: Capt. Thomas Fiske House, 189–190; Goldsmith-Pickering House, 190–191
Wenham Village Improvement Society, Inc., 189
Wesson, John, house leased to, 210
West, Catherine Lynn, 143
West Gloucester, Mass., Haskell House, 190–191
Westerwald ware, 52
Whaler's tavern, Great Island, Wellfleet: dating, 45; structure, 45–48; fate, 48–49
Wheeler, Benjamin, 151
Wheeler, Moses, 170
Whipple, John (carpenter), 137
Whipple, John (of Ipswich), 157
Whipple, Capt. John, 144
Whipple, Matthew, 144
Whipple House, Ipswich, 157–159
Whipple-Matthews House, Hamilton, 144
White, Cornelius, 205, 206
White-Ellery House, 142, 192
Whitefield, Edwin, 100, 149
Whitehill, Walter Muir, 4n
Whitred, William, 153

Whittemore, Benjamin, 160
Whittemore-Smith House, Lincoln, 160
Whittered, Thomas, 214
Whittier, John, 212–213
Willcott, John, 209
Williams, Caleb, Sr., 65
Williams, Caleb, Jr., 63–65
Williams, Charles, 63–65
Williams, Eunice (Mrs. Caleb), 65
Williams, Jane (Mrs. Caleb, Jr.), 63, 65, 67
Williams, John, papers relating to house of, 15n, 204–207
Williams, Josiah F., 63
Williams, Oliver E., 170
Williams, Roger, 171
Williams, Stephen, 210
Williams, Thomas, 170n
Williamson, Col. George, 81
Willison, George F., 115
Wills, Royal Barry, 139
Wilson, Shoreborn, 159–160
Wilson-Appleton House, Ipswich, 156, 159–160
Windows, sash, letters about, 195

Winslow, Edward, 58
Winter, Fred, 174
Winterthur Museum, Henry Francis du Pont, 117, 141, 150
Winthrop, Deane, 191
Winthrop, Deane, House, Winthrop, 191
Winthrop, Gov. John, 23, 172
Winthrop, John, Jr., 215–216
Winthrop, Mass., Deane Winthrop House, 191
Winthrop Improvement and Historical Association, 191
Witch House (Old Garrison House), Rockport, 169–170
Woodcock, William, 146
Woodcock-Langley House, Hingham, 146
Woolley, Charles, 148
Worthylake, George, land leased to, 210–211

Young, Alexander, 176

Zaharis, Peter, 141, 158
Zimmer, Edward, 61–74

*Design and
composition by
The Stinehour Press*

*Halftone photography
and printing by
The Meriden
Gravure Company*